Politicizing Islam

RELIGION AND GLOBAL POLITICS

SERIES EDITOR
John L. Esposito
University Professor and Director
Prince Alwaleed Bin Talal Center for Muslim-Christian Understanding
Georgetown University

Politicizing Islam

The Islamic Revival
in France and India

Z. FAREEN PARVEZ

OXFORD
UNIVERSITY PRESS

OXFORD
UNIVERSITY PRESS

Oxford University Press is a department of the University of Oxford. It furthers
the University's objective of excellence in research, scholarship, and education
by publishing worldwide. Oxford is a registered trade mark of Oxford University
Press in the UK and certain other countries.

Published in the United States of America by Oxford University Press
198 Madison Avenue, New York, NY 10016, United States of America.

Library of Congress Cataloging-in-Publication Data
Names: Parvez, Z. Fareen, author.
Title: Politicizing Islam : the Islamic revival in France and India / Z.
Fareen Parvez.
Description: Oxford University Press : New York, NY, [2017] |
Includes bibliographical references and index.
Identifiers: LCCN 2016034017 (print) | LCCN 2016035305 (ebook) |
ISBN 9780190225247 (hardback) | ISBN 9780190225254 (updf) |
ISBN 9780190225261 (oso) | ISBN 9780190651176 (epub)
Subjects: LCSH: Islamic renewal—France. | Islamic renewal—India. |
Islam—France. | Islam—India. | Islam and politics.
Classification: LCC BP60 .P37 2017 (print) | LCC BP60 (ebook) |
DDC 305.6/970944—dc23
LC record available at https://lccn.loc.gov/2016034017

Sections of chapters 5 and 6 are revisions of material that appeared in "Recognition and
Antipolitics among Muslims in France: Representing 'Islam of the Banlieues'" (in *Muslim
Political Participation in Europe*, ed. Jørgen S. Nielsen, Edinburgh University Press, 2013)
and "Debating the Burqa in France: The Antipolitics of Islamic Revival" (*Qualitative
Sociology* 34, no. 2 [2011]: 287–312).

For my parents, Zaheer and Kausar Parvez,
who made the journey

Study me as much as you like, you will not know me, for
I differ in a hundred ways from what you see me to be.
Put yourself behind my eyes and see me as I see myself, for
I have chosen to dwell in a place you cannot see.

JALAL AL-DIN MUHAMMAD Rumi

Contents

Contents

Acknowledgments

I BEGIN MY acknowledgments by thanking the men and women in Lyon and Hyderabad who, by welcoming me into their lives and communities, made this book possible. For their generosity and open hearts, I thank the women in Hyderabad's training centers who brought me into their worlds and shared with me their stories, dreams, and disappointments. For confidentiality, I have changed most of these names. I offer my heartfelt *shukriya* to Rahman and Anwar in Shanthi Colony and the activists in Zohra Bagh whose courageous work is to me the highest vision of public sociology. Many individuals in Hyderabad may think I forgot them. In truth, I have carried our memories and conversations with me all this time. This includes my time with Dr. Hasanuddin Ahmed, who shared many afternoons, analyses, and a wealth of insights into Hyderabad's Muslim history. I am indebted to Mr. Haq, Kulsoom apa, and to Mirza Mustafa Khan, whose generosity remains a source of awe. My aunt Naveed Haq passed away at the end of my fieldwork. From her unconditional love to delicious tiffins, her support in Hyderabad made all things seem possible. Her memory remains with me.

The women of Mosquée Hasan in Vénissieux altered my path in important ways, and it is their words that give life to sections of this book. In keeping with their pious practice they would not want me to thank them. I acknowledge Yassin and Mounir, with a full heart, and the Mosquée Hijra community for their trust and kindness. Several friends in Lyon over time made this city feel like home: Rachid Kssiouar, Sabrina Rieu, Giovanni D'Andrea, Laurent Chignier, Shubhra Chakravarty, Taysir Rekaya, and Sylvain Lagrand.

It gives me great pleasure to thank Michael Burawoy, who nurtured this book since its inception as a dissertation in the Department of Sociology at the University of California, Berkeley. Michael did not join the chorus of voices back then that discouraged the comparative angle of the research or that claimed Islam in France was a nonissue. Instead, he trusted my intuitions and supported every step, reminding me why this work mattered when I could no longer see it. If his influence is at all recognizable in the pages of this book, I will be serenely satisfied. Likewise, Raka Ray and Loïc Wacquant profoundly shaped my sociological thinking, and they made crucial marks on my understanding of politics in India and France. I am indebted to each of them for the many ways they supported me. And I thank Cihan Tuğal for reading early drafts and insisting on the need to struggle more with my concepts.

While I was at UC Berkeley, Saba Mahmood's seminar on liberalism and secularity challenged me in ways I would not fully appreciate until years later. I am grateful to have briefly crossed her path. I thank Olivier Roy, who saw the value of my research in Les Minguettes and whose seminar made me think more critically about the meaning of secularism. This book absorbed the early comments and ideas of my intellectual community of fellow Berkeley graduate students: Tom Medvetz, Barry Eidlin, Xiuying Cheng, Silvia Pasquetti, Ofer Sharone, Laleh Behbehanian, Cinzia Solari, Adam Reich, Marcel Paret, Emily Brissette, Mike Levien, and Jon Norman. James Lamb has been my comrade since the day we met in Gil Eyal's theory seminar, and in dialogue with him I still find my political and intellectual compass.

Since moving on to the University of Massachusetts, Amherst, I have treasured the mentorship and friendship of Robert Zussman. Robert commented on multiple drafts of the manuscript and supported me in all ways as I journeyed through the process of revising this book. I thank Mike Levien at Johns Hopkins University for carefully reading every page and helping me to sculpt this into a better book. And I am grateful that Jessica Cobb could step in at the eleventh hour to guide me through important revisions. Many other friends and colleagues engaged parts of this book and added insights as it developed. I especially thank Damon Maryl, Peter van der Veer, John Bowen, Charles Kurzman, Anna Korteweg, Melissa Wilde, Jon Wynn, and Claudia Casteñeda. Whatever failings or shortcomings remain are entirely my own.

I enjoyed opportunities to present my work to colleagues and mentors at several institutions who deepened my knowledge of Islam and politics in France and India. I am grateful to Camille Hamidi and Nancy Venel at the University of Lyon, Raphaël Liogier at SciencesPo at Aix-en-Provence, Anwar Alam at Jamia Millia Islamia University in New Delhi, and Samir Amghar. I benefited from conversations with José Casanova and colleagues at the

Religious Pluralism Workshop organized by Irmgard Coninx Foundation, Social Science Research Center Berlin and Humboldt University in Berlin. Peter van der Veer, Charles Hirschkind, and many fellows of the Social Science Research Council's New Direction in the Study of Prayer expanded my conceptualization of religion, ethnography, and comparative work as we shared our research. A number of institutes generously supported the research for this book including the National Science Foundation, the University of California Institute on Global Conflict and Cooperation, and the University of California at Berkeley's Center for Race and Gender, Center for Middle Eastern Studies, and Institute of International Studies. The Social Science Research Council supported the final phase of research in France and periods of writing. I would like to thank staff at the University of Massachusetts Department of Sociology for patiently assisting me during this time: Karen Mason, Wendy Wilde, Maureen Warner, and Cindy Patten. I thank Oyman Basaran for his excellent research assistance, and Aftab Ahmed for his Urdu translations. I had the privilege of working with Cynthia Read and her team at Oxford University Press, and I extend my gratitude to the anonymous reviewers who commented on the manuscript.

My colleagues at the University of Massachusetts, Amy Schalet, Anna Branch, Steve Boutcher, Jon Wynn, and Millie Thayer morally encouraged me through the trials of writing this book. I thank them for their sound advice, camaraderie, and urgings onward. As the book drew to a close, the curiosity and energy of students in my sociology of religion course helped me discover and articulate the complexities of what we call religion.

My family weathered the storms and distances this book summoned into their lives. I thank the Brummett family, my sister Farah—to whom I owe everything—and my parents, for the immense sacrifices they made and the beautifully complex attachments they gave me. This book is dedicated to them. For too long, Arman and Feroz took a backseat to this book, even as they filled my life with love and joy. Perhaps one day they will understand. Finally, I thank Brad Brummett, whose unassuming grace and wisdom carried me through and impacted every phase of this work.

Abbreviations

FRANCE

CCIF   Collectif Contre Islamophobie en France (Collective Against Islamophobia in France)

CFCM   Conseil Français du Culte Musulman (French Council of the Muslim Faith)

CRCM   Conseil Régional du Culte Musulman (Regional Council of the Muslim Faith)

CRIF   Conseil Répresentatif des Institutions Juives de France (Representative Council of French Jewish Institutions)

CTAM   Conseillers Techniques pour les Affaires Musulmans (Technical Advisors for Muslim Affairs)

EMF   Étudiants Musulmans de France (Muslim Students of France)

FN   Le Front National (National Front)

FSQP   Forum Social des Quartiers Populaires (Social Forum of 'Popular Neighborhoods')

HLM   Habitation à Loyer Modéré (subsidized public housing)

IESH   Institut Européen des Sciences Humaines (European Institute of the Humanities)

JMF   Jeunes Musulmans de France (Young Muslims of France)

PMF   Parti des Musulmans de France (Party of Muslims in France)

UJM   Union des Jeunes Musulmans (Union of Young Muslims)

UMP   Union pour un Mouvement Populaire (Union for a Popular Movement)

UOIF   Union des Organisations Islamiques de France (Union of Islamic Organizations of France)

ZUP   Zones à Urbaniser en Priorité (Urban priority zones)

ZUS   Zones Urbaines Sensibles ("Sensitive" urban zones)

INDIA

AIMPLB	All India Muslim Personal Law Board
AMU	Aligarh Muslim University
AP	Andhra Pradesh state
BJP	Bharatiya Janata Party
BPL	Below Poverty Line
IACR	Islamic Academy for Comparative Religion
JIH	Jama'at-i-Islami Hind
MIM	Majlis-e-Ittihad ul Muslimeen
MLA	Member of the Legislative Assembly
RSS	Rashtriya Swayamsevak Sangh
SIMI	Students Islamic Movement of India
SIO	Students Islamic Organization
TDP	Telugu Desam Party
VHP	Vishwa Hindu Parishad

Politicizing Islam

Politicizing Islam Across North and South

IN THE SPRING of 2004, the French Interior Ministry arrested Abdelkader Bouziane and deported him to Algeria on charges of posing an urgent threat to public order and security. Bouziane had lived in France for twenty-five years and was an imam of a mosque in Vénissieux, one of Lyon's drab working-class suburbs. The deportation was triggered by Bouziane's interview in the April edition of *Lyon Mag*, where he unwittingly confessed his wish that the entire world would become Muslim because people would be happier if they were closer to God. He also claimed that the Quran permitted a man to hit his wife in certain situations, especially adultery, and that men may live polygamously. "But pay attention," he added. "It's four wives at most, and there are conditions!" Interior Minister Dominique Villepin, who had been tracking Bouziane for months, said that France could not accept such an affront to human dignity. According to Villepin's lawyer, Bouziane preached hate and violence and promoted Salafist ideology.[1] The deportation stunned and scared local mosque-goers and neighborhood residents. Muslim leaders in Lyon denounced the state's actions while also calling Bouziane's remarks "stupid and unacceptable."[2] Bouziane was one of several imams expelled from France in the last decade over vague accusations of threatening security and inciting hatred.

Three years later, in May 2007, a pipe bomb exploded at Mecca Masjid, a 300-year-old mosque in the heart of the Old City in Hyderabad, India. As worshipers frantically tried to rescue victims and transport them to the local hospital, Hyderabad police fired on the crowd, killing five Muslims. In the days that followed, police questioned, harassed, and arrested dozens of young Muslims for their alleged involvement in the explosion and collusion with Pakistani terrorist groups. This was the second instance in 2007 alone of Hyderabad police illegally detaining numerous Muslim men. The Central Bureau of Intelligence later released its post-investigation position that right-wing Hindu groups, not Muslims, planted the bomb at the mosque.[3]

These two episodes occurred in vastly different societies, but they reflect a global trend toward the routine surveillance of mosque communities and arbitrary policing of persons associated with Islam. This surveillance rests on the assumption that Islamic piety has grave political consequences. Yet neither the Mecca Masjid worshipers nor Imam Bouziane had any intention of making a political statement. In each case, the state politicized Islam by criminalizing religious participation and expression. Bouziane, a member of an insular religious community isolated from politically engaged middle-class Islamic associations, was expelled from France in the name of security and protection of women's rights. By 2010, the French state would criminalize the act of wearing a "burqa," a choice made by some women of Bouziane's former mosque as a symbol of radical separatism and an attack on the principle of citizenship.[4] In Hyderabad, the dozens of Muslims who were arrested after the explosion were assumed to have terrorist affiliations because of their mosque activities or simply because they lived in certain neighborhoods of the city.

The surveillance and politicization of Islam constitute the backdrop of everyday religious life for Muslims in France and India. Given this backdrop, how do Muslims, as denigrated minorities, mobilize to improve their situations through their Islamic revival? What types of claims do they make on the secular state that has targeted them as threats to the nation? Contrary to what most literature on Islamic movements would suggest, Islamic revivals in the cities of Lyon and Hyderabad are not aimed at Islamizing state or society. Instead, at the very moment that the global War on Terror has voraciously politicized Islam, many Muslim communities, such as in Vénissieux and the Old City, have withdrawn from the state. Their withdrawal challenges the very concept of a political Islam in secular states.

France and India are two secular states that host the largest Muslim minorities in Western Europe and Asia. Yet these minorities are among the poorest and most marginalized sectors of their respective societies. Over 4 million Muslims reside in France (7%) and 172 million (14%) in India.[5] Suffering extreme rates of poverty and unemployment, they are widely suspected of disloyalty to the nation. They are stereotyped as adherents of shari'a intent on "Islamizing" the state and infecting the public sphere with their religious practices.

This research provides insight into the everyday lived experiences of religion and politics of Muslims in Lyon and Hyderabad during the post-9/11 era of the global War on Terror. As in many Muslim societies, French and Indian Muslim communities have undergone vibrant Islamic revivals in the last twenty years, marked by increased women's veiling, the opening of neighborhood mosques and Islamic schools, everyday participation in informal Islamic study circles and charity activities, and greater emphasis on Muslim "identity." The revivals in Lyon and Hyderabad share features with Islamic revival movements across the globe, but they also have distinct social consequences based on their interactions with the state and with historically embedded class structures. This book explores and explains these interactions and describes the specific types of politics that have emerged among religious Muslims in each city. In both Lyon and Hyderabad, Muslims were engaged in a struggle with the state over resources and religious rights, as well as internal struggles over political strategy and the meaning and interpretation of Islamic principles. Each city's struggles had consequences for debates within the Islamic tradition, the potential for minority participation in an open democratic sphere, and the situations of Muslim women. For largely poor and subaltern Muslims, these implications are of fundamental material and spiritual importance.[6] The question of how minority Muslims make political claims on the state and improve their situations departs from the dominant and problematic question of how to *liberalize* Muslims. This latter question is playing itself out through a struggle within Muslim communities that is closely tied to social class—a critical dimension of the Islamic revival that scholars often ignore.

Class, Claims, and Divergent Politics

Throughout my research in both Lyon and Hyderabad, I found that middle-class Muslim communities were conflicted over how to protect the community and the religion, as well as over what types of claims to make on the state and through what means. A major point of tension was whether to focus on economic redistribution or greater state recognition of Muslims and Islam.[7] Some parties worried that an agenda based on religious recognition either misused Islam and manipulated the poor or depoliticized the larger community, undermining an alternative, radical redistributive agenda. The political and economic structures middle-class Muslims faced and the types of claims they made impacted their relationships to low-income Muslims and, in turn, influenced the ability of the poor and subaltern to mobilize any form of politics.

The middle-class Muslims I knew also contended with a form of Islamic revival among the poor that they found deeply troubling, and even in contradiction with Islam. The issue of women's veiling was at the core of this class division over Islamic practice. Middle-class communities had a strong aversion to full-body coverings and especially the niqab, a facial covering, which they viewed as a regressive misinterpretation of Islam. How they managed this disagreement reflected the deeper nature of Muslim class relations in each city.

In Hyderabad, middle-class and elite Muslims engaged the poor through patronage, paternalistic affection, and disciplining. Distribution to the poor and to women in particular was central to their politics. Through philanthropic projects such as women's training centers, they hoped to transform the community by promoting their secular convictions, injecting or suppressing religion in their projects as a means to this end. Reacting to government neglect of the Muslim population's high poverty rates and low education levels, the middle-class and elite political field was riven by competition for legitimacy, where the measure of success was welfare distribution and support for private welfare programs.

With the backing of elites, subaltern Muslims in Hyderabad's slum neighborhoods pulled together to practice collective autonomy, refusing to direct their hopes at the state and instead building political communities. Women figured centrally in these political communities, creating alternate forms of honor by seeking skills and self-employment, and by using principles of shari'a to target social issues affecting women in particular; poor and subaltern men stood on the sidelines. Women sustained these political communities while adhering to strict gender segregation and confronting the moral disapproval of the same elites who facilitated their movements.

The relations between middle-class and working-class Muslims were strikingly different in Lyon than in Hyderabad. Here, too, the middle class had great disdain for the specifically sectarian Islamic revival that gained popularity in stigmatized urban peripheries like Vénissieux. But in Lyon, this divide paralyzed middle-class Islamic associations. Battling discrimination and state surveillance, these associations lacked the resources to promote political participation among poor and sectarian Muslims.

Reacting to state obstacles to everyday religious practice and widespread discrimination against religious Muslims, associations dreaded state control over Islamic institutions while negotiating with the state for religious rights and recognition. As in Hyderabad, the field was tensely divided between those who accepted the need to "integrate" and work with the state and those who thought focusing on recognition neglected the needs of the poor and working class.[8]

Isolated from middle-class Muslims in Lyon, sectarian Muslims in the working-class banlieues lived in a state of precarity. They made no claims on the state, withdrew from public life and institutions, and cared more for their individual relationships to God than all else. What I saw was not radical or political Islam but, instead, looked like the expulsion of politics altogether. The mosque community of women I came to know here worked to protect and nourish their private spheres, build a moral community, and achieve serenity and acceptance of divine will. They did this in a context of social mistrust, overall desolation, and collapse of civil society in their neighborhoods. Far from creating political communities, they practiced what I call antipolitics.

Given the similarities in the religious dynamics across these cases, why did the politics diverge so dramatically? I argue that these variations are explained by different models of secularism. Specifically, each nation's model of secularism set the conditions for the types of political claims that religious minorities emphasized and their potential to mobilize across class toward social justice. In France, the assimilationist model of secularism stigmatized religion in the public sphere, leading to middle-class claims for religious recognition. It also erected various barriers to cross-class identification and organization among Muslims as a religious group. As a result, working-class Muslims in Lyon's banlieues were isolated and disconnected from politics. In India, a pluralist model of secularism guaranteed and celebrated religious liberties, leading the middle class and elites to instead focus their efforts on economic redistribution to the poor. The recognition—indeed, solidification—of religious communities in India allowed for cross-class mobilization. With middle-class and elite patronage, subaltern Muslims in low-income neighborhoods were able to work toward community autonomy, social change, and the advancement of women. A flexible secularism—one that accommodated religion in the public sphere—allowed for stronger cross-class relations, which in turn facilitated greater political potentiality for the poor and subaltern.

Why France and India?

The vast majority of Muslims live in secular countries: almost half of Muslim countries are secular states, and 20 percent of the world's Muslims reside in countries where they are a minority.[9] Minority Muslims' political claims and marginalization reveal that secular democracy is in crisis. The longstanding Muslim populations of both France and India remain mostly at the bottom of the class hierarchy, and the prevalence of hate crimes against Muslim victims in these countries calls into question the meaning and effectiveness of secularism. In France, several hundred "Islamophobic acts" occur every year, with the vast majority of aggressions and assaults occurring against women.[10] In India, violence against Muslims is tragically endemic, culminating in the 2002 pogrom in Gujarat that displaced 100,000 Muslims and took over a thousand lives (see Ghassem-Fachandi 2012).

At first glance, France and India seem to present very different national contexts for Muslim minorities. France is an advanced industrial European state ranked twentieth on the Human Development Index; India is a member of the global South ranked at 135 (UNDP 2014). France is predominantly Roman Catholic while India is predominantly Hindu and far more religious, according to survey research (World Values Survey 2005).[11] The two nations stand on opposite ends of a colonial past. France has a long history as a centralized monarchy and is currently a member of the Group of Eight (G8) and United Nations Security Council. India has an even longer history of territorial kingdoms and tribal chieftains, and today the country struggles to attain international power.

Yet France and India are experiencing a similar crisis of secularism. Both states have failed to protect their Muslim minorities from discrimination and violence, and to contain the growth of religious activity and transnational Islamic movements. Both countries have also suffered major terrorist attacks perpetrated by Muslim individuals that stoked widespread fears of Islam and led to reactionary violence, exacerbating tensions with an already beleaguered minority. The 2015 killings at the Bataclan theater and other sites in Paris came seven years after terrorist attacks in Mumbai of nearly the same scale and nature.[12]

In France, Muslims are suspected of disloyalty to the nation and of secretly harboring loyalty to Algeria and other Muslim countries. The French discourse against *communautarisme* tends to focus on Muslims, whose allegiance to community is considered irrational and dangerous.

Communautarisme refers to ethnic or religious sectarianism and the submission of individual will to community authority that weakens allegiance
to the state (Salvatore 2007).[13] The specter of *communautarisme* hangs over
most demands for specific religious rights in France, such as halal food,
Muslim cemeteries, and Islamic schools. It also heavily influenced the official perspective on the headscarf, which the state banned in public schools
in 2004. In 2010, it went on to ban the niqab in all public space. In the city
of Lille in 2003, when Muslims requested separate swimming pool hours
for men and women, the UMP (*Union pour un Mouvement Populaire*) party
denounced the request as "communautariste." In fact, municipalities had
granted such provisions in the past to Jewish associations without any
denunciation or media uproar (Bowen 2007: 109–10).

While municipalities frequently meet religious demands with accusations of *communautarisme*, the media sometimes wrongly present periodic
urban rebellions against socioeconomic exclusion and police harassment
as religious conflicts. Every few years, episodes of violence against youth
in the banlieues instigate rebellions, marked most prominently by the
burning of cars. In 2005, an uprising outside of Paris spread to other cities
and lasted nineteen days. Triggered by the deaths of two teenagers hiding
from the police, it stemmed from frustration with police interrogations
and youth unemployment.

In India, accusations of community allegiance employ the label of
"communalism." *Communalism* refers to political organizing by religious
communities for their own purposes, "usually in a hostile way" (Tejani
2008, 116). In its earliest usage, the term indicated any irrational attachment to ethnic or religious ties that went against modern national identity,
but by Independence in 1947, it referred specifically to Muslims and the
threat they supposedly posed to secularism. Today, Muslims continue to
be accused of loyalty to Pakistan instead of to the Indian nation-state and
thus, communalism (Pandey 1999).

Unlike in France, religious minorities in India enjoy robust religious
rights such as the freedom to practice Personal Law, in this case Muslim
family law based on shari'a. Yet these rights are precarious, as they draw
particular scrutiny from Hindu nationalist administrations. In the cultural sphere, intellectuals and community leaders have impassioned
debates over the teaching of the Urdu language in schools (the language
predominantly spoken by Muslims), the nature of curricula in madrasas,
and affirmative action policies for Muslims. As in France, the government
and media depict urban rebellions and nationalist riots over resources as

religious conflicts. Hindu-Muslim riots, often related to political and eco- nomic inequalities, have increased in frequency in the last few decades.[14]

These parallel phenomena in France and India make for a productive comparative study, even though Islam has existed in India for a millen- nium, whereas Muslims from the French North African colonies started settling in France in the mid-twentieth century. It is tempting to explain differences between these cases through this migration history, but the lens of immigration is no longer adequate to understand Islam in France.[15] Some young, practicing Muslims of North African origin come from fami- lies who have lived in France for three generations. The immediate social issues and ethnic distinctions that mattered to their immigrant grandpar- ents have little salience for these young Muslims. Instead, my participants in both Lyon and Hyderabad aired similar grievances related to discrimi- nation, education, employment, and social respect.[16]

And Muslims in both countries have long been racialized, even though the dominant racializing frames have shifted over time. For example, in France earlier modes of marking difference centered on immigration (immi- grés) and foreign nationality (étrangers), referring particularly to Maghrébins (those from specifically Algeria, Morocco, and Tunisia). This shifted during the 1990s toward the dominant marker of "Muslim," often conflating reli- gion, culture, citizenship status, national origin, and even residence in the banlieues (Fassin 2006). Although this discursive shift took place recently, in fact the French state used religion in tandem with other racializing prac- tices in the management of its colonial empire. Today, Muslims are racial- ized as they were before, depicted as having innate cultural tendencies that make them fundamentally unable to assimilate to French life.[17]

In India, the dominant frame highlights religion and problems of "communalism," or less commonly, casteism and other ways of exploiting difference. But as in France, few frame inequality and violence as prob- lems of racism (Baber 2004; Chakrabarty 1995). Yet Hindu nationalist writing that depicts Muslims in racial terms dates back over a century, when it drew on orientalist scholarship to argue that Muslims as a racial group threatened the "Hindu race" with their overbreeding and mores (see Baber 2004). Today, in India these racial fears remain in place.

Comparing Lyon and Hyderabad

Lyon and Hyderabad are both cities that have experienced intense Islamic revivals. During my fieldwork, my participants emphasized an increase in Islamic religiosity in each region. Each city also has one of the highest concentrations of Muslims in its country. Hyderabad's population is 43 percent Muslim, and Lyon's regional population is approximately 10 to 15 percent Muslim origin, though the absence of official statistics on religious background makes it difficult to accurately cite a number.[18] Yet the two cities remain underresearched compared to their larger and wealthier counterparts of Mumbai and Paris.

Three hundred miles south of Paris, Lyon is France's second largest metropolitan region. Situated close to the Swiss and Italian borders, its picturesque landscape is marked by a mix of modern and medieval buildings that line the banks of the tumultuous Rhône River and serene Saône River. The two rivers converge south of the city, creating a peninsula. East of the downtown plazas, numerous small mosques exist in various arrondissements. Lyon's Grand Mosque (*Grande Mosquée de Lyon*), inaugurated in 1994, lies a few miles from downtown.

Moving several miles east of the city and beyond a major freeway, the scene gradually shifts toward suburban desolation. Concrete tower-block housing projects loom in the distance. Taking a combination of the Metro and tramway or bus, it takes almost an hour to travel to the eastern working-class banlieues. Vaulx-en-Velin, Bron, and Vénissieux once housed thousands of migrant factory workers in the auto, metallurgy, and electrical equipment industries. In the 1970s, the loss of factory jobs and the decline of labor unions in Lyon's banlieues eliminated the primary vehicle of stability and citizenship for many immigrants of Muslim origin. Today, these areas remain predominantly working-class territories with several stigmatized neighborhoods, referred to as *les quartiers*.[19] These neighborhoods are infamous for urban uprisings and their high concentration of immigrants. Approximately 40 percent of the people living in Les Minguettes, a quartier in Vénissieux, are of immigrant background.[20] Clearly segregated from Lyonnais space and culture, Minguettes residents under twenty-five years old suffer an unemployment rate of 40 percent (Voisin 2005). Lyon's urban periphery overall represents a case of "advanced marginality," which Loïc Wacquant (2007) defines as territorial stigma, spatial alienation, and loss of a community or space of refuge.

Vénissieux appears to have the highest regional concentration of Salafist Muslims, estimated to total only a few thousand in all of France. Salafism refers to a theological reform movement within Sunni Islam to return to the original teachings and practices of the Prophet Muhammed and the Quran.[21] Salafi reformism is only one type of movement within the larger Islamic revival, but it is the most condemned and politicized because of its ambiguous relationship to anti-state ideology and violence. French Salafist Muslims, however, are by and large quietist, meaning they shun politics, let alone terrorist violence.[22]

Salafists stand out because of their dress. Women wear djelbabs, a dark or neutral-colored loose dress that covers everything but the face. A small number wear the niqab, despite its illegality. Though not to the same extent as women, Salafist men might stand out for their beards and ankle-length pants. This public manifestation of a sectarian Islamic revival in the area caught the attention of politicians. The former mayor of Vénissieux, André Gerin, proposed the national ban on "the burqa" in his position as National Deputy based on his observations of Salafist Islam in and around Lyon.

As in many parts of the globe, women actively participate in the Islamic revival.[23] In Lyon's mosques they are just as active as men, attending prayers, holding classes, and arranging special events.

OVER FOUR THOUSAND miles to the east of France and a thousand miles south of New Delhi, the city of Hyderabad is equally as historic, pictur-esque, and segregated as Lyon. India's fourth largest city, it is located on the Deccan Plateau, in the newly formed state of Telengana.[24] The Musi River, disastrously polluted as of recent times, runs through the city, split-ting it into two sections known as the Old City and New City. The New City houses the city's middle-class and wealthier populations, holds the gate-way to the burgeoning IT center, and has recently welcomed numerous shopping malls and real estate developments. But the historical and archi-tectural draw of Hyderabad lies south of the Musi River in the Old City. Narrow streets and bazaars selling traditional artisan goods from metal work to bridal jewelry radiate from the late sixteenth-century Charminar monument that marks the center of the Old City. Near the Charminar is the Mecca Masjid, a mosque built in 1694 during the Qutb Shahi dynasty.

Continuing south past the crumbling architectural gems that dot the landscape of the Charminar area, dozens of impoverished enclaves spill into each other. They are generally classified as "below poverty line," or BPL. They reflect the decline of Hyderabad city and the extraor-dinary wealth that once was concentrated in the hands of Muslim royal families and administration in the pre-Independence period. In post-Independence Hyderabad, the state expelled many Muslims from military and administrative positions, pushing them into informal economies and slum neighborhoods (Leonard 2003). Hyderabad's unique postcolonial legacy shapes the kind of marginality seen in its poor neighborhoods. One observes poverty, precarity, and territorial stigma but not the same kind of spatial alienation and loss of community that characterizes many cities of the industrial North.[25] Instead, neighborhoods are densely populated, and people are embedded in social networks both in the city and in rural villages of origin.

Today, many of the BPL enclaves in the Old City are predominantly Muslim. Some sport visible signs of remittances from the Gulf countries—one enclave even earned the nickname "Little Dubai." Among these signs are ornate neighborhood mosques financed by remittance money and donations from Arab patrons. Women in these neighborhoods typically dress in black burqas, the term local residents use, when out in public. Some religious men grow their beards and wear an Islamic cap (topi) and traditional chemise and pant (kurta pajama).

The Islamic revival in these Old City enclaves is less clearly associated with a movement than the Salafist movement of Vénissieux, but it overlaps with Salafism in that worshipers seek to reform everyday Islam by purifying it of cultural rituals—in this case, rituals borrowed from Hindu practices. At the same time, the sectarian group, Ahl-e-Hadees, has influenced a minority of subaltern religious communities by promoting more rigid gender segregation and full-time madrasa education.[26] Working alongside associations like the Jama'at-i-Islami Hind (JIH), they have also drawn women into their fold. Unlike in France, Muslim women in India typically lack access to mosque space, but they meet in informal spaces and homes for their religious study and increasingly form communities through girls' madrasas. As in Lyon, women actively participate in collective religious activity.

Diverse Beliefs and Practices

In doing comparative research across Lyon and Hyderabad, I encountered an enormous diversity in religious practice and beliefs among self-identified Muslims. In my earlier periods of fieldwork, this diversity disoriented me. In Hyderabad, I met auto-rickshaw drivers who regularly drank alcohol and never attended a mosque, but they would never deny their faith and identification as Muslim. In Lyon, I commonly encountered people of Muslim origin who said they were not religious or not believers, but who participated in Ramadan. Ilyas, a French Moroccan immigrant rights activist in his thirties, described himself as an agnostic and Marxist, without faith in Islam despite his family's Muslim origins. I was taken aback one afternoon when he told me he was fasting for all thirty days of the Islamic month of Ramadan because in Hyderabad, the many Indian Muslims doing hard, manual labor viewed fasting during all of Ramadan as a serious test of faith. Thus, the meanings of faith, Islamic practice, and Muslim identity varied both within and across individuals, socioeconomic classes, and national contexts.

One of the skeptical questions I have consistently encountered, both within and outside the field, is "What do you mean by Muslim?"[27] This is a complicated and sometimes rhetorical question that has generated substantial academic research. Surveys and focus groups seek to uncover some essential quality that defines Muslims.[28] These surveys sometimes assume internal consistency between beliefs and behaviors; but in reality, this relationship is not so simple. Through my research, I came to understand that faith is a deeply private matter and one that is excruciatingly difficult to articulate. Few Muslims I met directly discussed faith, and none saw it as something discrete and measurable. Likewise, in Jocelyne Césari's focus-group interviews of Muslims in Europe and the United States, participants were reluctant to discuss the issue of belief.[29]

But when I say that faith was deeply private, I do not necessarily mean that it was based in an inner state of mind. Such a conception of faith does not resonate with the Islamic tradition (Asad 1993), but is a "typically Protestant and hence historically situated religiosity" (Houtman and Meyer 2012, 2).[30] Instead, informed by Talal Asad, we might think of "the objects of belief" as material practice and life activity that changes as the world changes (1993, 125). Belief was a difficult or inapt topic in isolation, and I did not choose participants based on this type of categorization. Instead, my participants were part of the Islamic tradition "that includes and relates itself to the founding texts of the Quran and the Hadith" (Asad 2009, 20). Asad writes, "Islam is neither a distinctive social structure nor a heterogeneous collection of beliefs, artifacts, customs, and morals. It is a tradition" (2009, 20).[31]

Despite the myriad ways in which Muslims inhabit their religious identification and relate to the Islamic tradition, most of my subjects met standard, Western definitions of religious individuals. They joined Islamic associations, belonged to mosque communities, or actively worshiped through prayer and fasting.[32] Faith was undoubtedly an important part of their lives. Further, most had some understanding of and belief in the

Muslim *ummah*, or global community of believers (Césari 2013). Even for them, however, the relationship between faith and practice was complex. Faith, as I learned, is not a fait accompli, a state that someone is proud to achieve. Rather, striving to attain faith in Islam is a continual process and one that might involve doubt, sinning, and redemption, in addition to ritual practice.

Politics Across State and Class

Table 1.1 summarizes the findings in this book. It shows four types of political movements I saw across the two cities and across the poor and the middle class. These movements emerged at the meso level from the nature of Muslim class relations and at the macro level from the type of secularism the French and Indian states pursued.

To understand the politics around Islam in either country, it is imperative to first understand its model of secularism.[33] One is a fundamentally pluralist model and the other is assimilationist. Indian secularism, or "composite nationalism," accepts religious laws in matters of family, finances, and property, and embraces the principle of noninterference in the affairs of religious communities (Madani 2005; Rajan 2000; Hasan 1998, 1997). The state built religious recognition into its constitution. Composite nationalism allowed Muslims to mobilize around religious identification, regardless of their religiosity or lack thereof, and build cross-class alliances as an ethnic group. Such use of identity was relatively free of stigma, as well as legal barriers, despite national discourses around communalism. By contrast, French *laïcité*, rooted in the Jacobin tradition, rests on assimilation to a dominant culture, language, and political ideology, and opposes recognition of religious or ethnic minorities (Scott 2007; Laborde 2001).[34] Unlike the Indian case,

Table 1.1 Politics Across State and Class

		STATE	
		Pluralist	Assimilationist
		Hyderabad	Lyon
CLASS	Middle-class (relations)	**Redistribution** (paternalism)	**Recognition** (opposition)
	Subaltern	**Community**	**Antipolitics**

French secularism sought to keep religiosity out of the public sphere and to uphold national values of *liberté, egalité, et fraternité*. Islamic associations had to restrict mobilization along lines of identity to receive state approval and obtain public funding, as well as to compete with secular associations that also tried to represent immigrant minorities (Leveau 1992). Class politics based on a unified Muslim category was highly unlikely in France because of the strong incompatibility of ethno-religious identity (negatively marked as *communautarisme*) and French conceptions of citizenship.

These opposite models of secularism account for the types of demands middle-class activists made of the state. In India, the politics of Islam almost always invoked distribution and not religious rights, which were legally safeguarded. In France, the repression of religion in the public sphere led to a middle-class politics of recognition.

Muslim class relations constitute the meso level of explanation for divergent movements, as shown in table 1.1. Elites and the middle classes have the power to attract political attention and provide critical resources to movements of the poor and subaltern,[35] but their interest in doing so depends on whether they view themselves as part of the same minority community (Pattillo 2008). This identification depends on historical factors and structural conditions.

In Hyderabad, elite and middle-class philanthropists possess a highly paternalistic relationship to subaltern, low-income communities. A history of charity and patronage and a keen cultural attachment to the Old City provide impetus to share their private wealth and remittances from abroad. They distribute welfare while promoting liberal forms of Islam and disparaging sectarian practices. Ultimately, through paternalistic protection and financial support, elites encourage the subaltern to participate in political life through independent Muslim civil societies. By contrast, in Lyon, Islamic and some secular associations that were once active in the banlieues have retreated from working-class neighborhoods, largely owing to the state's successful attempts to defeat them. While class relations in the past were stronger, the Muslim middle class had neither the legal and discursive space nor the inherited wealth for a sustained immigrant or racial-justice movement. Today, middle-class Muslim activists in Lyon regret their growing distance from Muslims in the working-class quartiers. This bifurcation maintains Muslims' political isolation in places like Les Minguettes and prevents avenues for cross-class dialogue about Islam.

Most attempts to understand Islamic movements overlook this critical importance of state secularism and class relations. Perhaps the best known of these attempts are orientalist approaches such as Huntington's "clash of civilizations" that still find their way into journalistic accounts and popular perception (Huntington 1996).[36] These focus on Islamic doctrine, treating it as inherently political and potentially violent (Lewis 2002, 1990; Huntington 1996), ignoring the diversity of interpretations and relationships to religious texts and history, as well as the fact that the same texts are associated with very different sectarian traditions and politics. This literature reduces the complex variations between secularisms like those of France and India to geopolitics and homogenized civilizations, and it has little to say about the effects of class differences within Muslim societies, whether minority or majority. It describes the sectarian forms of Islam I experienced in Lyon and Hyderabad as no more than radical ideology, or "fundamentalism," en route to terrorism.[37] The preponderance of this type of thinking about Islamic movements has led to an explosion of efforts to dissect and understand Islamic doctrine and texts. Would-be "jihadists" have been caught with copies of *Islam for Dummies*.[38] In concentrating on cursory examinations of doctrine, these attempts to understand Islamic movements remove all social and economic conditions and specificities.[39]

Even scholarly literature that recognizes the diversity of Islamic movements, making distinctions such as "moderate," "radical," or "jihadi," overlooks the importance of secularism and class.[40] This literature collapses the complexity of what different movements hope to achieve, such as religious rights or material redistribution, instead assuming that revival movements all seek the same goal of making state and society more Islamic.[41]

By contrast, some literature on Islam and globalization attends to class inequalities. Some document how mosques and madrasas provide jobs, shelter, and welfare in the context of state retrenchment, which I saw clearly in Hyderabad (Toth 2003, 557–58; Turner 2003, 144; Vergès 1997, 295; Riesebrodt 1993, 194; Zubaida 1989). Others focus less on class inequalities and more on the cultural effects of globalization and migration. Most prominently, Olivier Roy (2006, 2004) argues that younger generations of minority Muslims in Europe are alienated from both the dominant culture and their parents' immigrant culture, leading them to a "neofundamental" form of Islam, specifically Salafism. This bears some resemblance to the community of Salafist women I observed in Vénissieux. But, regardless of whether the object is the cultural or class effects of globalization, these studies present a deterministic view of global economic changes. This determinism obscures the importance of class relations among Muslims in shaping Islamic movements. It cannot fully explain how different types of movements emerge across countries with similar forms of Muslim marginalization and dislocation.

Politics of Redistribution

The major players in the middle-class and elite politics of Hyderabad were the Majlis-e-Muttahadil Muslimeen (MIM) political party and private philanthropists. The MIM worked in opposition to the state to defend the material and religious needs of Muslims. Philanthropists advocated for reservations (affirmative action) from the state, but otherwise sought to maintain their autonomy.[42] These two groups competed for political legitimacy on the terrain of welfare distribution to subaltern Muslims. Their efforts included, above all, youth education and skills training for women but also health, banking, and advocating reservations for Muslims in education and government. In general, redistributive politics tend to de-emphasize group differences, but Hyderabad activists and elites firmly viewed political-economic redistribution as the remedy for injustice against Muslims in particular (Fraser 1997).[43] For this reason, I call their movement a politics of redistribution.[44] The object of their politics, however, was primarily welfare, not a fundamental restructuring of the economy.

These forms of redistribution were types of political patronage. Politicians and elites used distribution, through channeling of social funds or promises of jobs, to secure votes or build constituent networks. In academic literature, "clientelism" has been largely portrayed as corrupt, inefficient, or as a vulgar form of material exchange (Stokes 2007; Kawata 2006; Sandbrook and Barker 1985; Gellner, Waterbury, and Silverman 1977). But these judgments overlook the redistribution accomplished through clientelist networks, as well as the social bonds, identities, and cultural practices that congeal into the everyday political culture of the urban poor (Ansell 2014; Tarlau 2013; Gay 1998; Burgwal 1995). In his study of Peronist survival networks in an Argentinian shantytown, Javier Auyero (2002) argues that dominant, stigmatizing images of political clientelism obscure rather than clarify the workings of these political cultures. He labels such practices instead as "personalized political mediation" and "problem-solving networks of survival." Likewise, in Hyderabad, the long history of royal patronage shaped a culture of paternalistic giving that created networks of survival alongside attachments and loyalties.

Clientelistic redistribution is relatively common in societies with high income inequality, especially in postcolonial societies where state bureaucracies were imposed before the development of civil society and democratic institutions, and where colonial divide-and-rule tactics led to disadvantaged educated groups that had to struggle for representation in the bureaucracy (cf. Wimmer 1997). In today's neoliberal era, the deterioration of welfare has forced the poor to employ self-help methods to meet basic needs, lending greater significance to patronage (Auyero 2002).

Patronage operates on a foundation of class domination. Individual brokers and members of the elite ultimately seek to advance their own power (cf. Piliavsky 2014). Material "problem solving" reinforces the role of political authorities, who personally symbolize the benefits they distribute (Auyero 2002, 114). Politicians and brokers perform their love for the poor and their willingness to sacrifice for the welfare of others. This symbolic labor, as Auyero calls it, does more to secure the relationship between elites and the poor than the material benefits per se. These performances reproduce a particular political culture while masking domination. Yet patronage is not simply a static transaction between parties. Rather, it is part of the moral economy that underpins South Asian politics but remains poorly understood.[45]

In three principal ways, Islam was intertwined with the politics of redistribution in Hyderabad. First, part of the conflict between the MIM and other elites pertained to the extent to which they either politicized religious identity or put their efforts into redistribution politics. Second, for elites and middle-class activists, Islam provided the ethical foundations for their charitable work. Third, philanthropists made clear their desire for a liberal Islam, which they promoted through their paternalistic relationship to the poor, characterized by a combination of affection and disciplining.

Political Community

In some slum neighborhoods of Hyderabad, poor Muslim women in particular created what I call political communities. These were extraordinary politics in that their means and end were community rather than the state. The women involved in these projects possessed a radiance and optimism that infused their participation in women's training centers, neighborhood activism, Islamic study circles, madrasas, and women's conferences. Through these activities, women undertook a number of projects with material, legal, and symbolic goals. With the help of Muslim philanthropists, poor Muslim women and men built civil societies through their mosques, madrasas, and other institutions, reinforcing notions of community responsibility.

In all three dimensions of activity, community served as both means and end. Material projects included educational opportunities and women's self-employment training, in which women mutually supported each other. The legal project I observed used Islamic law and community ties to support women securing divorce from abusive husbands. It also included campaigns against the distorted marriage practice of dowry and its devaluation of women. Symbolically, women created value in the form of honor and moral community.

I argue that these three dimensions of practice—material, legal, and symbolic—are the foundations of belonging to a political community because they are key to building civil society. Inclusion in a strong civil society is a precondition of the fundamental right to citizenship, or the right to recognition as a moral equal. I derive this framework from Hannah Arendt's conception of citizenship as the "right to have rights" (Somers 2008; Arendt 1951/1979). Civil society, balanced between the state and market, requires material provisions (such as employment), legal mechanisms, and state supports to resist being conquered by the market or by the state itself (Somers 2008, 25–34). Communities build civil society through participation in material, legal, and symbolic projects.

The subaltern communities in Hyderabad claimed their citizenship and the right to have rights in a few different senses. First, ties of mutual trust and obligation sustained women's courage to enter the public realm, which historically they were unable to do. Individual women were able to reap material benefits from their participation, but their reciprocal obligations were also ends in themselves. In religious study circles, welfare activities, and mosque communities, they held each other mutually accountable. Whether financially or through prayers, they expected all members to contribute. Mutual reliance for material and spiritual needs required trust,[46] especially in interlocutors such as mosque leaders, women *alims* (religious scholars) who led study circles, and activists who guided their religious pursuits and educated them about social issues. The freedom and independence women experienced in acquiring education, skills, and literacy only took meaning through trust in local leaders and community bonds. Using Arendt's language, members made and kept "promises" to one another, and the power of those promises was superior to the freedom of individuals unburdened by community (1958, 244–45).

Contrary to depictions of Islamic movements and associations as incompatible with democracy, women and men mobilized their religious identification in ways that nourished and enforced democratic public spheres (see Calhoun et al. 2011; Bayat 2007). The liberal demand that religious arguments must translate into secular terms to participate in democracy in this case appears out of place (Rawls and Kelly 2001). Or more broadly, the line between religious and secular, when it comes to debating normative commitments, is far from clear (Taylor 2007).

The term "civil society" has particular connotations given its Western bourgeois and bureaucratic antecedents, its many exclusions, and its location as the site of struggle for hegemonic domination (Somers 2008; Eley 1994; Fraser 1990; Gramsci 1971). Here, I use the term to refer to the space between the state and the market that can protect citizens from domination by either the state or the market. This protection is exactly what these political communities consciously attempted. Through religious movements in Hyderabad, women in particular constructed a world outside their private selves, exercising citizenship.[47] They did so without making demands on the state and despite their increased adherence to gendered norms and interest in veiling.

Politics of Recognition

In Lyon, the middle-class Muslim community was actively involved in a politics of recognition. Muslim political and cultural organizations invited dialogue with the state, protested actions by the state, and held public events to raise awareness of Islam and of religious needs, such as the construction of mosques and the defense of women facing discrimination owing to wearing the headscarf. Competition within the field of Islamic associations was not as fierce as in Hyderabad, but activists in Lyon still disagreed over which path to take: working with the state toward recognition or engaging in radical critique of the state and rejecting the language of Muslim "integration."

The term "recognition" is complex. In France, it sometimes evokes American movements of ethnic pride and multicultural celebration, which have little value in French political culture. I use the term to refer to respect as a moral equal (which does not necessarily imply appreciation or celebration) and religious liberties granted by the state.[48] As Islamic groups struggle for greater religious rights, they are seeking to overcome their "institutionalized status subordination."[49] To participate as full members of society, Islamic groups must overturn the cultural values that constitute Muslims as inferior and dangerous, and that inform discriminatory policies and practices, such as blocking construction of mosques.

Nancy Fraser (2000) warns that recognition struggles face the pernicious problems of "displacement" and "reification." They displace redistribution struggles and reify simplistic group identities. This displacement of redistribution troubled the French Muslim activists who rejected the path of working with the state. They claimed this path led Islamic associations to neglect issues of class. I also found the hardening of religious identification to be a real problem in Lyon, to the point where the sectarian divide appeared as an insurmountable barrier to cross-class organizing among Muslims. In Hyderabad, by contrast—where Islamic beliefs and practices were just as diverse as in Lyon—activists mobilized Muslim identity toward social, economic, and gender justice. My participants in both cases identified strongly as Muslim, but this does not mean they necessarily saw themselves as sharing much in common with other Muslims. That is, they shared an "affinity and affiliation," but they understood the weakness of Muslim identity in terms of a "sense of belonging" to a "bounded group" (Brubaker and Cooper 2000, 19–20). The difference between the two cases is that in Hyderabad, people knew and accepted the substantive weakness of the category "Muslim," but nonetheless used it as a basis of mobilization in response to state violence and disadvantage. In Lyon, identities were more rigid and were experienced as insurmountable.

These problems of displacement and reification were not due to the spontaneous choices or mistakes of activists. Rather, they resulted from the structural conditions created by the state. Discrimination and structural barriers to everyday Islamic practice in France left middle-class associations with little choice but to focus on recognition. But middle-class Muslims in Lyon also mourned the absence of a redistributive agenda, finding their lack of relevance to and contact with working-class Muslims in the quartiers demoralizing and even spiritually upsetting. Their sense of identity and piety suffered as they struggled with their political project.[50] I argue that this dynamic sheds light on the relationship between the *material* moment of social justice (i.e., redistribution) and the *subjective* moment (i.e., recognition)—a relationship that theoretical debates tend to obscure by portraying the latter, dismissively, as identity politics.[51] Simply put, the absence of a redistribution struggle undercuts the fulfillment that recognition struggles, or identity politics, ultimately strive for.[52] The case of Lyon suggests that religious individuals feel this tension especially acutely. For my participants, true Islamic piety required struggle for social justice.[53] While France's young Muslims are often depicted as having an identity crisis, I argue that their crisis was less about self-definition and more about how to be true to their faith while facing discrimination and a state that cut them off from redistributive politics.

Antipolitics

The foundation for antipolitics in Lyon's banlieues was set by the absence of strong Islamic civil societies and major obstacles to economic stability. Communities of mostly Salafist women in the banlieues retreated from the state and from public institutions to carve out a space and set of activities to protect their faith. The differences between the antipolitics of Lyon's periphery and the political communities of Hyderabad's poor areas are striking. Instead of participating in social programs to confront poverty, women in the banlieues struggled with precarity and hoped only for salvation. In lieu of legal projects to improve women's welfare, there was a resignation to, or exodus from, the family. In the place of circulating new forms of honor, women searched for serenity in a life defined intrinsically by suffering.

Antipolitics consists of three components. First, women struggled to defend, expand, and reconfigure the private sphere against an intrusive state that sought to "protect" Muslim women in the French public sphere. In their defense of the burqa, for example, women viewed all matters of the self and body (along with family and intimate relations) as private, and claimed the practice as an integral part of their private sphere, though one that they must inherently practice outside the home (cf. Scott and Keates 2004). This assertion of the burqa as private directly countered the claims of the French state, which insisted that the burqa's presence in public space harmed society because it is anti-social and symbolizes sectarian loyalty. I argue that these women sought to de-territorialize the private sphere and define it more through social interaction than by physical space (see Dupret and Ferrié 2005). This glorifying of the private realm starkly contrasts to the Arendtian value placed on the concept of the public that characterized the political communities of Hyderabad.

Second, Salafist women retreated into "unorganized private life" (Konrád 1984, 204–206). Their antipolitics prioritized moral community among individuals as opposed to formal associations or institutions. State regulation and control of public life, from mosques to youth associations, led to a retreat into less organized communities. The *mosquées des caves* (basement mosques), provided spaces of informal religious gatherings in contrast to the more structured and visible larger mosques. As a form of unorganized private life, Salafist Islam in the banlieues operated through informal networks of friends. Decentralized and lacking clear leadership, it relied instead on teachers and sheiks.

Third, antipolitics emphasized spiritual conditions, truth, dignity, and inner states of being that could avoid the heavy hand of an overwhelming state. In seeking serenity and dignity, Muslim minority antipolitics was not about hope for the future but, rather, as George Konrád had written of East European antipolitics (1984), "respect for the present" (185) and "push[ing] the state out of our nightmares, so as to be afraid of it less" (230). This particular ethos contrasted to the forward-looking "world building" of the Arendtian political community.

The term "antipolitics" has been employed in a few different ways, most notably to refer to the depoliticizing effects of the development project (Ferguson 1990). My analysis of Salafist Islamic revival outside of Lyon is inspired by the concept of antipolitics that developed in the 1970s and '80s in the context of East European dissidence, whereby antipolitics referred to the rejection of state engagement in favor of the valorization of private life. Private life served as a substitute for democratic political participation (Renwick 2006; Goven 2000; Havel 1985; Konrád 1984). The movement was promoted and practiced by intellectuals and artists, and provided ideological momentum toward the reconstruction of autonomous civil societies. While there were different variants of antipolitics and dissident thought, in Lyon I found a radical version of antipolitics that rejected all forms of state engagement and actively rejected labeling as political (Renwick 2006). Hungarian writer George Konrád distinguished antipolitics from being "apolitical," arguing that apolitical individuals were merely "dupes" of professional politicians, the "young people who can always be brought out for parades" (1984, 227, 231). Antipolitics, in contrast, implies a degree of conscious opposition to the political realm. Likewise, Salafists in the banlieues were aware of their status and the politics that obstructed and denigrated their way of life. But instead of confronting the situation, they turned away.

Politicizing Gender

The women in this study had numerous concerns and interests; because these were not all about their role as women, the movements I describe are not exactly women's movements (Molyneux 1998). At the same time, because many Muslim communities practice some form of gender segregation, at minimum during ritual prayer, gender was an important part of the movements I studied. Women participated in different ways, and the consequences of these politics for feminist movements varied.

Both the French and Indian states have politicized Muslim women. So have Muslim communities themselves, as they debate and conflict over interpretations of veiling. As feminist scholars have argued, women are viewed as symbols of ethnic communities and nations (Radhakrishnan 2011; Yuval-Davis 1997; McClintock 1995); therefore, the struggle to define the nation and to define Muslim communities from within invokes the roles and practices of women.

The French and Indian states have targeted veiling and family law on the basis of security and in the name of women's rights. For at least two decades, these controversies have embroiled Muslim women. These topics are most fraught in France, where veiling is a frequent subject of national debates and women in headscarves or burqas face severe marginalization. In India also, local controversies over the burqa erupt on occasion. The main controversy there, however, remains whether to continue to allow shari'a in marriage and divorce matters.

Among Muslims in Lyon and Hyderabad, gender was the object of a cultural class struggle over liberalizing Islam. While I found disagreement across class on issues like the relationship between Islamic and secular education or the meaning and value of minority integration, the clearest point of conflict had to do with gender. It manifested in interviews, everyday conversations, and arguments that took place in the main city mosques and in Muslim schools, in the case of Hyderabad.

Notwithstanding the politicization of women by the state and other Muslims, women stood at the forefront of the Islamic revival in both Lyon and Hyderabad, increasingly wearing and defending the headscarf or other forms of veiling, leading mosque classes and teaching circles, and mobilizing along the lines of their identification with Islam. While sociologists of religion have long argued that women are more religious than men owing to various factors ranging from biology and gender roles to socialized risk aversion (see Collett and Lizardo 2009), I focus in this book on the local political and economic factors that placed women at the center of Islamic movements and made their participation personally meaningful. In doing so, I emphasize the intersection of gender with class.

Among my middle-class participants in both cities, men and women worked together in relationships of collaboration and mutual support.

I observed few barriers to gender mixing outside of religious ritual practice. In Hyderabad, middle-class men and women shared the redistributive
agenda of education and welfare. This was perhaps unusual in that in many
societies, women dominate positions related to welfare or social work, reinforcing maternal expectations (Rousseau 2009; Auyero 2002). Especially
in the school setting, I sometimes saw women enact an explicitly maternal role, but generally, both men and women shared a focus on social welfare. Likewise, whereas men tend to dominate leadership positions, some
middle-class Muslim women in Hyderabad had their own Islamic and welfare societies and private social welfare projects in rural and urban areas.
Women also participated alongside men as philanthropic board members,
teachers, volunteers, and in the case of the MIM party, neighborhood "corporators" or electoral candidates. Women and men together ardently supported feminist discourses about education, literacy, and income-generating
opportunities, and advocated that poor Muslim women delay marriage. In
supporting and leading such projects, they also disciplined their poorer
sisters and brothers by critiquing the burqa and other gendered practices.
Elite women's own veiling practices varied from none to a hijab, and many
practiced the custom of sometimes lightly draping a scarf (orni or dupatta)
over their hair. Somehow, it was clear that elite women were exempt from
the types of practices that subaltern women rarely questioned.

In Lyon, too, middle-class men and women worked cooperatively in
recognition politics and in running mosque activities. In terms of veiling
practices, women had an immense and colorful variety of dress and hijabs,
but the rules appeared stricter than in Hyderabad in terms of properly
covering the neck and hairline. And unlike in Hyderabad, I heard little
debate about the role of women or the larger need for gender justice.[54] One
of the main concerns of middle-class Muslim women in Lyon, however,
was the problem of finding a good marriage partner. In France, women
faced such pressure from discrimination that religious rights outweighed
other concerns, including gender justice within their community. Nearly
every young woman I knew shared a story of employment discrimination or harassment against herself or a close friend—not getting hired,
getting fired, being told they had to stop wearing their headscarf to keep
their jobs, and being interrogated as to why they chose to veil. They also
complained that the courts generally refused to assist them. In addition,
because middle-class Muslim women in Lyon interacted little across class,
I observed no cross-class debates about the status of women.

Among my poor and subaltern participants, an extensive practice of
gender segregation meant that men and women worked together only

minimally in both Hyderabad and Lyon. But the two cases had inverse dynamics. In Hyderabad, subaltern men assisted women's political communities and tried to protect the community's autonomy from the state. Men were excluded from local educational and welfare projects that benefited women, and women's centrality developed alongside subaltern Muslim men's social dislocation. A significant percentage of poor Muslim men escaped poverty through work as migrant laborers in Gulf countries (Rao and Thaha 2012; Ali 2007). Their wives and female relatives were left behind to manage the home and play a role in local community efforts, including building political communities. Men were marginalized in the local economic sphere, while women gained empowerment through political community and entering the public sphere.

In Lyon's banlieues, working-class Salafist men were as withdrawn from politics as women. But while the women were estranged from the world of education and formal employment, men turned to small enterprises and developing business networks (Amghar 2011). Lyon's working-class Salafist men worked together to establish an economic base and provide for their families while women turned away from such activities and from the public sphere altogether.

What is the impact of the different politics and their gender dynamics on the potential for feminist movements? While the French state made gender hypervisible, within Muslim communities themselves, recognition politics and antipolitics rendered gender invisible. In Lyon, the absence of cross-class dialogue, in addition to the state's hostility, diminished people's willingness and desire to have conversations around gender or the need for gender justice. Contrast this to Hyderabad, where gender was visible from above (from the perspective of the state and elites) and below (from the perspective of the subaltern), and political communities laid the foundation for feminist projects with the help of middle-class and elite Muslims. To be clear, I am not implying that poor and subaltern women need spiritual or moral edification from their middle-class sisters. Nonetheless, middle-class activists might offer material resources as well as hope. My subaltern participants made this explicit to me, as a middle-class, educated researcher.

Conceiving Politics

Far from seeking a unified goal of "Islamizing" state and society, Islamic movements take different forms, and these forms imply different possibilities for gender relations and for social justice. The forms I observed in Lyon and Hyderabad illustrate the difference between instrumental and noninstrumental politics—the difference between trying to obtain something from the state and trying to enact a form of public life as an end in itself. Each has its own goals and normative stakes.[55]

The middle-class movements I describe are partially directed toward the state and are thus a form of politics in its most traditional sense (Weber 1946). In their articulation of demands for recognition and redistribution, they invoke Nancy Fraser's conception of politics as a practice of claims-making, articulated along these two axes of justice (1997). Such politics are instrumental in that they seek institutional inclusion or resources from the state. But among poor and subaltern Muslims, their collective desires and goals are not oriented toward the state. In the case of Lyon, my participants withdrew from politics entirely, while in Hyderabad, they embraced a noninstrumental vision of politics, as they created community and bonds of reciprocity as ends in themselves. This type of politics, in Hannah Arendt's unconventional use of the term, is about creating community and transcending individual selves. It is superior to the instrumental goal of securing material or legal concessions from the state.[56]

Distinguishing between these two dimensions of politics as focused on either state or community—or instrumental versus noninstrumental—allows for a sharper but expansive view of what politics is and can be, in contrast to the dominant conflation of Islam and politics *tout court*. It also departs from recent literature on piety movements, which argues that Islamic revival is inherently political because it shapes individual subjectivity.[57] Subjectivity in turn shapes public space and political desires, to which the state is forced to respond. With in-depth ethnographies, taking seriously people's pious practice and desires, this scholarship has accomplished the important work of taking on orientalist conceptions of Islam. But for societies where Muslims are minorities, this theoretical perspective needs unpacking. The literature's conflation of piety with politics coincides with the view of the state, but not the view of many Muslims.[58] Analytically, it becomes difficult to distinguish between a private and public (political) sphere if all life activities that shape subjectivity have political effects. What are the limits of these effects in a secular, non-Muslim country? If everyday practice itself is made political, either willfully or by the force of the state, there is no private domain that religious minorities can discuss or defend.[59] In the French case, it is precisely the politicization of pious practices like the headscarf and the curtailing of the private sphere of faith that produced antipolitics and the social disempowerment of Muslim women. Rather than taking the perspective that everyday Islamic practice is inherently political, I instead address politics as either an instrumental practice of making claims of the state or a noninstrumental practice of community. The potentiality and limits of both types can then be examined in all their specificity and nuance.

Ethnography Across North and South

Between 2005 and 2014, I conducted a total of two years of ethnographic fieldwork in Lyon and Hyderabad, traveling back and forth between the global North and global South. The method was global ethnography in that I was looking at the effects of global forces, as well as people's global connections.[60] I used a cross-class design in each city to see how Islamic revival differed across class and to look at the places most politicized in public discourse for sectarian radicalism.

In addition to ethnographic fieldwork, I conducted thirty-nine in-depth interviews with mosque activists and leaders, madrasa teachers, Muslim working-class and slum residents, politicians, Muslim philanthropists, and Islamic association leaders. I list the details of these interviews in appendix B. Unless noted otherwise, I have changed the names of all individuals and mosques in Lyon and Hyderabad, as well as the names of neighborhoods in Hyderabad.[61]

I arrived in Hyderabad in the fall of 2005 and rented a flat in the New City. I soon connected with Muslim elites, Mr. Haq, Mr. Akbar, and Mr. Husayni, who introduced me to their numerous women's training centers and educational projects in low-income areas and slums. Through them, and eventually MIM workers as well, I gained a broad overview of the political field and access to poor enclaves in the Old City. Alongside spending time with them in the local Muslim philanthropic world, attending their board meetings, and witnessing conversations in their headquarters and press offices, I visited their schools in slum neighborhoods throughout the city on multiple occasions. Several times a week, I visited Mr. Haq's women's training centers, some of which also shared space with madrasas. At these centers, I took a spot on the floor with the women, observed their work in tailoring and other skills, and talked with them for many hours. Occasionally, they held graduation ceremonies and board appreciation ceremonies, which I helped them organize. I interacted with over a hundred poor women at these centers and developed close relations with five young women.

In total, I visited centers in eight different BPL areas in the Old and New Cities, but the centers where I spent the most time were Zohra Bagh, a BPL enclave at the border of the Old City, and Faiz Nagar, one of the poorest neighborhoods in the Old City notorious for crime, trafficking, and terrorist sleeper cells. The Faiz Nagar center housed a private primary school for Muslim children from the area, funded by Mr. Haq. In Zohra Bagh, I regularly visited with Nasr, a civil rights activist, whose family ran a school, a girls' madrasa, and a neighborhood Islamic study circle for women. His home was also connected to a women's training center. I spent time with three activists who worked with him and participated in the Islamic study circle every week, coming to know approximately twenty women in the group. Once a week, I also participated in the Al Muminoon study circle, a middle- and upper-class women's Islamic study circle that met for Quranic and hadith explication. This gave me insight into elite women's Islamic teachings and political conversations. I also met several times with women members of the Jama'at-i-Islami Hind (JIH) and attended their weekend regional conference.

I connected with a third neighborhood through Rahman, my regular auto-rickshaw driver. Shanthi Colony, Rahman's neighborhood, is a predominantly Muslim slum area oddly located inside the New City. I regularly went into Shanthi Colony, spending time with residents and Anwar, the leader of a mosque I call Masjid Arabiya. Rahman also introduced me to local activists with the MIM party, whom I visited several times. Figure 1.1 provides a layout of the city and shows the enclaves where I spent the most time.

Unlike in India, in France, women freely access mosques, so mosques served as my principle point of entry into the field. In 2006, I arrived in France and made connections to a mosque in Lyon by attending the annual conference of Muslims in Le Bourget, outside of Paris.

Mosquée Hijra was situated in a municipality adjacent to Lyon. It welcomed a vibrant and relatively young community, and its leaders had years of experience with various Islamic associations. I attended special events, prayers, and evening Arabic classes at the mosque, where I came to know activists and a community of women who held leadership roles. Some of these activists worked at Tawhid, an Islamic bookstore in downtown Lyon that had recently begun hosting Islamic classes.[62] Of these members, I became close with four women and seven men.

Residents' suspicion of outsiders posed an immense obstacle to access to mosque communities in the working-class quarters in the banlieues. Through trial and error, I joined a community of Salafist women in Les

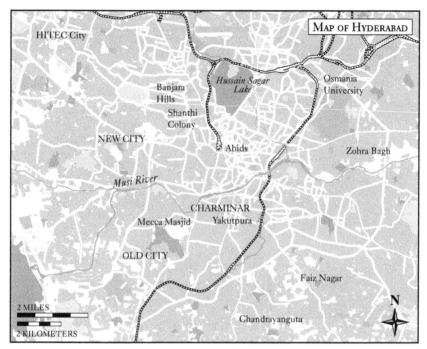

FIGURE I.I Map of Hyderabad.

Minguettes in the town of Vénissieux. Two to three days each week, I commuted from Lyon to Vénissieux to Mosquée Ennour and mostly Mosquée Hasan, where I attended prayers and took informal classes. I also studied Quranic recitation with women in their apartments in Les Minguettes or a nearby working-class neighborhood. I became close with five Salafist women and came to know many others throughout the fieldwork. I also became close with two working-class Muslim men from the banlieues, spending many hours in conversation with them in public places, such as parks and halal sandwich shops. Figure 1.2 of the Lyon agglomeration shows the location of Les Minguettes in relation to downtown Lyon.

I spent the majority of my fieldwork hours among women. In both sites, they call each other some variant of "sister" in the local language (*soeur* in French, *oukthy* in Arabic, *baji* in Urdu, and *apa* in Urdu). Gender segregation limited my ability to achieve the same depth of observation among men, especially among low-income communities. Ultimately, I was able to develop close relationships with both women and men in all settings. I refer to these principal participants and others with whom I regularly spent time as my research "companions," following Teresa Gowan's (2010, 9) lead in

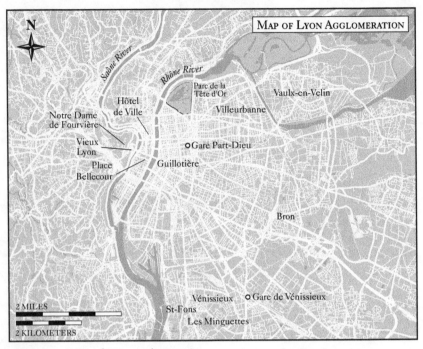

FIGURE I.2 Map of Lyon agglomeration.

her ethnography of homelessness in San Francisco. The standard terms of "subjects" and "participants" better describes the short-term transactions of survey methods while the anthropological term "informant" is laden with connotations of surveillance and breaching trust that I wish to avoid.[63]

I worked to embed myself in the communities I studied, dressing as my fieldwork companions did, including veiling. Since veiling practices varied across my field sites, I sometimes wore a burqa (with niqab), often a hijab, sometimes a light scarf (orni), and sometimes did not cover my hair.[64] I discuss the inconsistency of my veiling practices as well as the challenges of the fieldwork related to my crossing boundaries of class, nation, and, above all, epistemology in appendix A.

A final discussion on methods involves my use of the term "class." As I distinguish my observations among middle-class and elite Muslims from those among the poor and subaltern, it is useful to have a sense of the main class positions in these cities. In Hyderabad, the distinguishing characteristics of individuals I describe as upper and middle class included home ownership; ownership of consumer goods such as cars and jewelry of gold and precious stones; employment of servants and/or domestic workers; and some family household member(s) with higher education. The Hyderabadi elites I present owned multiple properties and had philanthropic projects and political connections. Some very wealthy families lived in palatial homes in the Old City, and many affluent Muslim women married young and did not pursue higher education, thus minimizing the significance of neighborhood and education. Elites also constituted a status group in the sense that they enjoyed social esteem and an awareness of themselves as part of the city's Muslim elite. On the other end, the poorer classes of Muslims rented small homes in neighborhoods officially designated as BPL, reported struggling to meet monthly expenses, had parents or spouses working menial labor and informal jobs, and generally did not complete secondary schooling. They typically lacked consumer items like cars and refrigerators, and some lived in makeshift housing. Subaltern location in Hyderabad also had an obvious subjective element: low-income Muslims saw themselves clearly at the bottom of the social structure (see Wright 2004, 717).

In Lyon, middle-class and poor or working-class Muslims were similarly situated in relation to capital, which they did not own. The primary characteristics that differentiated their life chances (Weber 1978, 302) were place of residence, education, and access to employment. Unlike in Hyderabad, where wealth inequality dwarfed the significance of neighborhood, in Lyon, neighborhood mattered a great deal. Residents of Les Minguettes suffered the stigma and extremely high unemployment rate associated with the quartiers. My participants and companions generally engaged in domestic work and caretaking, and they found even these job opportunities limited. Those in middle-class neighborhoods were more likely to have finished secondary education or some university education and to have stable jobs. Finally, while some successful individuals of Muslim origin had a presence in French politics, entertainment, athletics, or business, I was not aware of a unified or significant wealthy, Muslim-origin elite or status group (Leveau and Schnapper 1987, 870–73), though statistics point to the integration and upward mobility of many Maghrébins.[65]

Overview of the Book

Politicizing Islam disentangles the common conflation of Islam and politics. It offers a more refined understanding of Islamic revival movements, especially those judged as fundamentalist, contributing a new perspective on the politics of Islam in secular states. By providing a cultural class

analysis, it brings attention to the central role of class relations, which previous work has largely neglected. Middle-class Muslims and elites mobilize and politicize Islam to challenge the state's discriminatory policies,
focusing on redistribution in Hyderabad and recognition in Lyon. Poor
and subaltern Muslims politicize Islam in Hyderabad to promote community and women's education, while in Lyon's banlieues they practice antipolitics in the struggle to defend and reconfigure a private sphere, or to
protect the sacred from the profanity of politics. The relationship between
religion and politics is therefore contingent. The following chapters provide an analysis of the conditions under which religion is politicized to
think through the meaning and implications of different forms of minority politics in a post-9/11 world.

Chapter 2 focuses on the histories of French and Indian secularisms
and situates Lyon and Hyderabad within these trajectories. It analyzes
the contradictions of secularism that laid the foundations for the marginalization of Muslims and, consequently, the politics of Islamic revival
movements. These contradictions find their origins in British and French
colonial administration, which constructed Muslims as a homogenous
religious group despite their immense diversity. In both cases, Muslims
were largely segregated and suffered disproportionately the upheavals of
economic crises as the nationalist right wing in both countries steadily
gained strength and targeted Islam specifically. Ultimately, France resisted
the integration of Islam and treated it as an exception to its secular doctrine, while India embraced it to the point of reifying religious identity.
The secular model each state pursued determined the types of political
claims Muslims would make, as well as the possibilities for them to forge
an identity and movement across class.

Chapter 3 delves into the redistributive politics among middle-class
and elite Muslims in Hyderabad, showing the struggles between the MIM
party and philanthropists. While both were disillusioned with the state, or
even viewed it as nefarious, they conflicted over what kind of relationship
they should foster with the state and whether to mobilize Muslim identity
among the poor. They competed fiercely, sometimes violently, for political
legitimacy, and this competition in turn politicized the welfare of Muslim
women. The second half of the chapter explores the respect that elites
gave to the poor in the women's training centers and schools, a heartfelt
performance of symbolic labor to secure their relationship, alongside the
paternalistic discipline they imposed on these same women that stemmed

from their own culture of poverty thesis. As they disciplined poor and subaltern Muslims, they tried to enforce a more liberal Islam that "stays in the heart."

Chapter 4 looks at poor and subaltern Muslims in Hyderabad, highlighting how small mosques and madrasas enforced a sense of collective responsibility to preserve Islamic institutions and support the community's welfare. I examine how men and women participated differently in community projects before focusing on the political communities of subaltern women. Intertwined with religious teachings and movements, in political communities, women strived for independence through mutual reliance, exercised legal empowerment through community, and subverted their dishonor by creating alternative forms of honor. I argue that their political communities built civil societies and cultivated a desire to practice citizenship.

Chapter 5 turns to the French case, examining how middle-class Muslims in Lyon participated in recognition politics. As they faced everyday obstacles to Islamic institutions, lifelong discrimination and racism, and educational setbacks, recognition politics had deep emotional resonance for middle-class Muslims. They chose one of two paths: to either work cooperatively with the state or to radically critique the state and the agenda of recognition. This choice marked the main point of tension within the field. The second half of the chapter focuses on the post-9/11 disconnect from working-class Muslims in the quartiers. Activists acknowledged this detachment and attributed its persistence to the growth of Salafism. But they also regretted it deeply, seeing the abandonment of the quartiers as fundamentally impious.

Chapter 6 presents the movement of antipolitics in the working-class banlieues of Lyon, where individuals led precarious everyday lives and worked more for their salvation than any collective project. I discuss how Salafist men participated in neighborhood life while women retreated from the public sphere, and I describe how rediscovering Islam provided a turning point for men and an alternative to drugs and prison. The chapter then focuses on women's antipolitics, whereby women strived to protect the private sphere given the recent history of surveillance, the decline of civil society, and bans on veiling. Estranged from schools and uneasy in public space, they tried to form a moral community and placed utmost importance on achieving serenity as part of their work toward a perfect faith.

The book concludes by discussing the implications of these movements for social justice, deep democracy, feminist struggle, and the
War on Terror. I hope this book will succeed in reversing the common
understanding of the relationship between Islam and politics in secular
contexts; rather than seeking to Islamize the state, many Muslims have
actually retreated from the state.[66] I hope also that the commonly asked
questions, "Why do they hate us?" and "When will they have a liberal reformation?" will be replaced by broader questions about the potential for
social transformation and justice.[67]

2

Secularism and Muslim Marginality

THE ISLAMIC MOVEMENTS I observed in Hyderabad and Lyon emerged out of the contradictions and crises of secularism and the extreme economic dislocations of minority Muslims in both India and France. Hyderabad and Lyon are microcosms of their countries' larger political and economic histories. The broad trajectories of Islam and Muslims in both countries and cities reveal several common themes. Each state crafted its relationship to religion in general, and Islam in particular, as a central part of the process of building the nation (and empire). The construction of Muslims as a homogenous group was born out of colonial administration and attempts to secure elite privileges. This categorization eventually produced the instability, disproportionate poverty, and social exclusion of Muslim communities in both countries. And in recent years, right-wing nationalism gained power in both France and India by exploiting the rhetoric of secularism and targeting Muslims as the source of the nation's urban and economic problems.

In France, after disestablishing the Catholic Church, the secular state eventually came to accept and support Catholic institutions on "cultural" grounds. Islam, however, was tied to France's imperial ambitions and therefore was treated as the exception to *laïcité*'s rules of engagement. Colonial logic and administrative practice followed North African immigrants who traveled to France for work, implementing their designation as Muslims and their segregation in public housing. While immigrants had lived and worked in industrial zones, the economic crisis of the 1970s subjected them to extremes of unemployment and xenophobic violence. Although an immigrant activist movement took hold in the 1980s, the social distance between the few Maghrébi elites and poor residents in the banlieues weakened the movement. In the 1990s, political debates started

targeting Islam, conflating religious activity with problems of employment and urban marginality, while encouraging the integration of Islam
in a top-down fashion. Women's veiling took center stage in the state's
relationship to Islam, as the state increasingly called into question the
national loyalty and belonging of minorities.

In India, the anticolonial movement valorized religious traditions in the
struggle for independence from the British. The newly independent nation
defined its secularism as composite nationalism: the equal preservation and
facilitation of all religious communities.[1] Protecting Muslims in the new state
was central to these political debates. But in the process of defining "minority–
majority" communities, the low socioeconomic status of many Muslims was
dismissed, and their concerns were detached from issues of caste and class
"backwardness." This was built upon a longer history of British administrative practices of census enumeration and fixing the boundaries of communities. The Partition of the subcontinent in 1947 saw an exodus of Muslims to
Pakistan, the loss of Indian Muslim professionals, and severe political-economic dispossession of many who remained in the country. Despite eventual recoveries, Muslims are still disproportionately poor and marginalized.
In terms of rights to religious practice, the state has generally protected
their community rights, although right-wing Hindu nationalists periodically
threaten them. The profound shift to the right in Indian politics and society
in the contemporary period has led to tragic episodes of anti-Muslim violence,
which in turn have shaped the trajectory of Islamic movements.

To summarize, the contradictions of secularism laid the foundations
for the marginalization of Muslims and, thereby, the politics of Islamic
revival movements that would develop. In the French case, *laïcité* in theory
should have guaranteed state neutrality and the privatization of religion.
Instead, Islam was never allowed to be a private affair of the community
or to be supported as a cultural tradition, and Muslims were treated as
foreigners in need of special treatment and control rather than as equal
citizens. In the Indian case, composite nationalism sought to preserve
communities and social harmony, but the reification of religious identities
ignored the extreme material inequalities that lurked within "communities," exacerbating the deprivation and marginality.

French Secularism:
From Disestablishment to Laïcité

The early secularization in France was intended to overturn the economic
and political power of the Church and its Catholic clergy (Baubérot 1998).[2]

In the *ancien régime*, prior to the French Revolution, the monarch ruled by "divine right" and profited from the backing and legitimacy of the Roman Catholic Church. The revolutionary zeal of the late eighteenth century was driven in part by the need to wrest the state apparatus from the Church. The Church did not depend on the state, which had an incoherent administrative structure, but, rather, controlled its own fiefdoms and possessed numerous legal and political powers. The Church wielded immense wealth: in 1788, 130,000 clergymen possessed a full third of the country's wealth (Weil 2007, 10). In the years following the Revolution, from 1800 to 1804, a series of decrees in the French civil code disestablished the Church, and various decrees in the nineteenth century eliminated religion from public institutions.[3]

The revolutionary imperative to disrupt the Church's power marginalized religion itself. Republican ideological fervor supported a strong anti-clerical and anti-religious culture among certain classes and led to the suppression of religious congregations. In nearly every province, anti-religious sentiment clashed with the conservatism of faithful Catholics (Bowen 2007, 23). French elites and important Enlightenment writers like Voltaire and Rousseau asserted religion's incompatibility with modernity (Kuru 2009, 138). Diderot famously wrote, "Men will never be free until the last king is strangled with the entrails of the last priest."

The principles of French secularism, *laïcité*, were put into law in 1905, though the French constitution would not officially incorporate them until 1946. *Laïcité* emphasized state neutrality and the elimination of religion from all public institutions in favor of civic culture. The main principles were freedom of conscience, separation of church and state, and the free exercise of religion (Weil 2007, 16). The 1905 law passed after contentious debates as to whether *laïcité* should apply to colonized Muslims and as to the status of the German region, Alsace-Moselle.[4] Because the law forced the Church to hand over all its properties to "cultural associations" of laypeople, clergy and activists demonstrated in large numbers, and protests in several regions turned violent. As conflict ensued, religious congregations lost their right to free association, and religious institutions were shut down and prevented from teaching (Baubérot 1998, 115). Supporters of *laïcité* targeted the cultural realm and everyday life. Their hostility toward the religious establishment and its will to exclude religion from the public sphere became deeply rooted in France's political culture.

Yet *laïcité* did not fully live up to the principles of state neutrality, or of the separation of state and religion. In time, the state found ways to support Catholic institutions. In 1959, the Debré Law resolved the longstanding conflict between Catholic schools and supporters of religion–state separation by allowing state financing of private schools as long as they accepted students of all faiths and met a number of curricular requirements.[5] Since 1908, the vast majority of Church properties have been state-owned and have been able to benefit from public funds (Bowen 2007, 27). Because of legal accommodations, demands for public funds for church restoration are no longer controversial. Public funds are now used to support the restoration of churches and municipal "cultural" (formerly religious) structures as historical and cultural sites (Perrin 2007). The state also pays the salaries of chaplains (and now imams) in prisons, hospitals, and the army (Weil 2007, 16). Catholic "culture" thus merits preservation and protection from the state, though state–church conflicts still occur, such as with the availability of contraception in the 1980s (Baubérot 1998,121).

According to Raphaël Liogier, in France, "interference in religion by public authorities is the norm rather than the exception" (2009, 25). "If one goes deeper, it soon becomes obvious that the history of laïcité by no means took its cue from a movement towards separation, but was imbued from the start with a particular administrative mindset, one of control and public valorization/devalorization of religious phenomena and groups" (26). Beneath the façade of neutrality, the state intervenes in religious organizations and has a history of policies that favor some faith groups over others. For over a century, the state has exploited legal loopholes in order to create, finance, shape, and ultimately, control religious institutions. The state even defines the boundaries of religious groups; the Conseil d'État, a state body with many juridical functions, determines eligibility for the status of religious association. State definitions of religion or religious tenets are not typical in secular countries.

Islam as the Exception

In recent decades, the French state has broadly accepted Catholic institutions, and since the 1970s, the state has provided broad support for Jewish integration.[6] Islam, on the other hand, has faced a more difficult path, largely because France historically exploited Islam to support its imperial ambitions (Frégosi 1998).[7] When laïcité was instituted in France, officials decided to not apply the law in Algeria, to avoid undermining imperial legitimacy (Weil 2007, 3). Though officials desired the spread of laïcité as part of France's civilizing mission abroad, they applied it unevenly across the empire. French officials viewed Islam as a regressive force that kept Muslims chained to religious dogma and daily, embodied rituals (Davidson 2012; Achi 2007, 243). But rather than remove Islam from the political realm, France tried to control it. When Algerians demanded state secularism as part of their opposition to colonial rule, the colonial state declared *laïcité* and Islam incompatible—based on a notion of Muslims' inherent inability to live under a secular system. To avoid empowering anti-colonial organizations, the state opted to maintain its control of Algerian Islam, funding and intervening in religious property and institutions. It made Islam an exception to *laïcité* in the early years by funding institutions like La Grande Mosquée de Paris. The state proudly created separate social assistance services, including medical care, specifically for "Muslims" in the metropole, thereby legitimizing segregation in the guise of religious sensitivity (Davidson 2012).

France used an orientalized understanding of Islam as a lens and tool to manage its North African colonial subjects, overattributing Muslim identification and practice to enormously diverse societies.[8] This colonial view of North Africans, with its mix of surveillance and benevolence, left its mark most dramatically on French housing policy. Colonial rule had produced brutal ruptures in the Algerian economy and the proletarianization of Algerian workers, who began migrating to the metropole. Though some migrated even prior to World War I, most came after World War II and through the 1960s, responding to the need for labor in France (Sayad 1984).[9] Immigrants, including those from Portugal, Italy, and Spain, had long been organized in factory towns built around heavy industry. This produced the widespread segregation of immigrant zones of work from commercial and intellectual centers (Noiriel 1988/1996, 130). In certain cases, employers grouped immigrants into precise zones according to ethnic criteria—despite official government discourse that objected to ethnic categorization. In 1975, only 17 of 300 immigrant housing "dormitories" were multi-ethnic (Diop 1988, 78). The segregation of Algerians, in particular, was even more extreme.[10]

In the immediate postcolonial period, the state tasked the Interior Ministry (police services) with welcoming Algerian workers and providing housing and social assistance that followed the logic of colonial order (Kawar 2014; Viet 1998, 188–89). In the colonial era, government committees were formed to assist Algerian workers. Into the 1940s, they had charge of not only securing spatial order but also of curbing Algerian tendencies toward "cabaret" and other immoral activities. After Algerian independence, in terms of housing management, colonial administrative categories were simply imported to France, where officials continued to designate Algerians as *Français musulmans d'Algérie* (Dikeç 2007; de Barros 2005; Noiriel 1988/1996, 145, 186–87). Indeed, the colonial administrative corps, struggling to preserve its legitimacy in the aftermath of Algerian independence, converted its previous role into that of managing housing for all foreigners in France (de Barros 2006, 2005). This cadre of "experts" on Muslim affairs, the Conseillers Techniques pour les Affaires Musulmans (CTAM), had been attached to the Ministry of Interior and was responsible under colonial rule for separating Algerians from Europeans while controlling Algerians and promoting French mores. The CTAM existed until 1966, and was a powerful force in constructing Algerian Muslims as an ethnic group, leaving their imprint on housing policy and the broader structures of immigration into the 1970s (de Barros 2005, 28–31).

As a result of their categorization as *musulmans* (and eventually, "Maghrébins"), Algerian families, among all immigrant groups, were the most segregated into low-income housing, known as HLM (Habitation à Loyer Modéré). Though numerous government reports tried to promote ethnic integration (*mixité sociale*) in HLM housing in the 1960s, this goal remained elusive (de Barros 2005; Sayad 1984, 187). Algerians, more than any other group, were consistently treated and classified as foreigners and as Muslims despite their long history and knowledge of secular France (Hargreaves 1995/2007, 192–93; Sayad 2004, 141–43). Clearly, French secularism and Republican ideals were rife with contradictions that would lead to the contemporary crisis of secularism.

Economic Crisis and Immigrant Activism

The explosion of unemployment in the 1970s profoundly shaped the social and political trajectory of Maghrébi immigrants. The economic crisis that began in 1973 with the Gulf oil embargo "traumatized" the immigrant population, subjecting it to new forms of precariousness and racism (Courtois and Kepel 1988, 34). Between 1970 and 1984, the number of unemployed Algerians multiplied tenfold, from 8,000 to 80,000, such that the unemployment rate among French Algerians was 25 percent, two and a half times the national average (Sayad 1984, 129, 145). Unemployment exacerbated tensions within immigrant families, including a loss of paternal authority and regret over the decision to emigrate. Since the crisis, many Algerian families suffered great precariousness, periods of return to

Algeria, insufficient schooling, and informal sector work (Zehraoui 1999, 280–87).[11] In 1973, the French government temporarily suspended all immigration because of the crisis, and the Algerian government stopped emigration to France in response to episodes of xenophobic violence against Algerian workers. The late 1970s and early '80s saw heightened anti-immigrant violence. This period marked the development of xeno-phobic activism and the rise of the French right wing.

Partly in response to the popularity of the right-wing party, Le Front National (FN), French immigrant-rights activism flourished in the 1980s (Dikeç 2007, 58–59). After the election of the socialist government in 1981, legislation allowed foreigners to form associations, which facilitated the *"beur* movement," named after a slang term for the French-born children of North African immigrants.[12] While immigrant activism in the 1970s was generally limited to labor struggles, this second phase of activism focused on anti-racism and discrimination. Second-generation immigrant activists, working closely with mainstream and media-savvy associations like SOS-Racisme and France Plus, tended to dominate the movement.

Immigrant activism enjoyed an intense but short-lived era of vibrancy. Despite the *beur* movement's prolific cultural productions, its lack of struc-ture and tenuous bonds with mainstream associations contributed to its decline. Disappointment with SOS-Racisme's assimilationist ideology and attitudes toward Middle East politics led to rifts between associations. Less-educated activists in the poorer banlieues felt that the major *beur* and other organizations did not represent their needs (Baillet 2001, 165–67, 199, 282). Indeed, a wide social distance separated Maghrébi elite leaders from most working-class residents in the housing projects. Only 10 per-cent of the children of Algerian immigrants who arrived in France prior to 1975 achieved middle-class jobs (*professions intermédiares*). The few who had access to higher education generally had parents who spoke French and had arrived in France with urban or property-owning backgrounds. They also managed to avoid public schools and, importantly, their parents had enough capital to leave HLM apartments to buy houses in residen-tial areas (Geisser 1997, 79–81). Although such elites supported Maghrébi activists in the banlieues, at least superficially, they remained disconnected from Islamic practice and religious community leaders. Community lead-ers viewed such elites as *Arabes de service*—co-opted by political parties and inadvertently legitimizing the notion of an Islamist threat in the banlieues (Geisser 1997, 151–63).[13]

Laïcité and Islam, 1990s to the Present

After Maghrébi residents' permanent settlement in France became clear in the late 1980s, debates over *laïcité* dramatically shifted to limiting the public visibility of Islam. To this end, municipalities systematically obstructed or delayed the opening of mosques (Frégosi 1998: 118–120). But increasingly, the state has reluctantly approved and facilitated Islamic institutions, especially as it seeks to intervene and regulate community needs.[14] It uses legal loopholes when required, and in some exceptional cases has manipulated the boundaries of private and public in order to allow, for example, a Muslim section of a cemetery. On occasion, the central government has stepped in to dismiss local opposition to Islamic institutions. Clearly, French secularism is not monolithic but, rather, represents a dynamic process that is transforming with changing social realities.

Despite these shifts, Islamic leaders and activists view the controversies and inconsistencies around Islam as replaying colonial tactics and attitudes.[15] For example, the state generally demands centralized and "representative" interlocutors and institutions, which are not supported in the Islamic tradition. In 2003, President Nikolas Sarkozy instituted the Conseil Français du Culte Musulman (CFCM) to constitute the primary centralized body of Muslim representatives that negotiates with the state on policies toward Muslims. It consists of members chosen by the state in spite of perfunctory elections; for many, its structure of appointed ministers and leaders is reminiscent of colonial rule (Bozzo 2005; Frégosi 2004). CFCM frequently touts the positions of the state, including the 2009 endorsement of a national commission to debate the burqa (niqab). It eventually stopped short of endorsing the anti-niqab legislation that the National Assembly passed in 2010, but it maintained the position that the niqab is not an Islamic practice.[16]

Targeting Muslim women's veiling has preoccupied the state in its management of Islam.[17] While colonial interest in Muslim women's veiling has a long history, the state's recent politicization of veiling unfolded alongside a crisis over the very conception of Europe and the European Union (Berezin 2013). In the midst of such uncertainty, the burqa symbolized a violation of French citizenship. In 2008, the Conseil d'État (Council of the State) upheld a ruling denying citizenship to a Moroccan woman married to a French citizen on the grounds of her wearing the niqab. Her veiling practice was taken as a sign of her "failure to assimilate" and her rejection of the values of the Republic.[18] It was the first time religious practice was used to refuse nationality.[19]

During the same period, Eric Besson, the minister for immigration and national identity, launched town hall conversations on the meaning of French identity. The initiative was widely considered a failure because it stigmatized immigrants and minorities by questioning whether citizens and residents of immigrant background were loyal to France. Social science researchers also devoted serious effort to exploring this question and found that in various ways, most individuals do "feel French" or "feel at home" in France (Simon 2012).[20] While this field of study generally endeavors to normalize Islam and lessen the stigma applied to immigrants, it inadvertently reinforces the idea that minorities bear a special responsibility to articulate something as private as one's emotional attachments and belongings.

In addition to repressive legislation and accusatory national discourses, hundreds of incidents of anti-Muslim violence and mosque vandalism have occurred since 2010 (Blua 2013). Various sources report an increase in cases every year. These include physical assault, cemetery desecration, vandalism, and right-wing militant plans to gun-down mosque worshipers. The most disturbing acts increasingly involve violence against veiled women. A 2013 set of incidents in Argenteuil, northwest of Paris, involved beatings of several Muslim women. One of the victims, a twenty-one-year-old, suffered a miscarriage immediately after the attack. A spokesman for the Collective Against Islamophobia in France (CCIF), stated: "Unfortunately, we see a banalization of certain ideas from the far right that are being spread in much more conventional parties and that are then taken by average citizens who act in terms of discrimination, insults, and, unfortunately, physical aggression."[21] Anti-immigrant violence is certainly not new in France. The 1973 murder rampage that killed at least fifteen Algerians in Marseille is a grim reminder of this fact.[22] But what is perhaps newer is the use of specifically anti-Muslim symbolism such as vandalizing with pig blood and pig remains, Quran burnings, and the specific targeting of veiled women.

The "banalization" of ideas from the far right, or the "normalization of the right" (Berezin 2013), has real consequences for Islam and *laïcité*. After the 2014 European elections, le Front National (FN) gained control of eleven municipalities, including a district in the city of Marseille. As one example of its use of *laïcité*, Marine Le Pen announced in 2014 that the party would seek an end to pork-free lunch menus in school cafeterias. Unlike socialist and UMP (Union pour un Mouvement Populaire) mayors, Le Pen declared, her party would proudly ensure the "application of *laïcité*." Muslims have a long history in France of requesting accommodations for things like dietary restrictions and prayer space, and although these issues always caused contention, such requests were not framed as violations of laïcité per se.[23] This particular political discourse emerged only recently, indicating how the right-wing agenda has become normalized. Muslim activists disagree with this framing, presenting their claims not as opposing laïcité but as invoking principles of freedom of worship and association without state interference. Increasingly, Islamic associations declare their support for laïcité in terms of these ideals using a specifically Republican language based on individual rights, thus creating a uniquely "French Islam" (Bowen 2010).[24]

Conflating Urban Marginality with the Problem of Islam

While the practice of Islam in public was becoming framed as a violation of laïcité, the media started presenting urban marginality in the banlieues as a problem of Islamism. Maghrébi immigrants in the banlieues continued to grapple with unemployment and labor market discrimination, even as the second-generation middle class made great strides toward upward mobility. By the 1980s and 1990s, those of Maghrébi origin had fully entered into public spaces, housing, schools, and social services. Some immigrants assimilated into French society after family reunification, with relatively high intermarriage rates and school success (Tribalat 1995). Today, the majority of Maghrébi immigrants and their descendants do not live in precarious neighborhoods in the banlieues or les grands ensembles (complexes of buildings with at least 500 apartment units), cheap housing built in designated zones in the 1960s. However, their rates of poverty and poor housing conditions far surpass those of native-born French citizens and those of other immigrant groups.[25] Table 2.1 summarizes some of the salient features of the living conditions and poverty rate among Maghrébi immigrants, using figures for European immigrants as comparison.

Spurred on by the economic crisis of the 1970s, the FN began to manipulate public opinion toward seeing immigration as a threat to national identity (Berezin 2009; Noiriel 1988/1996, xv). The successes of the FN coincided more broadly with the fragmentation of the working-class and the decomposition of working-class territories (Wacquant 2008). These were amplified by changes in the political/electoral field that shifted the overall terrain to the right. At the same time, the decline of the left-wing media and left-wing parties allowed for new media tactics that encouraged French nationalism.[26] According to Noiriel (2007), the media created links in the public's perception between such disparate phenomena as the wars

Table 2.1 Comparison of Living Conditions between Maghrébi
and European Immigrants

Living Conditions	Region of Origin	
	Maghréb (%)	Europe (%)
Residing in "sensitive urban zones"	27	6
Residing in public housing with many immigrants*	19	5
Residing in "uncomfortable lodging"[†]	42	17
Renting "dilapidated housing"*	26	10
Below poverty line	43[‡]	24

Sources: Observatoire national des zones urbaines sensibles (2011); Jauneau and Vanovermeir (2008); Lombardo and Pujol (2007); and Simon (1998).

Notes: Figures for Turkish and sub-Saharan African immigrants are generally higher than for those of Maghrébi immigrants. None of these figures includes the descendants of Maghrébi immigrants, though they live in ZUS at roughly the same percentages.
*Includes only Algerian, Moroccan, Portuguese, and Spanish immigrants.
[†]"Uncomfortable lodging" was defined either by overpopulation or by a number of indicators, from plumbing and heating conditions to square footage.
[‡]The 43% figure includes all African immigrants. The estimated probabilities of being poor for Maghrébis versus black Africans are the same (Lombardo and Pujol 2007, 42–44).

in the Middle East, Islamist terrorism, and juvenile "delinquency" in the French banlieues. Young French Maghrébins were equated with Islam, violence, crime, and sexism. By the 1990s, a virtual right–left consensus emerged that no politician could win an election without denouncing *Islamisme* and *communautarisme* (Tissot 2006).

These trends coincided with the first Gulf War, the war in Algeria, and other events that FN supporters seized upon to politicize any trace of religiosity among youth in the working-class banlieues (Baillet 2001, 74–77). People of North African descent were perceived through the lens of Islam, regardless of their identification with Islam (Béatrix 1988, 90). The banlieue thus morphed in the 1990s from an administrative concept to a "journalistic category" (see Wacquant 2008; Dikeç 2007, 7–8, 72–79) that now stood for the violence of young Maghrébi men *and* the problem of Islam's supposed incompatibility with Republican values.

Government policy reports throughout the 1990s acknowledged that the primary concern in the banlieues was not religion but simply the desire for jobs and better schools. But plans for job creation mainly involved tax concessions to businesses and were unsuccessful (Dikeç 2007, 104–105).[27] New laws for the expansion of low-income housing met local resistance, as neighborhood adminstrators preferred to pay fines rather than provide housing for immigrant communities. Meanwhile, unemployment continued to increase (Dikeç 2007, 112–16).

As attempts at job creation in the urban peripheries remained unsuccessful in the early 1990s, the question of urban violence fell under the purview of the Intelligence Service (Renseignements Généraux) and the Ministry of the Interior. The categories of urban violence and "sensitive neighborhoods" (les quartiers sensibles) breathed new life and legitimacy into the Intelligence Service, marking the beginning of intensified surveillance and tracking (Dikeç 2007, 81). Several new laws aimed at security in the 1990s were followed by increased police powers in the post-9/ 11 years, culminating with the 2015 state of emergency declared after the ISIS attacks in Paris.[28]

Situating Lyon

The city of Lyon has been a major site of these developments in laïcité, Islam, and the poverty and exclusion of immigrants and their descendants. In the early years of laïcité, a solid network of supporters, secular intellectuals, and "militants" flourished in Lyon, eager to make the city a "laboratory" for secular culture. The election of Mayor Edouard Herriot in 1905 dramatically strengthened the cause of laïcité, as he encouraged numerous associations and activities to foster Republican values of free thought and liberty. These included festivals and celebrations, especially among youth. Secular education, sports, and the arts were all promoted as part of the campaign to support laïcité and shape citizenship (Dessertine 2007; Dessertine and Maradan 2001).

Lyon was also the second most important hub for immigration after Paris (Grillo 1985, 30). North Africans made up over half of all foreigners in the Rhône region in the 1970s and were concentrated in the working-class banlieues, where they were employed in heavy industry. For example, in 1975, North Africans constituted the majority of foreign workers and over one-fourth of semi-skilled workers (ouvriers specialisés) at the Berliet-Renault automobile factories, a major employer in Vénissieux (Grillo 1985, 37–38). With the economic crisis, jobs in Lyon's banlieues suddenly declined, replaced to some degree by part-time positions. In Vénissieux alone, seven companies shut down between 1975 and 1982 (Belbahri 1984,

108n3). In terms of housing, Algerians were concentrated in HLM housing more than any other immigrant group (Grillo 1985, 93–94). But they also faced greater difficulty finding coveted HLM apartments by the mid-1970s, as HLM buildings surpassed the "threshold of tolerance" for foreigners of 5 to 15 percent that was being implemented (as described in Grillo's ethnographic study of Lyon). Finally, in education, the system tracked the vast majority of North African children toward working-class jobs (1985, 170–71). As one schoolteacher in the eastern banlieue of Vaulx-en-Velin described to Grillo: "Many [especially North Africans or Portuguese] can't wait to reach sixteen to leave, and we can't wait until they are sixteen to get rid of them" (173).

The combination of social exclusion, unemployment, and police violence against Maghrébi youth led to the creation of an immigrant rights movement in the 1980s.[29] A crucial event in raising national consciousness was the 1983 Marche pour l'Egalité et contre le Racisme, dubbed by the media as "Marche des Beurs," France's first and largest national demonstration for immigrant and racial justice. The march was initiated in Les Minguettes following a series of rebellions in the neighborhood that erupted when police injured a local teenager.[30] The moment following the march marked the beginning of the *beur* movement, which thrived in Lyon.[31]

As the political terrain shifted from immigrant rights to Islam, Lyon's banlieues again were an important center of advocacy. One of the first second-generation Maghrébi associations to identify itself as Muslim, rather than *beur* or anti-racist, was founded in Lyon in 1987. The Union des Jeunes Musulmans (UJM, or Union of Young Muslims) had similar social welfare activities in the banlieues as other associations, but it emphasized piety and critiqued the *beur* movement for its distance from and embarrassment of Islam (Fernando 2014, 39–40). Lyon's banlieues became closely associated with Islamist terrorism following the 1995 Paris Metro bombings that killed eight people and injured more than 100. The bombings were organized by the Algerian GIA (Armed Islamic Group) and led by a resident of Vaulx-en-Velin.

HOW DID THESE historical developments lead to the forms of politics I observed in Lyon? These politics grew from the legacy of anti-religious sentiment that developed alongside disestablishment of the Church and the contradictions of *laïcité*. These contradictions would construct colonized North Africans as a homogenous group of Muslims unsuited to a secular political system and as violating *laïcité* with their *communautarisme* and disloyalty to the nation. French Muslims were placed in an impossible set of situations. On one hand, the state upheld a façade of state–religion separation, while on the other hand, it routinely intervened to set the very contours of religion. From these contradictions has grown a recognition politics in Lyon that aims to secure the equal respect, freedom of worship, and freedom to define Islamic traditions from the ground up that secularism should have guaranteed.

The continuation of colonial ethnic grouping in the management of housing and social welfare, combined with the assault of deindustrialization, segregated many North African immigrant families while concentrating economic insecurity and social exclusion in their communities. Despite these obstacles, by several markers, Maghrébi migrants achieved integration and forms of success, including the production of a middle class. But when immigrant activism emerged in the 1980s, the few existing Maghrébi elites remained disconnected from both working-class activists and those who identified more closely with Islam. Today's second and third generations are perhaps even more distanced from Maghrébi elites as civic activism has declined. In contrast to their predecessors from the 1980s, they are further removed from earlier leftist struggles, more likely to face long-term unemployment, and more engaged in Islamic practice, according to some researchers (Baillet 2001, 176–77, 287–90; Zehraoui 1999, 302). They are also more likely to be stigmatized as Muslims because of international events, including the Algerian civil war and the rise of ISIS. They live in the aftermath of the failure of the *beur* movement's demands for integration. In neighborhoods like Les Minguettes, economic dislocation, the collapse of civil societies, repressive legislation, surveillance, and a hardening of class bifurcation laid the groundwork for antipolitics. Given the region's history and contemporary conditions, a turn away from the state, from the middle class, and from the activism of the 1980s and 90s appears logical and inevitable.

Indian Composite Nationalism: Protecting Communities and Securing Privilege

Indian secularism unfolded under the unique conditions of national independence from the British in 1947. There was no *ancien régime* to parallel the structure of the Catholic Church in France, notwithstanding the existence of a Hindu religious upper caste and powerful Muslim ulema.[32]

Neither Hinduism nor Islam had a centralized authoritative body, so historically the Indian state provided important structures to manage religion. Yet the relationship between temples and the state was based on patronage rather than control (Copland 2010; Bayly 1983). The British continued the system of patronage practiced by the Mughal dynasties, but eventually abandoned it in favor of broad neutrality. But the long history of patronage was such that even atheistic political parties participated in the exchange between religious institutions and the state in the postcolonial period (Rao 2006). The stigma applied to religious figures that became so prominent in France never emerged in India, where decentralized religious spaces and individuals generally depended on the state and there was no centralized hierarchical religious authority.

The nationalist struggle led to the valorization of religious tradition in India. Gandhi appealed to Hindu identity and morality in the anti-colonial cause as powerful symbolic resources (Rao 2006, 51). His reverence for religion and his insistence on the principle of *sava dharma samabhava* (the equality and truth of all religions) provided a moral foundation for Indian nationalism, even if many of his contemporaries did not share these sentiments (Parekh 1991). Indian secularism was not a fight against religion or religious authority but, rather, a pragmatic approach to maintaining relations among diverse religious communities.

These diverse communities did not emerge *sui generis*. Instead, they were defined through a particular history that contributed to the contemporary politics around Islam. Communities became defined in terms of "minority–majority" relations, beginning with the colonial administration and elite manipulation of a society otherwise characterized by immense heterogeneity (see Hansen 1999). The British initiation of a census in 1871 fixed the boundaries of religious communities and heightened awareness of both caste and religious identity. The salience of caste in turn energized an incipient Hindu nationalism. Even when the British stopped enumerating castes in 1931, the effects were imprinted; Indian politics would henceforth be seen as a competition between numerical communities.

In 1909, with the Morley-Minto Reforms, the colonial government created separate Muslim electorates and reservations, officially constructing Muslims as a political entity separate from Hindus. The placement of Muslims into an administrative category solidified the identity as an axis of mobilization in a political field defined by patronage: any individual seeking patronage had to do so in the name of a bureaucratically recognized category. Self-appointed Muslim leaders claimed to represent the community and competed for political posts and privileges. Within a short period of time, the British colonial state and self-appointed Muslim leaders managed to construct a distinct Indian Muslim *community*, dismissing immense differences across region, everyday religious practice, sect, and language. By the time of Indian independence, the Muslim intelligentsia actively manipulated religious identity to avoid the real, material concerns of most Muslims. Although Muslim industrialists and elites were generally not religious, their fieldworkers used religious propaganda in the years leading to Partition (Hasan 1997, 87). The patronage prospects of the educated classes thus drove the "communalization" of Indian nationalism (1997, 47–49).

During the independence struggle, the principles of Indian secularism, or composite nationalism, developed explicitly to guard against majoritarianism and preserve the integrity of religious communities. Composite nationalism originated in Gandhi and Prime Minister Nehru's determination to protect the rights of Muslims in the post-Partition independent states. With Indian independence and the creation of Pakistan, Hindu nationalists began vehemently campaigning for a Hindu state. The Constituent Assembly debates at this time took place amid epic communal violence, forced evacuation of Indian Muslims, and suspicion of even those Muslims who rejected the idea of Pakistan. In response, Nehru's belief in a secularism that protected minorities became even more resolute (Ahmad 2009, 17–18).

Composite nationalism thus emerged from the embers of impassioned debates about caste, class, religion, the future of the postcolonial nation-state, and the violence of Partition. In contrast to *laïcité*, composite nationalism allows legal pluralism and seeks to preserve community rights and equal facilitation of religious practice in public and in private. The doctrine of legal pluralism allows every religious community to abide by religious laws in "personal" matters like marriage, divorce, adoption, and inheritance. Religious minority recognition also occurs through state funding of certain religious activities, such as subsidies for Muslim pilgrims, affirmative action policies for Muslims (that were recommended in 1979 but have only been partially implemented), and holidays. India has one of the highest numbers of public holidays in the world, thanks to minority religious recognition (Alam 2007b, 48; Rao 2006, 59). From one perspective, the Indian Constitution reflects classical liberalism, with its prohibition of discrimination based on ascriptive identities. At the same time, accommodation policies demonstrate how the Constitution sought to preserve community rights. This unique blend of individual and community rights marks the fundamental tension in Indian secularism (Parekh 1995; Madan 1993).[33]

Just as *laïcité* in the French case was never exactly about the separation of state and religion, composite nationalism in India was not directed exclusively toward the preservation of communities. Rather, it also was a process of securing privilege through caste and religious grouping. This happened through a definition of minority and majority groups. While leaders in the nationalist cause understood that minorities would require state protection, the questions at the time of independence (and to a large extent, today) were who constitutes a minority and what should be the scope of protection (Tejani 2008, 244). Until the Constituent Assembly adopted the Constitution in 1949, the signification of minority status had very little clarity (2008, 244). Prior to Partition, in the regions of Bengal, Sindh, and Punjab, Muslims were numerically dominant. Yet in the midst of nationalist politics, India's Muslim population was constructed as a unique threat to secularism and as a special minority group, rather than as fundamentally constitutive of the nation. What clinched the definition of secularism and minority–majority relations in India was the official separation of caste from religious considerations, which occurred with the 1946–50 Constituent Assembly debates (Tejani 2008, 235–36).

The counting of castes made clear to upper-caste Hindus that their numbers were relatively small and that their power in a future Indian state would be precarious. Motivated by a desire to maintain hegemony, they campaigned for a pan-Hindu identity that would absorb the lower castes. Around the same time, the Muslim League started lobbying for its own interests. Initially, the question of political recognition for Muslims was tied to debates about the Dalits ("depressed classes"). An emerging Dalit leadership argued that if Muslims constituted a separate electorate or deserved special protections, this should also apply to Dalits. But if Dalits and Muslims were both treated as separate groups from Hindus, upper-caste Hindus would become a minority. For Gandhi, politically recognizing Dalits would fracture the Hindu community, as well as foreclose the possibility of one day transcending caste. He famously undertook a week-long fast at Yerwada jail in protest of Bhimrao Ambedkar's struggle for political recognition of Dalits. The creation of an electorate for Dalits was defeated precisely because nationalists did not wish to divide the Hindu electorate. They instead absorbed Dalits into a pan-Hindu identity, preventing a Muslim–Dalit axis (Tejani 2008, 14–15). After Partition, the needs of Dalits became a question of social "backwardness" and were no longer connected to the needs of Muslims.

As a result of these debates about caste, class, and religion, as well as prevailing desires to achieve the universal citizenship of Western liberalism in the new nation, Muslims became defined only as religious minorities who were guaranteed freedom of worship. They would not receive special protections beyond religious rights because doing so would violate secularism and the ideal of universal citizenship, even though several members of the Assembly argued that what counted as universal was in fact particular (Tejani 2013). Accordingly, the Assembly created reservations for "backward classes" to the exclusion of religious minorities—despite the fact that most Muslims were poor and suffered discrimination. Several Census operations showed that approximately half of the Muslim population shared the same occupational groupings as lower-caste Hindus.[34] The process of correcting this exclusion of Muslims began only in 1979 with the Mandal Commission, which was established by the leftist Janata government to redefine "backwardness" and increase quotas for those who met the indicators. The commission declared eighty Muslim groups, or half the Muslim population, as backward based on occupational groups and lineage. It sanctioned reservations for these groups, but left the quota percentages to the states, few of which properly implemented the commission's recommendations (Hasan 2007, 23–24). Affirmative action policies for Muslims were thus stalled.

Exodus and Displacement

With independence and Partition in 1947, India lost much of its Muslim industrial and professional class in the exodus to Pakistan. Peasants and artisans lost their patrons (Sikand 2004), and the majority of India's remaining Muslim population hailed from the rural poor and urban proletariat (Hasan 1997, 8). Amid great confusion and refugee movement, authorities used accusations of Muslims' disloyalty to justify their forced migration. Thousands of Muslims who went to Pakistan to visit relatives returned to India to find their properties confiscated and homes occupied. "Evacuee" ordinances passed in a state of emergency legalized and facilitated their internal displacement and dispossession (Zamindar 2007). The government lifted these ordinances in 1954, but in the case of Delhi, for example, government records of ancestral homes were destroyed, making it impossible for Muslim families to reclaim their homes (2007, 122).

Scholars of India have provided various additional explanations for the decline of Muslims in the post-Partition era. The absence of business traditions among Muslims compared to other minority groups prevented gains in industry, and job discrimination against Muslims surpassed even the discrimination against Dalits. Above all, many scholars accuse the state of deliberately undermining progress and failing to implement policies, such as the promotion of the Urdu language spoken by many Muslims, that might have mitigated their displacement.[35]

Today, nearly half the Muslim urban population lives below the poverty line, compared to approximately one-third of Hindus. Muslims have low access to government welfare projects and almost no representation in major industrial enterprises. They work primarily in unorganized sectors, are underrepresented in the police force, and have achieved only about 5 percent representation in Parliament (Engineer 2007, 16, 241–50; Hasan 1997, 281–83). Table 2.2 provides salient social indicators vis-à-vis the Hindu population. Although rates of poverty, illiteracy, and child labor among Hindus are also dismal, Muslims fare significantly worse on most social indicators.

One of the significant factors that allowed many Muslim families to build some wealth and relieve their poverty has been remittance money from work in Saudi Arabia and other Gulf countries. The Middle East oil boom of the 1970s effectively had the opposite effects in India as in France, opening new markets in the Gulf and creating migrant employment opportunities (Gayer and Jaffrelot 2012).

Table 2.2 Comparison of Social Indicators between Muslims and Hindus

Social Indicators	Religion	
	Muslim (%)	Hindu (%)
Illiteracy rate	31	27
Workforce participation	33	41
Percent of workers aged 5–14	4	3
Children, aged 6–14, who dropped out of school or never enrolled	25	15
Below poverty line (urban only)	44	27

Sources: Ministry of Home Affairs (2011, 2001) and Sachar Committee (2006).

Note: Although the former state of Andhra Pradesh performed better than other states, Hyderabad district tends to reflect national trends. Illiteracy rates are percentage of population aged 7 and older.

Community Rights as Stable but Insecure

Muslims as a group have suffered economic inequality, but the state generally has protected their rights as a religious "community." Specifically, the state protected Muslim Personal Law even in periods when it came under attack. The Indian state refrains from interfering in religious or theological matters, leaving such debates to their respective religious communities. This also means that the state has never demanded a Muslim representative body. The All India Muslim Personal Law Board (AIMPLB), an NGO created in 1973 to defend Muslim Personal Law, acts as a self-appointed representative body that influences relevant judicial rulings in the country. Yet its political influence has been highly problematic because its leadership has excluded women and different sectarian communities. In response to this problem, Shia Muslim leaders formed their own Personal Law board, as did a group of thirty Muslim women leaders. In 2005, this group of thirty women formed the Muslim Women's Personal Law Board to defend shari'a and participate in its application to cases pertaining to women (Subramanian 2008, 656–57).

The state's noninterference has also produced tensions within women's movements seeking legal justice for Muslim women. This crystallized during the 1986 Shah Bano legal controversy, in which Islamic law came under attack and debates ensued over Muslim women's rights to alimony payments in cases of divorce. The case culminated in Muslim women's exclusion from postdivorce maintenance rights (through the Muslim Women's Bill), representing a major concession by the Congress Party to conservative Muslim leaders. Rather than instate a Uniform Civil Code that would override the customary practices of Muslim Personal Law, the state upheld legal pluralism and protection of community. In siding with self-appointed male Muslim leaders and institutions, such as the AIMPLB, the state supported the right of the "Muslim community" to practice its own laws, especially those regarding women and family. The polarization between those who supported legal pluralism and those on the Hindu right who advocated a Uniform Civil Code left little room for more nuanced debates about Muslim women and Islamic laws (Agnes 1999). Nonetheless, though the Shah Bano verdict presented a serious setback for the women's movement, Muslim women have used the bill's language to secure lump-sum alimony payments as required by Islamic law (Agnes 1999).

In addition to upholding Personal Law, the Indian government has supported minority institutions, even against opposition from the public and sometimes even from Muslims themselves. For example, in 2005, the Uttar Pradesh state government and central Congress Party government approved a 50 percent quota for Muslims at Aligarh Muslim University (AMU). AMU was established prior to independence and maintained its legal status as a minority institution, though from its inception it welcomed all potential students regardless of religious background. When the quota decision passed, controversy erupted over the "communalism" of AMU. But the government justified its financial support of the university by pointing to AMU's status as a minority institution. (The Indian Constitution allows state support of minority institutions.) This did little to quell popular and right-wing opposition, not to mention opposition from Muslim faculty members who found the quota unnecessary and demeaning.[36] The current Modi government, however, has called into question the status of AMU as well as of Jamia Millia Islamia University, once again threatening to undermine historically Muslim institutions.

The AMU quota clearly demonstrates how Congress and left-led governments promoted systems of reservations, but these remain insecure as the Hindu right casts them as "communalism" and argues that they violate secularism. With the rising tide of Hindu nationalism, minority claims have been increasingly suspect and interrogated. Overall, reservations in public universities and jobs have followed an incoherent trajectory.

Failed Secularism, 1990s to the Present

Many scholars agree that secularism in India has failed, or at best is in crisis, citing the steady and dramatic rise of Hindu nationalism, communal riots, and atrocities carried out against Muslims. To be sure, some scholars still defend India's secularism on the grounds of the legal protections it provides for religious minorities. Bhargava (2011) argues that Indian secularism has successfully maintained a "principled distance" from particular communities by intervening in substantive ethical questions of domination while otherwise maintaining a stance of noninterference. In contrast, for Bilgrami (1994), secularism has failed, largely because of Nehru's refusal to allow secularism to take substantive form through active communal negotiations around ethical questions. He argues that Indian secularism was nothing more than a "holding process."

Bhargava's positive evaluation of Indian secularism and its comparison to Western models relies mostly on the *ideal* of secularism. The Indian ideal has always been essentially flexible, with "porous" boundaries between state and religion precisely because managing social and religious diversity requires different policies for different contexts. Even for Bhargava, it is not clear that the Indian state or society has lived up to the ideal. From the perspective of the left, the Hindu right eroded secular democracy in tandem with the state, which came to play an active role in Hindu–Muslim riots and even supported right-wing networks in some instances (Ahmad 2009, 232). The 1998 election of the BJP-led coalition made Hindu nationalist ideology part of the state apparatus, and the 2014 landslide victory that brought Prime Minister Modi to power shifted the political center of gravity toward the Hindu right (Sridharan 2014; Needham and Rajan 2007). The state's acquiescence to the 1992 destruction of the Babri Masjid at Ayodhya (Ahmad 2009, 232) and the 2002 pogrom of Muslims in Gujarat tragically symbolize the failure of Indian secularism.

At the popular level, serious "communalization" has taken hold among educated, middle-class Hindus (Engineer 2007, 17). Ordinary middle-class citizens justified the persecution of Muslims in Gujarat in a "new politics of violence and intolerance" (Menon 2007; Pandey 2007, 174). Hindutva educational campaigns, revisionist history, and efforts to erase social difference in India (Prakash 2007) circulate through television and other media (Thapar 2007, 203; Rajagopal 2001). Since Gujarat, the communal situation has remained tense and unpredictable.[37]

The nationalist turn in Indian politics provided a foundation for the post-9/11 surveillance of Muslims. In the post-9/11 years, the government made plans to modernize madrasas, monitor their funding, and bring them all under the jurisdiction of the Ministry of Human Resources. In 2002, the Prevention of Terrorism Act (POTA) accepted self-confession as proof of guilt and allowed 180-day detention without specific charges (Singh 2007). The state eventually repealed the act, but Hindu nationalist organizations campaigned for its reinstatement (Engineer 2010, 117; Alam 2007a). POTA, like preceding legislation, was used distinctively to target minority communities (Singh 2007). With or without anti-terror legislation, following nearly every suspected terrorist incident, the police have conducted sweep arrests of lower-middle-class Muslim men, obtained confessions through torture, and held arrestees without granting bail (Engineer 2010).

Islamic Movements in Defense of Composite Nationalism

Despite the growth of Hindu nationalism and surveillance, Islamic religious parties are among the staunchest defenders of composite nationalism in contemporary India. They have been compelled to respond to Hindu nationalists' criticisms of secularism, which are intended to undermine Muslims. Some Hindu nationalists have fomented hostility toward the concept of composite nationalism, arguing that Hinduism is itself fundamentally tolerant and that a Hindu nation has no need for the Western concept of secularism (Rao 2006; Varshney 2002). The BJP, for example, notoriously argued that secularism only panders to Muslims and has prevented their assimilation, which would otherwise occur in a Hindu nation true to its ideals. Other members of Hindutva defend secularism and accuse supporters of Muslim protection as "pseudo-secularists" (Chatterjee 1994, 347). In their view, pure secularism would not allow special consideration for minorities. As Chatterjee (1994) points out, the Hindu right is not really against secularism—rather, its interest lies simply in using the power of the state to oppress Muslims.

Islamic organizations and activities have grown in response to Hindutva ideology. Political Islam and Islamic reformist movements have a long history in India that includes several shifts in focus from supporting Indian democracy to rejecting all politics outside of shari'a, to resignation to Hindutva domination (Osella and Osella 2008). Some of these organizations once advocated total separation from the state, but later came to politically defend the status of Muslims and composite nationalism.[38]

JIH in particular, which has hundreds of thousands of sympathizers, underwent a major transformation since its founding in 1941. JIH's founding constitution called for an Islamic state. Its leader, Syed Abul Ala Maududi, declared secularism *haram* (sinful) and promoted a boycott of all secular, government institutions. Over time, this position fell out of sync with the vast majority of Muslims and with the growing political organizing of the Hindutva movement. When the RSS began promoting the idea of a Hindu state, JIH switched its position to passionately defend secularism. No longer concerned with an Islamic state, it sought an intercommunal coalition to fight Hindutva campaigns (Ahmad 2009). The ultimate symbol of such transformations was the Islamic seminary, Darul Uloom Deoband's recent fatwa urging Muslims to vote as part of religious obligation (Engineer 2010, 84).[39]

While some organizations have sought mainstream political participation, others have turned against the state in response to the growth of Hindutva. The Students Islamic Movement of India (SIMI), for example, began calling for jihad, arguing that secularism was a fraud if the state could not protect Muslim lives (Ahmad 2009). Its radicalization was a direct response to the Babri Masjid campaign. The Indian government banned SIMI in 2002 during the advent of heightened surveillance of Muslims and Islamic institutions, arbitrary arrests, and police raids.

In response to and in spite of Hindutva and state surveillance, Islamic revival movements have flourished. Madrasas have proliferated, educating anywhere from 4 to 30 percent of Muslim children; Muslim associations have grown, and widespread interest in greater piety has developed. There is also a growing sense of surrender to a communalized government and a focus instead on the Muslim community's economic activity and autonomy (Alam 2007a, 140–41). The failure of Nehru's secularism has reinvigorated Islamic movements and has shifted politics away from the state.

Situating Hyderabad

During the colonial period, hundreds of princely states in the Indian subcontinent enjoyed a semi-sovereign arrangement with the British Crown. Hyderabad was the largest and wealthiest of these, ruled by a succession of Muslim princes given the title of Nizam.[40] At independence, the Nizam refused to meet the conditions of surrender to the new Indian government, leading to the forcible annexation of Hyderabad.

Prior to the independence movement, Hyderabad had been a stable feudal order that functioned almost entirely on the basis of the Nizam's patronage. The Nizam's government, known for its courtly culture and decadence, recruited immigrants of all classes and skill levels from the north of India and from Iran, central Asia, Arabia, and sub-Saharan Africa (O. Khalidi 1988, xi). It welcomed a steady stream of immigrants from North India after the 1857 uprising against British rule, and an additional influx of hundreds of thousands of migrants at the time of Partition, even as Muslim elites left en masse for Pakistan. This migration abruptly ended and reversed itself when India annexed the state in 1948. Following the violence of annexation, the Congress Party, representing the Indian state, succeeded in defeating the pro-Nizam army.[41] According to Theodore Wright, the Congress and the Majlis-e-Ittihad ul Muslimeen (MIM) party, which had formed years earlier to defend the Nizam's rule, wound up colluding to suppress a growing communist movement among both Hindus and Muslims (1963, 132–36). Within a year, the previous feudal order and its populist resistance were replaced by a new administration that would dramatically dislocate Muslims.[42]

Prior to annexation, the Nizam's government owned 50 percent of the capital invested in the state's main enterprises. Half of the state's population, including Muslim artisans and peasants, depended on some form of state patronage. The upper ranks of government and army officers were predominantly Muslim, while lawyers, businessmen, and other professionals were mostly Hindu (Smith 1950, 3). With the state's dissolution, Muslim administrators and military men were expelled and left unemployed. The new state overhauled the formerly Urdu educational system and legal apparatus, leaving educated Muslims who remained in the city with few employment options. These upheavals produced massive unemployment and destitution. A 1962 survey revealed that former state employees constituted nearly a third of the city's rickshaw drivers, and in 1956, 48 percent of the street beggars were Muslim (Khan 1971, 151). Although former Hyderabadi elites were not all reduced to pauperism, most struggled to navigate the new competition and political rule. They spent many years thereafter "wallowing in grief and nostalgic for the bygone era" (Hasan 1997, 182–83).[43]

Despite the bleakness of their poverty, Hyderabad's Muslims eventually formed new political coalitions to deal with the consequences of their losses following Partition. Notwithstanding the many forms of discrimination against them, India's democratic framework allowed them to claim a share in the country's political structures (Hasan 1997, 188, 219). Some Muslims who lost their wealth after Partition were able to build on family and political connections to again become prosperous, and a significant number of descendants of feudal landlords also built upon their family wealth (Hasan 1997, 8; U. Khalidi 1988, 193–94). Many middle-class Muslims who remained in Hyderabad hid their religious identity in order to become civil servants and attain executive positions (Ahmed 1985, 181). And in the 1960s, young men who built capital as entrepreneurs in Pakistan began returning to the city. In recent years, a new Muslim middle class emerged in Hyderabad, primarily among artisans (Engineer 2007, 105).

Labor remittances are arguably the most influential factor creating consumer affluence and allowing hundreds of thousands of families to subsist in Hyderabad's poorer Muslim neighborhoods (S. Ali 2007). The former state of Andhra Pradesh (AP) received the highest amount of labor remittances to India in the early 2000s ("AP Tops in NRI Remittances," 2006) and in 2013 surpassed all other states in sending migrant labor to Gulf countries.[44] The majority of remittance money goes to family maintenance, but a small but significant percentage goes to charity. Remittances have played a major role in the expansion of philanthropy among Hyderabad's Muslims, a phenomenon I argue is central to local politics and Islamic movements. A small but wealthy Muslim elite continued the Nizam's tradition of philanthropy in the Old City and slums of Hyderabad using private money and shrewd management of Islamic trusts (*wakf*) to fund schools and assist poor families (Kozlowski 1998, 294–95).[45] These elite philanthropists are driven by a keen nostalgia for the courtly culture of the Nizams and the "splendors" of the Old City (Luther 2006; Ahmed 1985, 185).

The MIM party competes with local philanthropists for legitimacy as the representative of the city's Muslims. After Partition, the MIM took on the role of protector of dislocated Muslims (Hasan 1997, 273, 295), helping to define the city's political terrain.[46] In its early years fighting Indian takeover, the MIM managed to solidify and politicize a Muslim identity, across a population deeply internally divided by sect, caste, and language (Kooiman 2002, 167). It drew on this history to command allegiance among Muslims in the Old City. But in constructing a Muslim electoral bloc that would support the party, it also reinforced the state's approach to Muslims as an ethno-religious minority.

HOW DID THESE historical developments in India lead to the contemporary politics among Muslims in Hyderabad? Nationally, the Constituent Assembly defined Muslims as religious minorities rather than through a lens of caste and class, setting the conditions for their economic neglect by excluding them from the reservations policy for over sixty years. As Tejani (2008) argues, whereas "backward classes" were defined as socially dynamic communities that would one day overcome their deprivation and difference, Muslims were defined as permanently "different." Because the national government guaranteed religious rights while marginalizing the economic concerns of Muslim communities, contemporary politics revolve around questions of redistribution. Low-income Muslim communities are drawn into a redistributive politics through cross-class identity bonds forged by a long history of patronage, and their own emphasis on community as an end in itself was able to take root in a secular democracy founded on the principle of preserving minority communities. I do not argue that their politics are deeply transformative (although they encompass some notions of financial and social restructuring), but Muslims in Hyderabad firmly assert that the political and cultural recognition of minorities is inseparable from material anti-poverty measures.

IN BOTH FRANCE and India, secularism unfolded as a paradox. *Laïcité* was intended to diminish the importance of religion or, at minimum, restrict it to the private sphere. Yet the secular state never allowed Islam to remain a private matter. Composite nationalism was intended to encourage communal harmony, yet India entered the twenty-first century with a pogrom in the state of Gujarat. Today's crises of secularism have their roots in British and French colonial power, which used religious categorization to administrate subjects. Each state continued to pave the path of Muslim marginality through its exercise of symbolic power, whereby classifications and public policies racialized groups and structured urban life (Wacquant 2007). Each state created the political-economic conditions that determined intracommunity class relations. Amid the upheavals of incendiary nationalist politics and economic crises, Muslim elites proved crucial to the poor and subaltern in terms of their ability to create or protect civil society.

France's particular history of disestablishment and *laïcité* produced the mistrust for and devalorization of religion, establishing a hostile cultural context for the integration of Islam. And France's simultaneously orientalist and colonial approach to Islam meant that the religious tradition would not benefit from state neutrality or noninterference, nor would it be integrated as part of the country's cultural heritage. Muslims would have to struggle for religious recognition, for basic institutions like mosques and schools, and for the freedom to inhabit their religious identity without shame and stigma. As the state took an increasingly hostile stance toward Islam, middle-class Muslims prioritized the struggle for religious recognition over cross-class coalitions and redistribution politics.

Though the Maghrébi second generation enjoyed a period of immigrant activism in the 1980s and '90s, this period left a bittersweet legacy. The few Algerian and other Maghrébi elites attained their positions by physically and culturally distancing themselves from Muslims in the quartiers. They were either created or co-opted by political parties concerned with their public image and disdainful of religion. When these elites appealed to a sense of Maghrébi unity for their own legitimacy, the results were awkward and unsuccessful (Geisser 1997). They lacked the discursive space and resources for a sustained immigrant or racial justice movement. Though cross-class associations achieved temporary success in the banlieues of Lyon in the 1990s, the barriers to closer class relations along an axis of identification with Islam proved too high. Facing greater state surveillance and economic precarity, and increasingly estranged from middle-class activists, Muslims in the working-class quartiers turned to protecting the private sphere and taking refuge in their moral teachings and community.

The particularities of Indian history produced a different set of outcomes because secularism was defined in a way that valorized religion and, in principle, the integrity of religious communities. Legal pluralism in the domain of family law and support for or noninterference in religious minority institutions meant that religious rights would remain relatively robust. However, the state's approach to Muslims as a religious group elided the population's dire material needs. Muslim elites and middle classes have struggled for economic redistribution and policies such as reservations for the most disadvantaged Muslims.

From India's birth as an independent nation, its population has included a Muslim intelligentsia and landowners who benefited from colonial patronage (Hasan 1997, 51). Though Muslims suffered great losses after Partition, many rebuilt their wealth and positioned themselves in fields of patronage. Elites in Hyderabad eventually created large philanthropic foundations to draw poor and subaltern Muslims into a network of charity and redistributive politics. Their politicized religious identity, set in motion by British colonialism (Hasan 1997, 236–37), alongside their attachment to the Nizam's practice of charity, provided a foundation for their strong paternalistic relationship to the poor. As the entire Muslim community faces greater surveillance and communal and state violence, the poor and subaltern are thus able to use elite resources and labor remittances from the Gulf to practice autonomy from the state and create a civil society through political communities in an effort to protect themselves. The pluralism that inspired India's early national imaginary meant less interference in religion and greater space in civil society for social mobilization and debate. Yet these debates remain a far cry from, in the words of Gyan Prakash, questioning "the nation as an organic, majoritarian space and envision[ing] it as an open, plural space of contingency and contention" (2007, 188).

3

Politics of Redistribution

"AS YOU CAN see, we've made a real difference here in the *basti* [slum].[1] The MIM put in all these roads you see here on the hill. Before, it was just dirt and rocks." Niaz pointed at the winding roads as we walked under the hot February sun. I tried to pay attention, but was distracted by the stench of raw sewage floating beneath the little bridge that ran through this part of Shanthi Colony. Niaz, a local MIM party representative (corporator), ignored several of these intolerably wretched lakes of sewage as he guided me around the neighborhood, showing off the party's achievements. Rahman, my steadfast auto-rickshaw driver with wild hair and a dirty button-down shirt, was at my side. We passed a large stone placard announcing the area as an official MIM constituency. Following accusations of distributive failures, the MIM had suffered a ten-year hiatus as the party representing the area. But the MIM worked to make infrastructural improvements to local neighborhoods and again won representative seats in Shanthi Colony in 2002.

"We try to respond to local needs, money for schools, help in issuing ration cards, applying for home loans and issuing loans, installing electric phones and high marks [large public lights]."

"That's great," I remarked. "What other projects has the party done here?"

Niaz grinned. "Mmm, well, we're putting a large drain pipe on Ahmed Nagar Road right now. Rainwater was flooding everyone's homes, so we're taking care of that. And you know, issuing loans is really important. There are no government jobs for Muslims, whereas Hindu families often have a family member with a government job. This means difficulty for Muslims in getting government home loans. The banks want guarantors, tax papers, bank statements, and most Muslims can't provide these.

Hindus, in comparison, are able to secure loans from family members. Home loans can be 10,000 rupees [$250]."

"We also buy almaris [trousseaus] for ladies at the time of their wedding," Niaz said. Rahman chimed in enthusiastically, "Madam [Parvez] is from America, bhai sahib [sir]. If you get any requests for wedding expenses, she can help." I glared at Rahman, who was pleased with his affiliation with this American researcher and readily offered my "services" for weddings, much to my annoyance. "In my years here," Niaz continued, "the ratio of girls to boys has increased, so young ladies are having trouble finding husbands. After age twenty-two, it's almost impossible. So the MIM tries to facilitate one marriage every month. We help them rent the local government function hall, and they just have to provide the food."

We continued our walk, passing shabby storefronts and small stone houses with people sitting on the floor, trying to escape the afternoon heat. Niaz took me into a government girls' school, a crumbling stone building missing half its tin roof. Three dank rooms held only a handful of ancient and rusty metal desks. The girls were all sitting outside on the dirt, in the sun. The teachers, unsettled by our sudden appearance, eventually recognized Niaz. One of the teachers explained that the school had no bathrooms, so the girls tried not to go to the bathroom during the school day. If they really needed to go, they did so outside behind a nearby bush, though boys roaming nearby sometimes harassed them when they did. "We don't even have chalk," she said. "I'm not sure what you're doing [with your research], but if you wish to donate something, we can use anything—a chair, a blanket." I asked Niaz why the school was so unusually impoverished, and he explained that a family residing in the United States privately owned the land. The owners refused to pay for any maintenance and refused to sell the land to the government, which in turn refused to offer a fair price or money for repairs. While the family and the state battled in court for the land, the girls made do with the school's poor conditions.

"This is the state of schools for Muslim children," Niaz affirmed as we walked back to the neighborhood MIM welfare office. Since the day I arrived in Hyderabad, I had been hearing about the sorry state of education in predominantly Muslim areas—and in turn, the multitude of private and MIM welfare projects geared especially toward education. A common sentiment I encountered with regard to the MIM was that no matter how corrupt the party might be, it was imperative to have Muslim representatives to ensure some modicum of distribution to Muslims. The party committees and individual neighborhood representatives, or corporators, like Niaz, recruited workers at the neighborhood level, conducted social work, inspected individual welfare needs, and fielded welfare requests through the coordination of private donations.

The MIM has had an antagonistic relationship with a network of private charity and philanthropic organizations that provide similar services in the city. Operating on the basis of Islamic principles, these organizations range from major foundations to smaller Islamic associations. Together, they educate many thousands of Muslim children, train and support thousands of low-income and semi-literate Muslim women, and spend millions of dollars on welfare projects. Elites, especially those with experience in government, practice as much autonomy from the state as possible in their work while making claims on the state on behalf of the poor. Their experiences with the state have left them gravely disillusioned.

This network of elites and the MIM party participate in a competitive politics of redistribution directed, first, at the state through claims and protest and, second, at the poor through service provision. Their redistributive efforts include social welfare in the form of education, health, family assistance, and skills training, as well as advocacy for reservations for "backward caste" Muslims in education and government. These redistributive politics are *clientelistic*. Politicians and elites use distribution, through channeling of social funds or promises of party jobs, to secure votes or build constituent networks.

In this chapter, I describe the two types of *clientelistic redistribution* that occurred in Hyderabad: electoral and paternal. The MIM party dominated electoral politics among Muslims, sometimes as an opposition party and sometimes as part of the ruling coalition in the city. Generally in exchange for votes, the MIM provided the types of services Niaz described in predominantly Muslim areas. Muslim elites and philanthropic associations dominated paternalistic redistribution. They focused especially on Muslim education and women's welfare schemes, and infused their projects with messages of autonomy from the state and paternalistic affection toward the poor. They interlaced this affection with moral judgment, as they hoped to reshape Islamic religiosity among the poor and subaltern. Though the practical stakes of the intense, sometimes violent, competition between the MIM and the elite philanthropic community were not always clear, they involved political legitimacy among subaltern Muslims and control over their social and economic fate. Aside from Muslim elites, numerous middle- and lower-middle-class Islamic associations also engaged in paternalistic redistribution with smaller welfare projects alongside *da'wa* (calling others to Islam) activities.

Electoral Clientelism

The MIM party was a major force of opposition in Hyderabad's tense electoral politics. Its fierce rhetoric and robust presence dates back to its early formation in 1927, when it supported the Nizam's state and opposed Hyderabad's surrender to India. In its early era, the MIM evolved into a militant organization deemed terrorist by the Indian state. By the 1960s, it had become a mainstream political party aimed at representing Muslim constituencies.

MIM ruled the Old City with an iron fist. My companions considered it both the defender and the oppressor of poor Muslims. As it relied on ethno-religious identity to establish its relevance and it sought broad support among Muslims in the Old City, party members were careful not to criticize sectarian practices among the poor, and they worked to enforce religious rights such as the right of women in burqas to be examined in public services only by female officials. MIM leaders made visible their religious affiliation with their choice to wear the traditional Hyderabadi Muslim sherwani and caps. During political events and processions, gigantic billboards displayed images of the MLAs (Member of Legislative Assembly) in their traditional dress, thereby mixing ethnic attachments with state politics.

But its major projects related to distribution and welfare, generally in exchange for electoral support. The party implemented hundreds of different welfare activities and built neighborhood offices, two major hospitals, a number of health centers, medical and engineering colleges for Muslims, and a large cooperative bank. The MIM ran various local infrastructure programs to address problems in areas like sanitation and road repair. In more obvious clientelistic fashion, according to some of my poorer companions, the MIM distributed cash and new auto-rickshaws right before elections. It served at the forefront of campaigns and demonstrations for the AP (Andhra Pradesh) Muslim Reservations Bill, which passed in 2010, and made other claims of the state in matters of redistribution.[2] The party persistently accused the state of diverting funds away from minority welfare schemes.

With the help of Niaz, I arranged a visit to the MIM's head office in Darussalam. The entire complex spanned several acres, housing the main office, the party's newspaper, a medical center, two colleges, and a main branch of its cooperative bank. Niaz took me straight into the main office and introduced me to Sultan Owaisi, the party president who served as a Member of Parliament for six terms. Before Owaisi passed away in 2008, he was one of the most powerful politicians in the state. He had been unyielding in his belief that Muslims had to gain as much autonomy from the state as possible.

Owaisi was sitting behind his desk reading a newspaper when Niaz and I walked in. Gigantic family photographs adorned the office, exemplifying the dynastic quality of the party's clientelism. He calmly looked at me and commanded me politely to speak only in Urdu. He was soft-spoken and gentle as he lectured me about the history of the party and its motivation to defend Muslims after their massive dislocation following Indian annexation. I found myself persuaded by his words, and by the clients who kept walking in and interrupting, bowing down and kissing Sultan Owaisi's hand and thanking him for one favor or another.

Unlike nonparty elites I had met, Owaisi had little interest in commenting on the nature of religiosity among poor Muslims, aside from asserting that Islamization had increased alongside state oppression of Muslims. He dismissed debates about reforming madrasas, asking, "How can poor people think about education when they barely have food in their stomachs?" "The government doesn't have good intentions with us [*inka zain saaf nahin hai*]. But at least they guarantee a few things, like Haj subsidies." As the political representative of Old City Muslims, the party carefully steered clear of criticizing the religious practices of the poor. It instead saw itself as the defender of poor masses of Muslims.

Owaisi told Mirza, one of his elected councilors, to give me a tour of the compound, where I visited the bank and the *Etamaad* newspaper house. The bank, which started in 1987, had 12,000 shareholders and four branches. It provided loans totaling 60 crore rupees ($13 million) for education, business, mortgage, and gold jewelry at the time of marriage. The bank's clients were predominantly Muslim, though Hindus also accounted for a small percentage of its membership. The organizing ideology behind the bank's business is that Muslims face discrimination when they apply for bank loans or request government assistance. At the bank, the staff completed all paperwork for its clients, defended the loan applications to the board, and accommodated clients who defaulted on their loans. During my visit, dozens of clients arrived and waited in line. The bank charged interest for its loans, so though it existed to serve the Muslim community, it was not technically an Islamic enterprise.[3] According to the bank representative who spoke with me, most Muslim institutions lacked the resources to operate interest-free.

On the way back to the head office, we stopped at the *Etamaad* building, which had been built three months earlier to house the newspaper's production. It was luxurious, with new computers, leather couches, and a European printing press. The MIM had officially entered the competitive field of the local Urdu press. Before I left Darussalam, Mirza urged me: "You can also write that we have colleges parallel to government colleges and offer almost the same number of degrees. No one else has so many. Minorities get 51 percent at these places, whereas there aren't even 1 or 2 percent Muslims in government colleges. Please be sure to write that."

Private Philanthropy

Parallel to electoral clientelism, elite and middle-class Islamic and secular associations wholly embraced the principle of charity, its religious foundations, and its moral legitimacy. This field of philanthropic giving included individuals who contributed to private schools or madrasas and wealthy elites with foundations that funded entire colleges, as well as dozens of women's welfare and training centers. These foundations had a visible presence in Hyderabad and were politically involved in struggling with the state for Muslim reservations. For large foundations, philanthropic organization offered an alternative to government bureaucracy. "I don't believe in always blaming government," said one prominent philanthropist. "Government is a bureaucracy that just slows down our work. We should just get on with our business."

Whether large or small, philanthropic associations strived to reduce child labor, construct health clinics, educate women, and promote communal harmony through interfaith projects. They also collected Islamic *zakat* funds (religiously obligatory annual donations to the poor), which one organization centralized and distributed throughout the city.[4] Wealthy men established the largest foundations, but middle-class and wealthy women also ran many charity projects.

Compared to philanthropic associations, religious organizations were more intent on encouraging Islamic study. But they also incorporated charity and educational programs. Even organizations that focused mostly on individual piety emphasized redistribution as critical to improving the situation of Muslims. "Why should everything be turned into a religious issue?" asked Saif, a long-time volunteer with the Islamic Academy for Comparative Religion (IACR), an organization founded immediately after the destruction of the Babri Masjid in Ayodhya in 1992. He continued,

> What we need is money for the poor, education, jobs, social security, a reduction of discrimination in government offices, private companies, and hospitals. . . . Religious rights are safeguarded in an environment where education and welfare needs are satisfied. Madrasas [for example] that cling to their institution and don't want interference will sacrifice all their worldly needs for their religion. But it doesn't have to be this way. Religious needs can be safeguarded only through welfare.

Even on the topic of women's equality in Islamic practice, Saif and his IACR colleagues saw economic issues as more important than religious questions. He supported women's equal mosque space, for example, but argued,

> If you think just giving space for women in the mosque will better their position, you're very naïve. Their basic health care and livelihood are more important. In the lower segments of our society, women are in desperate situations because their husbands aren't earning anything. Opening up all mosques to women is not going to give them what they need to raise their status. These debates are artificial issues.

IACR lacked the funds for large welfare projects but had begun a blood donation program aimed at gathering 5,000 volunteers to donate blood for poor hospitals, emphasizing redistribution despite its primary religious agenda.

"I was haunted by memories of poor children"

Mr. Haq, one of the most well-known business elites and philanthropists in the city, provided my entrée into Hyderabad's philanthropic world. Unlike many other elites, Mr. Haq was not from a wealthy family. His story reads like a true rags-to-riches tale. Mr. Haq grew up poor, in Hyderabad's Old City. Orphaned at the age of twelve, he earned a sports scholarship that allowed him to attend college and eventually move to the United States.

He earned much of his fortune from his years of work and business dealings in the United States, where he pursued certain fortuitous avenues
and invested well. Yet he remained "haunted" by memories of the poor
children in Hyderabad and images of child labor. He decided to return to
India late in life and commit himself full-time to philanthropic work.

In my time with Mr. Haq, he was often surrounded by various assistants and other board members. His driver took orders from him all day, and
managed his daily details. In business settings, Mr. Haq can seem formida-
ble and authoritarian, but I also saw a softer side that transcended the syco-
phancy that surrounded him. Rooted in deep compassion and moral resolve,
his work for the poor was more important to him than all other matters.

Mr. Haq's redistributive projects focused on education and training.
His political efforts and personal donations for legal expenses proved crucial to passing the 4 percent reservations for Muslims in education and
government employment. His foundation sponsored dozens of women's
training centers, where 25 to 30,000 women learned skills primarily in
textile work and began paving paths toward self-employment. It also sponsored alternative banking, cultural and athletic programs for poor youth,
and free primary schools for approximately 20,000 low-income children.
With these programs, he worked steadily toward his specific goal of reducing child labor.

Mr. Haq took pride in operating his educational institutions on solid
Islamic ethical foundations. He ensured that school fees were minimal—
as low as 10 rupees a month for some of the poorest families. He complained that some private Muslim foundations were run as profit-making
enterprises, a complaint I heard elsewhere as well. Like others, he enjoyed
remaining independent from the government. "If government gives
money, they'll try to control everything: . . . the hiring of teachers, reducing
the number of reservations for Muslims or eliminating them completely."
Using his own wealth was one way Mr. Haq could avoid state interference
in his distributive work.

As a form of patronage, his work created a wide network of Muslim
families who relied on his charitable programs. Mr. Haq personally symbolized the benefits he distributed, as he and the many students who
attended his schools performed a mutual love and appreciation. From time
to time Mr. Haq, like other elites, visited some of the women's training
centers and schools for low-income children. The teachers, schoolgirls,
and young women prepared appreciation rituals to express their profound
gratitude to him. On a few occasions, I sat at the dais with Mr. Haq and

board members as they handed schoolgirls various gifts for their scholarly achievements. In return, the young women and girls recited poems and speeches praising Mr. Haq and his generosity. They also took to the microphone to recite prayers (*duas*) for Mr. Haq, for his health and long life. Some even became tearful as they thanked him for their education.

"You are family to me"

Mr. Haq introduced me to Kulsoom apa, who managed most of his women's training centers. Kulsoom apa was from a middle-class family and lived in a modest flat with her husband and children in the New City. Dressed in her white salwar kameez with a sheer orni softly draped over her hair, and wearing at least eight different rings on her fingers, she arrived to pick me up to visit the centers in her old car, honking wildly and rushing me out the door to get started on her packed agenda for the day. Hundreds of low-income women and staff members anticipated her frequent visits and guidance on a regular basis. At the women's centers, Kulsoom apa delivered materials from chalk to fabrics, oversaw the instructors' methods, heard about what resources the women needed, and encouraged the women in their work. She also came to intimately know many of the women's individual situations and see the ways they coped with their poverty, offering counsel and sometimes relaying these issues back to Mr. Haq.

In many ways Kulsoom apa worked in the trenches of private philanthropy, regularly enacting a maternal love for the poor while simultaneously disciplining them when it seemed they were not taking their work or education seriously. As she said to dozens of poor women in the Faiz Nagar tailoring center, "You are like family to me." By articulating this, she created a sense of mutual rights, obligations, and attachment. The women at the centers affectionately looked to Kulsoom apa as a source of economic and moral support, but also of authority. Through her, they could access means of welfare and feel connected to Mr. Haq as their patron.

"I was a one-man commission"

Elite philanthropists also included those who had once worked for government and became disillusioned. Mr. Husayni was one of these men. Mr. Husayni reflected all the sophistication and grace of the old, aristocratic Hyderabadi culture. His grandfather and father were important members of the Nizam's court, and Mr. Husayni's own career and home reflected his inheritance of their work ethic and public responsibilities. He worked several terms in the national administration before retiring, was involved in the administration of *wakf* property (Islamic endowments set aside for public use),[5] and wrote scholarly monographs on Islamic reform. "I am a nonpracticing Muslim," he once confessed to me. "But I believe in the Quran."

With his academic background and family heritage of princely administration, Mr. Husayni had detailed knowledge of Hyderabad's political history. Far from defending the princely dynasties, he had a careful class and caste analysis of how Old City poverty came to be so entrenched after Hyderabad's surrender to India. Occasionally, in casual conversations with me he would unexpectedly throw in some cultural arguments seemingly for good measure. In his years working in government, he witnessed a gradual communalization of politics and concluded, "Government is not interested in long-term change." He joked that he had served on a "one-man commission," and that the lengthy government reports he wrote about the status of Muslims were simply gathering dust in the state archives. He spoke with the ease of someone who had left government service behind and who took great joy in his private endeavors, specifically his focus on children's education. Mr. Husayni managed components of Muslim endowments, making enough profit to finance his philanthropic projects: absolving debts for poor families, paying marriage expenses, and operating a number of free primary–secondary schools for hundreds of poor children. Aligned with his own secular sensibilities, these schools for Muslim children did not include mandatory Arabic or religious training, but focused largely on math and science. Mr. Husayni felt strongly that those with power, or those engaged in patronage, should not promote or manipulate religiosity among the poor but, rather, should promote secular education.

"I try to tell myself I'm doing a bloody great job"

Mr. Akbar was once a prominent politician in Hyderabad. His father had been a wealthy industrialist with major business dealings around the state and political connections with colonial officers and the prime minister. Mr. Akbar served in state government and held appointed posts before resigning to focus on philanthropy. He continued to lobby the state despite his disillusionment following his tenure in government. He believed that government was capable of making changes to protect Muslims, but that it lacked the political will to do so: "Muslims are killed like rats here, throughout the country. But they're also prepared to fight back. And this scares them [the state]. Government has proved that if it wants to prevent riots, it can. You [the state] don't do irrigation, industry, education, but you'll maintain law and order [if you're scared enough]."

Mr. Akbar noted that relative to the rest of the country, Andhra Pradesh state allocated substantial funds to minority welfare, but these funds were still insufficient to address the enormous poverty among Muslims. Unlike Mr. Haq, Mr. Akbar was not a proponent of Muslim autonomy because he believed Muslim institutions needed government facilitation and assistance. But he also believed that negligence of Muslims was an intentional government strategy to undermine Muslims by preventing their progress. He explained,

Wakf Board, Minorities Commission, Minorities Finance Corporation, Urdu Academy—we have agencies of the state to promote some aspects of welfare. I have noticed over the years that government tends to ignore these organizations to such an extent that if they are self-destructive, I believe they [the government] allow it deliberately. "Let them destroy themselves" is the idea. And Muslims are very capable of being self-destructive, and they have been.

According to Mr. Akbar, in the 1950s, just after Indian independence, Andhra Pradesh had 32,300 *wakf* institutions—more than any other state. These included lands, buildings, mosques, *dargahs* (saintly shrines), *ashurkhanas* (centers for Shia commemoration ceremonies), and graveyards, all of which were religious, cultural, or educational. By an act of Parliament, the Wakf Board is an autonomous party, though the state may exercise some controls. But, Mr. Akbar said, the state chose not to intervene when the board mismanaged the thousands of Muslim properties. He added,

We had over 32,000 buildings and acres. I don't think hardly anything was left unoccupied by government, hoodlums, politicians, Hindu societies, various Muslim societies. It's practically gone. Government is supposed to have some control over the board. But from day one, Muslims said, "Leave us alone, this is our autonomy." So we have destroyed it—*destroyed it!* In my experience, I saw there was nothing I could do because it's "autonomous." Parliamentary members, members of assembly, social people, *muthawalis* [trustees], religious scholars—each one swallowing, allowing it to be swallowed, making money out of it. It's a pathetic state of events.... "How to destroy Muslims?" I'm beginning to think it's a real strategy.

Mr. Akbar lamented that Muslims are dramatically underserved by and alienated from government schools. Urdu-language schools make up less than 3 percent of all schools in the state, and the government allowed the appointment of Telugu-speaking teachers to Urdu schools. When the school underperformed or the teacher retired, the state would then convert the position to a Telugu post, and the number of Urdu teachers would decline. In turn, Muslim students would stop enrolling in schools that did not meet their linguistic needs, at which point the state could justify the school's closure. Urdu schools also failed because the government refused to pay fair rent to the owners of the school facilities, and the owners refused repairs in response, as I saw first-hand in Shanthi Colony. When the physical infrastructure of these schools fell into extreme disrepair, the government shut them down or merged them with other schools. This problem of school infrastructure disproportionately affected schools serving Muslim students because Muslims had no avenue or will to request government repairs, Mr. Akbar explained, adding,

> And nobody cares. I myself went and met the chief secretary, armed with data I gather for all these fights I put up. I told him, "There is 2.2 percent enrollment in Urdu-medium schools, which are only 2.8 percent of schools. So unless there is some Muslim officer who is sitting at the head of the department, in the government, where he controls policy, things are not going to change." He listened to me very carefully, he took it well. But even when it's brought to the administration's attention, nobody cares. It's a *sham* democracy.

Mr. Akbar believed that the Muslim masses were willing to defend themselves in the context of riots, but that they were ignorant and passive when it came to politics. He insisted that Muslims did not see the value of education and refused to make serious demands of their representatives. He exclaimed,

> I am working for the welfare of the community. I use politics, I use my political platform, my connections. I know all the [state government] officers and they know me. So I think I can get a lot of things done. But not many people come. People just come to ask for minor

things, small things, charity. Nobody comes and says "Why don't you ask the government to open 1,000 schools in the villages?" Nobody, not one person! And I try to tell myself I'm doing a bloody great job. I'm a social activist, I intervene in the government regarding what matters. But nobody else cares, except my wife perhaps.

Although Mr. Akbar was involved in numerous enterprises and official minority programs, his disillusion with government and his disappointment with people's refusal to make claims on the state led him to concentrate on philanthropy. He helped establish self-employment programs for low-income women and numerous schools for children. And like Mr. Husayni, he had strong opinions about the need for secular education rather than religious.

Relationships to the State

Despite their disillusion, elites generally avoided inflammatory rhetoric against the state while contributing great wealth to the urban poor. As a result, philanthropists like Mr. Haq established legitimacy with and autonomy from the state. Non-MIM politicians even used philanthropists' legitimacy to advance their own careers. For example, politicians visited Mr. Haq's women's training centers on occasion to make promises and speeches, though neither they nor their political efforts had anything to do with the centers. During one women's center certification ceremony in an extremely poor neighborhood of the Old City, Mr. Gopal, the local police inspector, and Mr. Reddy, a Congress Party corporator, both Hindu, attended as guests of honor. Mr. Reddy announced his promise to secure a government loan from self-employment training funds for beauty parlor equipment for the center. He also promised to campaign for a junior college in the area because it was difficult for women to commute to other colleges. Mr. Reddy then launched into an impassioned speech that echoed the same discourses around the status of women that I had heard from middle-class and elite activists: "My sisters, it is your support and love [*pyar aur mohabbat*] that elected me as corporator. Our minority [Muslim] sisters are no less than anyone else and are worthy of the same rights to education and welfare!"

After the ceremony, the police inspector and Mr. Reddy joined everyone inside the center. The walls were covered with Islamic posters addressing prayer, FINDING A MARRIAGE PARTNER THE ISLAMIC WAY, plus how to perform ablutions after menstruation, and several other details about pious comportment. Beside these posters hung drawings of the henna designs the women were learning. One young woman stretched out her henna-decorated arms to show the appreciative inspector. Mr. Reddy and Inspector Gopal's presence lent political legitimacy to the foundation's work, and in turn, their association with Mr. Haq's redistributive programs validated the local Congress Party's interest in Muslim welfare. In this way, philanthropic work in slum communities took pressure off the state while providing Muslim elites with respect and autonomy—exemplifying the role of elite philanthropy in sustaining neoliberal state retrenchment.

The state's relationship to middle-class religious and activist groups was less sanguine. These groups were either primarily religious or highly critical of the state, which in turn did not benefit from them as they did from elites. Generally, my middle-class companions were educated and ran charitable activities, but they were neither board members of large foundations nor in any way connected with business and real estate, as were elites. Religious groups, like the Students Islamic Organization (SIO), were banned during certain periods. And in 2008, the police prosecuted Nasr, a prominent middle-class civil rights activist and one of my close companions, accusing him of conspiracy against the government after he spoke out against the detention and torture of Muslim youth accused of the Mecca Masjid bombing. Dozens of religious and political activists came to his defense. Before I left India after fieldwork in 2006, I was detained by the police inspector's office because I regularly met with Nasr, a fact the police could only have known through surveillance. After some investigation, they decided to leave me alone, but I left India worried sick for Nasr, who later assured me that this was routine business for him.

In sum, the relationships between Muslim groups and the state exist on a spectrum. Those who criticize the state on the basis of either religious or civil liberties have tense relations with the state, while elites with wealth and property enjoy autonomy and respect. All, however, participate in redistribution as the only way to circumvent the state and ameliorate poverty.

Competition Between Elites and the MIM

One of the defining features of the politics of redistribution is the competition between different groups; in the case of Hyderabad, it is between the MIM and the network of philanthropists. They competed for the allegiance of low-income Muslims in Hyderabad, who constituted a significant voting block that could provide elites with political legitimacy. The MIM had mobilized Muslims in the Old City for decades, but in recent years, the party faced increasing competition from other candidates. The result was greater mobilization and greater rhetorical support for welfare programs. This competition, which sometimes turned violent, played out in the local Urdu press, where popular and educated readers alike followed the issues and knew the newspapers' biases.

"He's just a troublemaker"

A major point of disagreement between philanthropic elites and the MIM involved the use of religious discourse and Muslim nationalism, or put differently, the role of recognition politics. The MIM vociferously opposed Hindu nationalism, at times taking its inflammatory rhetoric to an extreme. In 2012, the party's MLA was arrested for hate speech against Hindus and held in custody for over a month before being released on bail. His arrest galvanized his supporters but raised criticism from philanthropists. Speaking of a different politician, one philanthropist complained, "He's just a troublemaker. They [MIM] tell poor and uneducated Muslims in the Old City that the government is going to take away their religious rights. They create religious antagonism. Part of their stupidity is that they're always blaming government instead of doing things independently."

The party's ideology of defending religious rights developed in reaction to what it viewed as an upper-caste Hindu agenda of oppressing Muslims. My participants of all classes, including philanthropic elites, widely shared this view. But the MIM positioned itself as the primary champion of recognition for Muslims and held a near-monopoly on the staging of anti-government events and demonstrations related to religious identity. For example, every year on December 6, the anniversary of the destruction of the Babri Masjid, party members attempt to shut down activity at the state legislature. And in 2005, during the controversy over a Danish newspaper's publication of cartoons mocking the Prophet Muhammed, the MIM led major demonstrations after Friday prayer in the Old City. A fight erupted between protestors and police officers, leading to major rioting and police tear-gassing. The BJP joined the melee in a counter-demonstration to taunt the MIM. Police arrested and jailed MIM leaders, including Mirza, the MIM official who gave me a tour of the party headquarters. The MIM was also responsible for planning citywide celebrations of Milad-un-Nabi, the Prophet Muhammed's birth date. Between 2005 and 2010, the celebrations grew to an unprecedented scale, with flag displays, processions, and a mixture of religious and political speeches broadcast over loudspeakers in poor neighborhoods late into the night. In 2010, Hindu-Muslim riots ensued on the heels of the celebrations. Although evidence pointed to the VHP's (Vishwa Hindu Parishad) role in instigating the actual riots, many Muslims blamed the MIM for promoting large-scale public religious celebrations and for displaying their party flags over a period of several weeks.

By contrast, my elite philanthropist companions held strong secular convictions and opposed the public broadcasting of religious lectures and prayers, even though the sound of the *azaan* (call to prayer) had become integral to city life.[6] Mr. Haq explained, "The Quran says that you must respect your neighbors and you must respect all religions. Prayer is not meant to bother others." For Mr. Haq and other elites, MIM tactics misused religious identity for the purpose of political power.

"Why are your conditions still so terrible?"

The competition between the MIM and philanthropic elites meant that many of my participants offered devastating criticisms of the party. They accused the MIM of false promises, charging high interest to low-income clients for loans, and turning away sick patients for their inability to pay fees at the hospitals the party founded. Some even accused the party of deliberately keeping certain neighborhoods in the Old City poor, lest the subaltern gain political consciousness and demand new leaders. The dark side of electoral clientelism included alleged vote bribery in the Old City enforced by threats of violence. One of my companions in Faiz Nagar claimed that the MIM paid her friend to vote multiple times in the election—a strategy enabled by officials' failure to check the voter identities of women in burqas. Yet without another party to trust, many subaltern Muslims ambivalently supported the MIM (Rao and Thaha 2012).

These criticisms of the party, and the conflict between elites and party officials, did not just exist in the realm of discourse. Instead, they manifested in real, material ways. For example, I once found Mr. Haq sitting with a loaded gun on the desk in one of his offices. When I nervously asked about the weapon, he gave me a tired smile and said, "I have some enemies, people who don't like what I do." As he hinted several times, "Our main problem is that minorities are against minorities!"

Mr. Haq's loyal board members and supporters worried about his solitariness, long working hours, and safety. On one of our drives to Faiz Nagar, Kulsoom apa, the manager of Mr. Haq's women's training centers, and her friend fretted over Mr. Haq. "He's such a good man, an *angel*! God will protect him. The more you help people, the more good you do in the world, the more people will come after you to hurt you. God will punish them in the afterlife, although they sure seem to get what they want in *this* life. MIM thinks it can get by just distributing auto-rickshaws and cash hand-outs in time for elections!"

Later that day, during tea with Kulsoom apa and some of the staff at the Faiz Nagar school, Abidah, a caretaker of the school from the Old City, recounted her horror after reading about a physical assault on one of Mr. Haq's workers. Abidah sighed, "They've [the MIM] controlled the Old City for decades. Nobody can touch them. But Muslims vote for them because at least they're Muslim. Other parties, the Congress, TDP, they'd rather wipe out Muslims entirely." I did not ask Abidah whether she voted for the MIM to avoid putting her in an awkward position as a worker at a school sponsored by Mr. Haq. "[MIM politician] shows up at big functions and parties and complains about how pitiful (*ghareeb*) and barbaric we are in the Old City," she continued. "But then he comes to the Old City and begs us for votes. He holds out his kurta [shirt] like a beggar. Tell me, what do you call a man who begs from a beggar?" she asked resentfully. Misunderstanding Abidah's sentiments, Kulsoom apa's friend, a wealthier woman from the New City, chimed in. "Well, and why are they [in the Old City] so barbaric in the first place? Because you [MIM] don't help them!" This conversation reflected the animosity between "Mr. Haq supporters" and MIM supporters, but it also illustrates the disconnect between low-income people like Abidah and both the MIM and philanthropic elites. Through electoral clientelism and paternalistic philanthropy, Abidah benefits from both camps, even as they remind her of her inferior status.

In 2006, the MIM launched its own Urdu newspaper, *Etamaad*, which competed directly with the Urdu paper owned by Mr. Haq. According to media reports and some of my companions, MIM-affiliated thugs assaulted a journalist from Mr. Haq's paper and started a fire in the press office. On another occasion, I observed as Zaidi, one of the board members of Mr. Haq's paper, tried to convince Mr. Haq that they needed to concoct an advertising strategy to compete with *Etamaad*. Kulsoom apa interjected, "A few years ago there *was* room for several Urdu daily papers." But Zaidi was not dissuaded. "There's a limited number of Urdu readers," he said. "We have to be aware of the presence of a new paper like this." Mr. Haq broke his silence. "I don't care for such things. I just want to provide quality articles. Let people read what they want to read. Anyway, I'm not worried. MIM hasn't provided welfare or schools." Clearly, the measure of success in this competitive field of Muslim elites was not media influence, but welfare distribution.

Rather than backing down, Mr. Haq and his board members engaged in political rhetoric that indirectly challenged the MIM. I saw this most clearly at the inauguration ceremony of a women's training center in the Shanthi Colony slum. Mr. Haq's organization installed the center after Anwar, a longtime resident of Shanthi Colony, asked me to convey his desire for a center to Mr. Haq's staff. Anwar was about forty and strictly religious. He identified me as a possible connection to the organization after his young daughter saw my photograph in an Urdu paper from a graduation ceremony at the Faiz Nagar school.

A hundred community members attended the inauguration ceremony, and announcements were made from the neighborhood mosque, Masjid Arabiya. Dozens of young boys from the adjacent madrasa giggled and mis-behaved as Anwar anxiously prepared for the grand arrival of the founda-tion members. To the sounds of drumming and firecrackers, Mr. Haq and several board members arrived and took their seats on a makeshift stage.

After Anwar opened the ceremony with Quranic recitation, board members began their speeches. One member had previously campaigned against the MIM in local elections, and I had the strong impression that he still harbored electoral ambitions. Taking note of the severe poverty in Shanthi Colony, he spoke passionately into the microphone: "You must think about who are your political representatives! Why are your condi-tions still so terrible?" In an area ruled by the MIM, these were provoc-ative statements. "I say to you, Mr. Haq, poverty is not just in the Old City. It is here in the New City as well! Muslims must never be dependent on anyone—they *must* stand on their own. Mr. Haq, I request that you help build a college right here in this area!" The audience enthusiastically applauded. Mr. Haq stood up, took the microphone, and pleaded emo-tionally, "You have your representatives *right here*—you *must* hold them accountable! Don't be afraid to demand change from your representa-tives. The Minorities Finance Corporation has nearly 80 lakh rupees [U.S. $800,000] for Muslims, so you have every right to go and request money for local projects." He ended the speech by urging the community to avoid petty squabbles [*nafrath*]. "I've tried to stay away from fights, jealousies, the things that keep us divided. I am doing the work that God wants me to do."

The women's center, with its signage displaying the name of the philanthropic foundation, would likely not be welcome by the MIM, given that the enclave was one of MIM's electoral constituencies. In this way, elites and politicians alike politicized the center. The last time I visited the Shanthi Colony center, I was thrilled to see a number of women busily working in the nondescript building across from a lake of raw sewage. But my eye was quickly drawn toward a very large poster of another prominent philanthropist who worked with Mr. Haq's foundation. The philanthropist had promised to provide the women with a tailoring contract from a company based in Dubai. I learned that a board affiliate had stopped by the center to affix the poster to the wall some time before he was attacked by thugs and suffered stab wounds that left him in intensive care. The oddly placed poster served as a reminder of the intense politicization of the neighborhood. If Anwar saw the poster, he certainly would have disapproved on religious grounds of its glorifying images of men. But he also would have been powerless to take it down, because he had to abide by the wishes of the elites who funded the center.

Relationship to Subaltern Muslims

As elites competed for political legitimacy among the urban Muslim poor, they also sought to establish hegemonic control over subaltern Muslims through material projects and paternalistic disciplining. The respect they gave to the urban poor existed in tension with elites' embrace of negative stereotypes associated with low-income Muslims.

Like many of the women I knew from the Al-Muminoon Islamic study circle, Bilqis apa, a particularly charming and charismatic older woman, operated a preschool for young children in a predominantly Muslim slum. Even as she worked with poor urban Muslims, she also viewed them through the lens of stereotypes applied to racialized minorities throughout the world as lazy, backwards, aggressive, or lecherous. "Terrible!" She told me, "The conditions of Muslims are *terrible*. And you know why? Because they're lazy! Just look at these poor Hindu construction laborers, working all day, carrying concrete on their heads. Then look at the Muslim.... He's resting in the shade!"

The most common word I heard to refer to Muslims especially in the Old City roughly translates as cheap or petty (*chillar*), and many of my middle-class and elite companions thought of poor Muslims as fundamentalist and prone to communalism. They saw proper and liberal Islamic education as the behavioral solution to poor Muslims' social problems and vulnerability to political manipulation.[7] But these middle-class and elite Muslims also carried a paternalistic responsibility that I believe was strong and typically heartfelt. And with some exceptions, low-income families felt comfort and gratitude from the presence of Muslim elites.

"This is the first time we're treated with respect"

On one of my visits to the Faiz Nagar school, Abidah told me, "This is such a big deal for these girls, and they're performing well [in their training] because you [the board] are giving them respect [izzat], and you take them seriously. Usually, people from such poverty are ignored—we're told to sit in the corner, eat from separate plates. This is the first time that we're treated with respect from the outside world." Whenever I came to the school, the young women would kiss my cheeks, hold my hands, and stay close to me the entire time, perhaps in gratitude and astonishment that I treated them respectfully.

I witnessed many moments of affection and compassion from middle-class and elite philanthropists toward poor women and young students. Sometimes this meant waiving the minimal school fees for children and college students. At a different women's training center in the Old City, I was with Kulsoom apa when a burqa-clad mother and her daughter approached to confess that they could not afford the girl's school fees. They both started crying as the mother said she had to withdraw her daughter from the sixth class. Kulsoom apa was distraught, especially because the girl appeared very smart and promising. She told them there was a school sponsored by Mr. Haq's foundation in the neighborhood and that she would see to it that the girl could continue her education there.

Visits by board members also offered respect and mattered immensely to the children and the women. The most anticipated visit I observed was when some of Mr. Haq's American-educated family members visited Faiz Nagar from the United States. Kulsoom apa had frantically prepared for the visit, making sure the younger students had speeches and songs to perform, hand-made gifts to give, and other ways to impress the powerful visitors. For the first time in my visits to the center, I felt marginal. As I tried to blend in with the young women, wearing my burqa and sitting on the floor, Mr. Haq's relatives arrived, at ease, glamorous, and kind. His wife stood at the front of the room and spoke about how proud she was of all the young women and their progress. "This is all a blessing from God. You should begin each day with *Fajr* prayer [early morning prayer], remember God in everything you do, and be determined to work hard and make progress in your lives. I am so happy to see Haq's dream come true." Her son and daughter-in-law then spoke in English, also praising the women and offering advice. The women and male staff in attendance were honored, though they could not have understood the English. Kulsoom apa was relieved and satisfied with the successful visit.

Over the years, Mr. Haq's visits to the centers declined, as the political competition, legal harassments, and his own health concerns wore him down. One of the last times I saw Kulsoom apa, she was pleading with one of Mr. Haq's wealthy relatives on the phone: "Please, you know Mr. Haq hasn't been able to come in so long. If you'd just come to two of the centers next week, it would make the poor girls so happy. They would be thrilled. Even if anyone from the Foundation can come, it would mean so much to them, to show them that we give them *izzat*." In her maternal role at these centers, she worked hard to protect the women and maintain their motivation, partly by keeping them connected to board members.

Kulsoom apa was tireless in her management of the centers, arranging visits and encouraging the women to apply for government programs. At the Faiz Nagar school, I arrived one day to see her and assistants helping the young women with their applications to a state program that provided sewing machines to 200 of the poorest applicants. The atmosphere was hectic, as many of the women were confused and did not know their own addresses or government ration card status. We attended carefully to each application, helping them write and making phone calls to verify their information. Whether helping them attain state benefits, honoring them with visits from the wealthy elite, or waiving their school fees, elites infused their relationships to poor subaltern women with a genuine ethic of care.

"I'm a liberal. I want something to change"

Respect, care, and compassion coexisted with frustration, judgment, and disciplining. Even as my wealthier companions cared for the poor women and children they supported, they also subscribed to a culture of poverty thesis and disdain for the sectarian forms of Islam that were popular among low-income Muslims.

Though his primary frustrations were with the state, Mr. Akbar was also upset about the larger Muslim community. For example, he lamented Muslim attitudes toward education, which he viewed as apathetic and self-destructive:

> Hindus are also very poor but they send their children to school, they think there's a meaning to education. Muslims don't think so at all! If you ask a poor man [Muslim], why are you not sending your child to school, he says *"parkar kya karega?"* [what's the point?] "Will he get a government job?"
>
> Okay, there are so many poor Muslims self-employed, driving an auto-rickshaw, taking home an average of 8,000 rupees a month, and they're satisfied. I employ four drivers, and I think three of them can't read or write. They've come up in a class where they never thought education was important. They're twenty-two, twenty-three years of age, and they can't even write their own car number, can't read a bill or count money.... We have employees who are Muslims in the office—they're the ones who come late, who don't record what they've done, they don't do their work, they don't do anything accurately! The more you look, the more you see something is terribly wrong.

Among the things he found problematic, Mr. Akbar was especially concerned about the "fundamentalism" of uneducated Muslims. He argued that madrasa education was a "death knell" for children who grew up without math, language, and science. He dismissed as "rubbish" the claims of madrasa teachers that they freely chose to study at madrasas instead of at secular schools. His insistence on reform made him a target of attack by Islamic ulema (scholars of Islamic law), specifically for advocating birth control, curbs on polygamy, and regulation of madrasas. Confronting powerful religious forces left him feeling threatened and demoralized. He explained,

> I am a liberal, I want something to change, change drastically. But if I say a word, something about Islam, my opinion, there'll be ten swords drawn against me. Politically, because I have a political background, the mullahs, the politicians, and the ordinary man, using the Urdu media, will try to finish me off because they want to be correct about everything. Nobody can reform this community. Nobody can reform personal law, for example. You can't even ask for it, ask

for a reinterpretation.... It's popular to be on the right side, to be conformist. Nobody will stick his neck out and say, "let's think in a different way." Therefore, we are self-destructive. We refuse to look at things in a different way, and yet we are not even following the spirit of Islam. It's unpopular, it's like *blasphemy*. It *is* blasphemy. They'll kill you."

Mr. Akbar desired a reinterpretation of Islam and reform of shari'a in the domain of family law because he believed that existing interpretations were perverted versions of Islam that impeded the community's progress. His view was not only unpopular but also regarded by some as blasphemous and dangerous.

Other elites shared Mr. Akbar's desire for a more liberal Islam and his conviction that social problems among the poor stemmed from their fanatical religious ideology. Rather than speaking out publicly, they quietly worked in the trenches to discipline poor students and women in the centers. Specifically, they interjected—or suppressed—religion as they deemed necessary.

Like Mr. Akbar, Mr. Husayni argued that madrasa education was spoiling the future careers of Muslim children. He spoke many times with me about how young people had more concern for their outward religiosity than with their inner piety and character. "Our problems are mainly created by so-called religious-minded people.... It wasn't so fundamentalist fifty years ago in Hyderabad. Now, when I see young men wearing their Islamic caps, I just have an allergy to it. When my students wear it, I tell them, 'You shouldn't do this. You don't look like a student.' ... I don't want to make religion an institution. It should stay in the heart."

Mr. Husayni asked me on a few occasions to accompany him on visits to his schools in the Old City to help broaden the horizons of the young students. The first school I visited was a merit-based secular school. From the decorations on the wall to the dispositions of the teachers, the school's secular orientation was clear. Prayer and Arabic education were optional. The students spoke English and aspired to attend college. Given their isolated upbringings, they were thrilled to have a visitor from the United States and cornered me in droves. Mr. Husayni stopped to make conversation with a big group of adolescent students. "What do you want to do when you graduate?" he asked.

"Doctor!" one student shouted out. "Teacher!" shouted another.

"What about an advocate [lawyer]?" asked Mr. Husayni.

"This is against Islam," one girl interjected. He quickly disagreed and tried to convince her otherwise.

"Whom can Muslims turn to when they are in trouble? We have to have advocates to defend us." This one moment captured multiple dynamics central to the politics of redistribution: the secular orientation of elites; their paternalistic affection, concern, and disciplining of poor youth and families; and their encouragement of specifically women's education and work opportunities.

In other situations, religious disciplining was subtler. One late morning, Kulsoom apa picked me up to go to Faiz Nagar. She looked upset. When I asked what was wrong, she told me about the infighting at the center—which she attributed to the unruly, "interior" Muslims of Faiz Nagar. As soon as we arrived, we marched into the sewing room, where everyone was shouting. A number of the women, teachers, and the "Master sahib" who managed the income-generating aspect of the women's textile work, were anxiously waiting for Kulsoom apa to mediate. Apparently someone had started a rumor that the master and Zainab, one of the women who had begun to take charge of some of the textile projects, were having an affair. The master, a middle-aged married man, and Zainab vehemently and tearfully denied any affair. On top of this, resentment was brewing that Master sahib had not provided enough work for the last two weeks and had chosen only five women to sew garments.

Kulsoom apa, deeply upset and struggling in her managerial role, scolded the group and became tearful herself. "We are all supposed to be one family! This is why I volunteer, why I come here, because I want to help you. You are family to me. Islam doesn't teach us to be petty like this. You are here to concentrate on your work and make progress!" Later, I heard her say to one of the teachers, "this is exactly what you people do [ap logue karthe aisa]."

Kulsoom apa several times referred to hadith (teachings of the Prophet) about how to behave with others to create pause and agreement amid all the shouting. She relied on broad concepts from Islam to create discipline and community in the welfare centers. Soon after the conflict, she started a weekly Quranic recitation session, a subtle tactic to improve people's comportment at the center.

But the relationship between philanthropy and Islam was inconsistent. Mr. Haq, for example, preferred to keep all religious matters out of the training centers, believing they would be divisive. He felt poor Muslims needed more worldly engagement, not more religion. When Hafeeza, a madrasa teacher in the low-income neighborhood of Zohra Bagh, asked Mr. Haq if she could implement Islamic education in the center he founded next to her madrasa, he refused. He said that he did not want to deal with the competing visions and ideologies of different sects. Hafeeza recounted, "He said, 'I just want the women to learn some skills and that's it.' So I said, 'Okay, fine, if that's your wish.'"

Mr. Haq was attentive to the tendency of lower-middle-class leaders to add religion to material and political matters and he used his authority to curb it. Anwar also had grand plans of including Islamic education in the Shanthi Colony center, but he never followed through. Though I do not know for certain, I suspect that he knew it would annoy Mr. Haq and so decided to let it go. Anwar also had no choice but to interact with Kulsoom apa, the center's manager, even though Kulsoom apa did not wear a hijab, let alone a burqa, in violation of his fairly strict gender-segregated practices. I watched as he conversed with her politely but awkwardly, avoiding too much eye contact and keeping his distance.

"A burqa is not a school uniform!"

Perhaps no other issue caused as much disagreement between my subaltern and elite companions as women's veiling. Elites succeeded in inserting their opinions into the conversation in low-income communities—sometimes by facilitating dynamic debate about gender and other times by employing a top-down strategy of control.

Middle-class and elite discomfort with women's veiling revealed itself in numerous settings. During one weekend, I attended the regional conference of the women's wing of the Jama'at-i-Islami Hind (JIH). At one point during the weekend conference, several philanthropists' wives and elite board members visited as honorary guests and sat at the dais in front of the sea of 40,000 low-income, burqa-clad women dressed in black and sitting on the ground in the scorching heat. They appeared uncomfortable, with their hair only lightly covered under decorative scarves. One woman wore sunglasses throughout the speeches, which seemed to symbolize the vast chasm between her and the women on the ground. They made brief, dispassionate comments about elevating the status of women and then quickly left the conference. Their elite status and distinct veiling practices highlighted an unequal balance of power. Though they supported the poor in their welfare endeavors, these women appeared as exempt from the practice of burqas and as uneasy spending time among this population of poor, subaltern women.

Elite and middle-class women and men judged the burqa as regressive and unnecessary. When I met a prominent Muslim journalist in the city, without any prompting on my part, he said, "I like your kind of hijab, not this full burqa. They [women in burqas] are making a mockery of Islam." Like many middle-class women, I was wearing a light orni on my head, with much of my hair and neck uncovered. On another occasion, Mr. Husayni and I stopped by the Jamia Nizamia University campus to take photographs. I quickly covered my hair out of habit, and he laughed at me. "You are becoming orthodox because the occasion demands it!" Mr. Husayni, I knew, despised most forms of veiling.

After several months of visiting the Faiz Nagar school, I observed a major incident that involved the female principal. Madam Rabia was a petite, young, middle-class woman. Mr. Haq's foundation board chose her out of 150 candidates who applied for the position in the primary school. The school served 500 Muslim students, belonging to the poorest neighborhoods falling below the poverty line in the Old City. She lived most of her life in Secunderabad, north of the New City, and attended Christian schools and colleges. She spoke fluent English and refused to cover her hair, though she identified strongly as Muslim. With her resilient personality and forceful style, Madam Rabia had fought with local residents and parents for several years until she finally started to earn their respect. The mostly male philanthropic board members consistently supported her decisions, despite her controversial role in the neighborhood.

At a staff meeting one morning, the male teachers for the children's Islamic and Arabic classes raised the issue of Madam Rabia's uncovered hair. Ideally, they argued, she should wear a burqa. They also criticized her programs, such as celebrating students' birthdays and always speaking in English with them. The teachers had apparently campaigned around the Faiz Nagar neighborhood, defaming Madam Rabia and telling parents that the school had brought in an "un-Islamic" and "English lady" to teach their children. Led by a religious *hafiz* (an individual who had memorized the Quran) at the school, the teachers printed a pamphlet against Madam Rabia, which they distributed to hundreds of people at the neighborhood Friday prayer. As a result, some parents filed complaints against her.

Kulsoom apa tried to calm Madam Rabia's fury over the incident. She assured Madam Rabia, "Don't worry. They won't get their way. Mr. Haq is on your side and will fire them [the teachers] if we need to. They're ignorant. They don't understand Islam. They don't realize that wearing the hijab is an extremely personal decision, and no one's supposed to tell us how or when to do it."

Madam Rabia insisted, "I always wear the whole burqa when I go to Charminar [Old City center]. But my parents and in-laws were modern—they always encouraged me to work, learn English, have a life."

Kulsoom apa eventually left the office, and Madam Rabia said to me, "You see, after all, these teachers are so backwards, so ignorant [*jahil*]. They have no idea that these kids need to know English and learn science, or they'll never get jobs. This is why Hindus will always be better off than us. The Old City will always remain poor, as long as they keep this mentality about religion. They will only eat rice and sleep and read the Quran—and this is why Muslims will always be backwards!"

Later that spring, Madam Rabia's troubles resumed, culminating in "the worst day of my life that I will never forget." According to her, a male Urdu teacher harassed another female teacher and became inappropriate with her. When Madam Rabia called him in to discuss what happened, he became angry, asking, "Who are you to tell me what to do?" She decided to call the board and request that they fire him. The next day, the head office sent him a termination letter. In the middle of administering Urdu exams, the teacher stopped and gathered all the other teachers and students. They all exited the school and went "on strike," chanting slogans against her and locking her inside the school building. She called the police, who came and tried to arrest everyone, but Madam Rabia insisted that they release the female teachers so that the women would not have to interact with police. "They [male teachers] think because they're older than me, they don't have to respect my authority!" she cried. Two years after that incident, all of the teachers came to her and apologized for their complicity. Now, she says with authority to anyone who criticizes her refusal to wear a hijab, "Don't interfere in my personal matters! Why are you concerned with what I'm doing?"

Madam Rabia moved to Faiz Nagar eight years earlier when her parents, in a disappointing move, arranged her marriage with a man who lived there. Moving to the area from a solidly middle-class upbringing was a shock. "I used to think, if I stay here, I'll lose everything [about myself]."

But she decided to channel all her energy into her work and making a difference in the area, and her husband eventually became her "number one support" in encouraging this work. Even though Madam Rabia stood out in the neighborhood, she refused to surrender to local customs. "I don't believe in orthodox things, the burqa. This is the modern world. I believe in Islam, God, and his Prophet, but I don't have to show it. Whatever I have, whatever I believe, is within me. I don't need to wear the burqa and walk around and show everyone. I know everything [about Islam], and it's inside me." [8] As she walked to the school every day in her sari with a shawl wrapped around her shoulders and her hair showing in a long braid, she remained confident in spite of people's stares.

Madam Rabia instituted a number of controversial changes in the school, and things eventually began improving—the children were healthier and the parents valued what she wanted to achieve. But she lamented the parents' lack of education and crudeness. Some children came to school unbathed and starving, and some would vomit or faint in the middle of the day. "When you have six children, how can you care for any of them? About two years ago, I started bringing in soap and nail-cutters, and in the morning, I started cleaning up the kids. You would not believe how much it's changed since you were here before. Parents are starting to change and pay attention, but there's a long way to go." Later she added, "But these people will *never* change, Fareen. It's in their blood." She said male–female segregation exacerbated poor Muslims' narrow-mindedness, and that their backwardness was her greatest source of misery. Yet she learned to take it easier, to control her anger, and to deal more calmly with those who challenged her agenda. With the support of Mr. Haq's board, she ensured that only women taught Islamic courses at the school. Of twenty-two teachers in total, only four were men.[9]

Though she supported religious instruction and prayer in the school, Madam Rabia tried to reduce the presence of religion and banned women's wearing of the burqa among teachers and students. She explained,

I say to these teachers, "You are like second parents to these kids. If you don't understand this [if all you think about is religion], don't even come out to teach. It's better to just stay at home." The female teachers wanted to wear [the niqab] in the classroom, and I said no, that face-to-face contact is critical. We are a private Muslim school, but we are also accountable to the state. The district education officers visit the school a few times. I don't want them to visit and see all these teachers in the niqab.... There's no doubt there's been an increase in religiosity and the burqa since I've lived here. But I won't allow it among my students. They have to take it off in the school. Parents objected at first but then eventually accepted it. I still have critics. But a burqa is not a school uniform!

Madam Rabia continued to use English, despite earlier opposition, and enforced the language as much as possible. "I always tell [the students], 'You need to keep speaking English, and if you have no one to speak with, then stand in a mirror and speak to yourself.'" The unique blend of despotism and affection that Madam Rabia employed in encouraging her students to use English came through as she advised a burqa-clad mother and her daughter. She spoke Urdu with the mother and English with the girl, asking, "Are you scared to move on to the tenth class? Are you avoiding your exams?" The girl mumbled her response, and the mother was too diffident to speak. Madam Rabia firmly but affectionately replied, "Pass or fail, ma [my dear], you have to take the exam. Just see it as practice. Eat well, drink well. I already explained to you a number of times to not be scared. You have to get rid of this fear."

Like the elite philanthropists who supported her work, Madam Rabia believed that education was the only hope for Muslims in the Old City. She was happy to note that families had started to accept girls' education, and that some parents sent their children to the Faiz Nagar school *because* it had a "lady principal." In just a few years, she went from being defamed throughout Faiz Nagar to attracting students from all over the area, despite her lack of outward Islamic practice. "Now, I always try to motivate my teachers. 'See how great we ladies are! We're taking care of 500 children, as well as our own. Allah is always with you. Keep faith in him and the Prophet. Islam is all about your intention—so just be positive.'"

THE POLITICS OF Islamic revival among the middle class and elites constituted a politics of redistribution: leaders struggled with the state for reservations and distributed wealth to the poor and access to welfare through private means. Why did a politics of clientelistic redistribution develop? India's pluralist secularism protected religious rights, while government administration historically employed patronage and solidified ethnic categories. In this context, elites and the Muslim middle class logically focused on redistribution, rather than recognition, on behalf of the religious community. In Hyderabad especially, the memory of Muslim princely rule and the history of the Nizam's patronage fostered a keen sense of responsibility and paternalism toward the Muslim poor.

As the postcolonial state began undermining Urdu education and neglecting Muslim minority welfare, deliberately in the eyes of my companions, elites and the middle class stepped forward to provide material support to low-income Muslims. The MIM party provided parallel institutions to those of government, such as colleges, banking, and hospitals, and established small welfare offices to root the party in poor Muslim neighborhoods. As a political dynasty, MIM performed a familial bond with the poor, but it also firmly expected electoral support in these neighborhoods and relied occasionally on ethno-religious attachment to garner support.

Among elite philanthropists, Mr. Husayni felt that the government cared little about the status of Muslims, and Mr. Akbar lamented government neglect, as well as Muslims' political apathy. Like the MIM, they created alternatives to public institutions like schools and self-employment training centers, which provided skills to thousands of low-income women throughout the city. Many of these women demonstrated their profound affection and gratitude for board members and volunteers, offering to philanthropists both loyalty and legitimacy. Elite men like Mr. Haq symbolized the paternalism that defined the relationship between Muslim philanthropists and the poor; and middle-class women like Kulsoom apa worked untiringly in the trenches of private philanthropy, insisting that she and the foundation's low-income clients were family. Apart from elites, middle-class religious organizations also made redistribution central to their agendas. Even as they wished foremost to promote Islamic study and piety, their projects typically involved distribution, from blood donation to student tutoring.

On the terrain of redistribution and through venues such as the Urdu press, the MIM and philanthropists competed for political legitimacy. The competition between them increased overall support for welfare programs. Through this competitive process, the poor and subaltern received concessions from both electoral clientelism and paternalistic giving. While the MIM engaged in recognition politics to attract more clients, philanthropists disapproved of this approach as using religion to manipulate the poor. They instead tried to promote a secular culture among the poor and to maintain relations with the state based on mutual respect and autonomy. Struggles among elites, struggles between elites and the state, and struggles over Islamic interpretation all politicized the women's training centers. These centers became the symbolic locales where elites secured hegemony through material concessions and disciplining in addition to affection and respect.

For example, Kulsoom apa actively facilitated visits by elite board members in order to show respect to the women in the centers. These visits personalized the women's relationships to the philanthropic foundation, strengthening their loyalty to the elites. They also allowed the women to interact with leaders in the larger Muslim community and feel connected to a movement outside their individual lives. With an ethic of care and respect, Kulsoom apa and others kept subaltern women involved in a social world and prevented their isolation.

Minimizing women's social isolation coincided with the desire of elites like Mr. Haq, Mr. Husayni, and Mr. Akbar to promote a specifically liberal Islamic practice as part of the solution to social problems in slum neighborhoods. In their welfare projects, they interjected or suppressed Islam, as they deemed necessary. For example, while Kulsoom apa used hadiths to create discipline and a sense of community, Madam Rabia forbade the practice of wearing burqas among women teachers and students in her school. Some elites vocally opposed sectarian Islam while others, like Mr. Haq, quietly promoted a more private and liberal Islam through women's education. These philanthropic groups were united in their belief that women's education and support of women against patriarchal authority would improve the social conditions of poor Muslims.

Amid the erosion of public welfare and government neglect of poverty among Muslims, the MIM, middle-class activists, and elites willingly supported the poor and subaltern. They built cross-class alliances because they viewed themselves as part of a common Muslim community. The bonds they constructed, as well as the disciplining and debate around Islam and around gender, constituted the everyday political culture of Muslims in Hyderabad. Even as calls for a liberal Islam occupy international discourse, the on-the-ground reality of Muslim communities reflects complex struggles over religion and social practice that are embedded in simmering class tensions.

4

Political Community in the Slums of Hyderabad

Two hours into our study circle on a hot day, I started nodding off. Rehana baji was talking about the importance of worship while we're alive because there's nothing we can do to honor God after we die. "Dear God!" she raised her voice, startling me awake. "We are sinners, but we are your creations. We are weak!" she shouted. "So give us strength." "My dear sisters," she concluded the session and urged us cheerfully, "I hope you will remember to fear death and the afterlife. See you next time, insha Allah." I followed Rehana baji and Farzana outside, and we chatted. They were rushing off for the evening prayer. "Do you have plans to go see your husband in Jeddah?" I asked Rehana baji. "No," she looked at me and smiled. Farzana was carefully putting on her black gloves, part of the veiling she practices, and touched Rehana baji's shoulder. "You know, she manages everything by herself, housework, three kids. She works so hard." They both put on their niqabs and got onto Rehana baji's scooter. "Remember to come to the madrasa graduation on Saturday!" Their burqas were flying in the wind as they sped off down the street, leaving a cloud of earthy dust behind them. I could hear them laughing above the roar of the engine.

FIELD NOTES FROM HYDERABAD, India

REHANA BAJI AND Farzana were leaders in a political community of poor women in a slum area of Zohra Bagh. Together, they ran an Islamic study circle for twenty to fifty women every week, usually out of Rehana baji's home, around the corner and up the dusty street from an activist association, women's madrasa, and women's training center. Like a number of women in the city, their husbands lived and worked in Saudi Arabia. With her husband permanently abroad, Farzana was very rigorous in her practice of Islam. Her daughter studied full time at a madrasa and had already memorized twenty-two (of 114) Quranic chapters. Whereas Rehana baji graciously welcomed me into the study circle, my relationship with Farzana started off awkward and tense. She thought my presence might distract the other women. When Rehana baji engaged me in conversation in front of the study circle, Farzana would quickly interrupt, bringing us back to the religious topic at hand. Somehow, with time, Farzana warmed to me and started inviting me to local events. I felt I surpassed a big hurdle when she invited me to dinner in her home. After dinner, she showed me a framed photograph of her husband and started giggling, along with her daughter, as though he were a stranger to them. "My niece can't even bear to look at that photo, she's so scared of him!" she laughed. I simply smiled, noting to myself how mismatched he looked from Farzana's rather young and delicate face.

Farzana's father was a hakeem, a practitioner of traditional Islamic medicine, and her mother used to hold public Islamic lessons (*ustima*) for women, drawing as many as a thousand women in the month of Ramadan. Farzana continued her mother's tradition. She would arrive at Rehana baji's home, sit on the platform, place her notes and books on a small wooden half-podium, and methodically open the Quran to the right page, as we all excitedly waited for her to begin. One day during a lesson, Farzana said to the women, "If others make fun of you and call you a 'pakora,' tell them proudly, 'yes, I'm a pakora!'" I asked Rehana baji later what this meant. She said it was a demeaning term to refer to someone who practiced Islam in an orthodox manner.[1] "See," she said. "This is how they try to tear us apart."

Maintaining unity, especially when confronted with insults, was important to this group of women. They were part of a movement advocating religious practices and forms of veiling that middle-class Muslims and non-Muslims considered regressive, but they were also self-organizing for religious and worldly education, as well as social and economic mobility. They did all of this *in* community and *with* community as an end in itself.

It seems counterintuitive: these societies of women and men are judged as "fundamentalist" and/or actively targeted as potential terrorists. They are politicized this way, though they are not making claims on the state—and they sometimes even take pride in their refusal to do so. Their politics were not about Islamizing the state or otherwise transforming its secular foundations. Instead, they simply intertwined religious teachings with practices of citizenship that build social trust. Despite their poverty and marginalization, they used middle-class and elite resources to exercise their citizenship and practice a politics in a broadly democratic sense.

Part of the backdrop of community politics in Hyderabad was a strong sense of collective mission and individual responsibility to support the Muslim community. Neighborhood mosques and madrasas channeled this collective mission and enjoyed a relationship of give and take with local communities. Low-income Muslim men enforced these messages of responsibility as they tried to protect the community from the state by avoiding claims on the state and spreading messages of ascetic living. They generally supported women's political communities even as they saw few avenues for their own material progress other than migration to a Gulf country. As low-income, reformist women coped with their husbands' migration, some faced pressure to earn income and navigate the public sphere. In doing so, they emphasized preserving women's virtue and practicing strict gender separation.

In this chapter, I argue that despite strict gendered practice, poor and subaltern women in slum and BPL (below poverty line) neighborhoods created political communities through material, legal, and symbolic projects. In their material projects, which were supported by the middle class and elites, they sought independence through community, elevating a new model for women to emulate. They taught each other skills and pursued self-employment to alleviate extreme poverty. In the legal domain, rather than turning to civil law they turned to community to help them use Islamic law to secure their rightful legal status in marriage and divorce. Islamic teachers campaigned specifically against the marriage practice of dowry, a harmful inversion of the Islamic tradition regarding marriage gift-giving practices. Women also strengthened bonds based on mutual trust and accountability while recognizing alternative forms of honor through their Islamic education and skills.

Collective Responsibility

It was 4:30 in the morning when I was sharply awoken by the sounds of a snare drum and rhythmic singing. I peered out over my balcony onto the narrow dusty streets of Shanthi Colony, a predominantly Muslim slum oddly located in the New City across from my apartment building, and saw the outline of a thin figure walking around with his drum. It was the Islamic month of Ramadan, and as I would learn, this man held the honorable task of waking up the neighborhood in time for *sehri*, the pre-dawn meal with which one starts the daily fast. As his drumming continued, coaxing people out of their slumber, women lit their oil lamps and started fires to heat the morning water. In time, sounds of soft chatter floated in the air as young boys and men hurried to the little blue mosque, Masjid Arabiya, for the morning prayer. The call for prayer (*azaan*) echoed from the mosque minarets, as the sun started to rise and the roosters crowed.

Madrasa Arabiya sat adjacent to the little blue mosque. Every morning at six a class full of young boys were learning Arabic, reciting the Quran, and struggling to memorize verses. The teachers were men in their twenties and thirties, devoted to their work, and of the same poor background as their students. Attached to the madrasa was also a women's "stitching center," which was started during the course of my fieldwork and that has now trained several hundred semi-literate women in self-employment skills. By early afternoon, dozens of burqa-clad women walked to and from the center.

Mosques, madrasas, and women's training centers were the institutional anchors of political communities. They circulated announcements, literature, and imperatives to provide various forms of support for the community and for these institutions. The idea that the larger Muslim community had a responsibility to preserve Islamic institutions and support Muslim welfare arose in numerous diverse settings. For example, walking into a small photography studio in Shanthi Colony, I spotted a bumper sticker on the wall: TO HELP JAMIA NIZAMIA IS THE FOREMOST DUTY OF MUSLIMS. Jamia Nizamia is India's second largest Islamic university, training hundreds of men to be Islamic teachers and leaders each year.

After months of passing an old hakeem who worked on the street near Masjid Arabiya in Shanthi Colony, I decided to stop by one day. He poked around my face with his frail hands and suggested herbs to improve my health. When I politely refused his services, he launched into a long diatribe against the government's deliberate undermining of Islamic medicine (*unani*). "The only way this system [*unani*] will survive is if Muslims support it," he scolded me. He lamented the poor state of his "office," a stone hut located next to a "jaundice treatment center," and complained: "government will never give even one rupee!" As many diverse individuals often repeated to me, "government doesn't do anything." Thus, individual

Muslims had the responsibility to uphold the community whether by supporting Islamic institutions or by giving charity.[2]

Neighborhood mosques promoted this message of collective responsibility. All throughout the city, small mosques in Muslim enclaves amplified their announcements.[3] Announcements from Masjid Arabiya blared
through the loudspeakers several times every day. Many of these were
requests, or imperatives, to give money or provide physical assistance for
a Muslim family. Typically, these were burial or wedding expenses. The
imam would announce a local resident's death, its hour, and the immediate start of collections for his burial. He would also call for extra prayers
that local male residents were expected to attend. Residents could hardly
ignore the sense of obligation toward community members when these
announcements commanded such a powerful presence.

Mosque and local leaders also coaxed people to pray and read the
Quran. They collectively disciplined children in particular. Sometimes, as
once occurred in an accidentally amplified and amusing set of announcements from Masjid Arabiya, the imam scolded young boys for rushing
through their prayers or skipping their prayers in favor of playing outside the mosque or running home. I once heard him yelling at dozens
of giggling boys, running out the door of the mosque: "Get back here,
children! If you don't learn to pray properly now, you'll never develop the
habit. You have to make it a *habit!*" The task of instilling in children the
bodily practice, desire, and habit of daily prayer belonged to every par-
ent, but the authority, possession, and affection with which Masjid Arabiya
additionally undertook such disciplining was striking. Many young people
felt accountable to Anwar, Madrasa Arabiya's caretaker and a beloved local
leader in Shanthi Colony. As he hurriedly walked down the street one evening, several young boys shouted out to him before he even noticed them.
"Yes, yes, we already did our prayers!" they exclaimed. "See, we all have to
remind each other," Anwar confirmed.[4]

Part of the religious ethical teachings and discourse emphasized supporting the Muslim community economically. Efforts toward local economic sustainability took place above all during the month of Ramadan.
Many shopowners and workers I knew made most of their yearly sales
during Ramadan, when they expected families to purchase their goods
from Muslim merchants. Donating to the neighborhood mosque was
also an obligation, especially when funds go toward local charity projects and needy families. Generally, small neighborhood mosques have
scarcely enough funds for their own operations, so leaders make weekly

or bi-weekly announcements requesting funds for infrastructural projects. When the imam announced the need for repairs for Madrasa Arabiya and a future women's center, a number of people volunteered and completed the construction.

In turn, mosques and madrasas gave back to the community in important material ways. During Ramadan, Masjid Arabiya frequently provided *iftar* dinner, the meal to break the daily fast, to the neighborhood children. I would see volunteers light lamps, roll out carpets on the street, and bring out large vats of rice and curries, which the children hungrily devoured as they sat on the rugs. Madrasas also generally provided free lunches for their students, an enormous benefit to the many families who might otherwise send their children to beg on the street or work odd jobs.

Because prayer is required five times every day, mosques also provided physical space and respite for many poor residents. Most families in slum or low-income neighborhoods lived in cramped, one-room, rented homes. Mustafa, an elderly resident of Shanthi Colony, attended Masjid Arabiya every day. After decades of supporting his family as an auto-rickshaw driver, Mustafa suffered a stroke and partial paralysis. He was one of seemingly many men in the neighborhood left unable to work after suffering an injury or medical crisis. Most of these men could not afford the costs of proper treatment or rehabilitation. Mustafa's seven-person family lived in a one-bedroom home. Masjid Arabiya played an important role in his life, as he hobbled to the mosque five times daily. There, he prayed, enjoyed the *qhutbas*, and begged for money. Because everyone at the mosque bore a responsibility to give him small amounts, he received enough money to survive.

Mustafa's daily routine at the mosque also had an important gendered aspect. When men went to the mosque to spend hours with the community, women enjoyed more privacy and physical space in the home. While his wife, daughters, and daughter-in-law appreciated his brief absences, I could also see that Mustafa's daily routine of walking to Masjid Arabiya provided him with a sense of independence in an extraordinarily emasculating and dependent state.

Gendered Differences in Participation

Though the political communities I explored were groups of women, men had important, but different roles in these neighborhoods. They actively encouraged women to participate in local projects, and I saw men of nearly

every age raising money for women's centers and helping with tasks like
façade work or cleaning. Yet the men did not participate in or directly benefit from the kinds of skills training and education reserved for women.
Instead, they enforced a wider collective responsibility and tried to protect Islam and the institutional anchors of political communities from the
state.

"We are poor, and we want to die as poor persons"

Men tried to protect Islam and the community by protecting madrasa education, promoting ethical behaviors around ascetic living, and avoiding
politics. For example, Anwar and the teachers at Madrasa Arabiya decided
to not pursue subsidized electricity rates, though all nonprofits and
schools technically qualified for this benefit. They argued that the savings
were not worth the bureaucratic hassle or the risk of inviting government
interest in controlling the school. Anwar proclaimed, "We don't need your
subsidies! We don't need your scholarships. We are capable on our own."
"Anyway," he said to me, "money and income for mosques is ultimately
bad for the mosque because then people start arguing over salaries and
budgets."

To maintain the autonomy of these institutions, members had to strive
for asceticism and to avoid the hazards of materialism. Local leaders spoke
out against *riba*, or usury, and debt and encouraged subsistence living and
community forms of wealth. Anwar charismatically promoted such teachings in Shanthi Colony. His ethical teachings resonated with his own life,
as he had to quit his education at age thirteen. He worked as a sweeper at
a hotel in Saudi Arabia for several years before returning to Hyderabad to
care for his widowed mother. He used what savings he had from his work
abroad to expand the full-time Madrasa Arabiya. Crucially, he avoided giving or taking interest payments his entire life, refusing bank loans in both
India and Saudi Arabia. "It's a matter of faith to accept what doesn't seem
to make sense, such as the idea that you'll gain more [wealth] without
interest than with interest."

In our many conversations and in his occasional *qhutbas* at the Masjid,
he emphasized that exploitation and excessive materialism violated Islamic
principles. He explained:

The Quran says, "We will destroy the banks and promote charity."
If a man knows how to live, he can live on 1,000 rupees. If you're

earning 3,000, and you think you need 5,000, where will you get this extra money? You'll lie, cheat, steal, take interest, do anything. Interest [credit] is the one thing that is spoiling the whole world. Allah hates lavish living. If I have a headache I go to the pharmacy, take a tablet, and I'm fine. For a rich person, they'll bring an ambulance, scans, a day in the hospital. And then what? After thousands of rupees, they'll say "Congratulations, there's nothing wrong with you!"

Leading by example, Anwar applied his personal ethics to his politics and rejection of political parties. According to Anwar, a few years after the opening of the Shanthi Colony women's center, Mr. Haq approached him to see if he had any interest in a political appointment. Mr. Haq was contemplating the idea of an independent political party, and a post for Anwar could have dramatically improved his social position. Anwar politely refused, asserting that he had no interest in party politics. Years before, during the inaugural ceremony of the Shanthi Colony women's center, he even refused to be photographed for the local newspaper, because he did not want people to associate him with any type of politics. He insisted that a new political party would merely divide the Muslim vote and ultimately benefit the majority Hindus. Anwar's overall distrust of wealth and of the state led him to focus squarely on the community and its autonomy. "We have to think this way," he told me, "because we are so-called minorities."

One of the main reasons Anwar and other men of the community wanted to shield the madrasa was to preserve the integrity of Islamic education and not dilute it with worldly subjects. Teachers insisted that specialization in Quranic study, for example, was necessary and superior to an education fractured by various and secular interests. Hafiz Azmath, a graduate of the famed madrasa at Deoband, had memorized the Quran by heart at a young age. He taught occasionally in Shanthi Colony. He argued that large madrasas that accepted government management in favor of promoting English and secular courses were mediocre by every measure. "The result of these madrasas is nil. If you are studying four hours of English and then four hours of Arabic, you can't be a professional in either subject." He and others at the school passionately invoked the unique complexity of Arabic, the vital importance of *tajwid* (art of Quranic recitation), and the many years of study required to gain a deeper understanding of the Quran. For these reasons, they rejected the imposition of

secular education on madrasas as an undermining scheme of the state
and those hostile to Islam.

Hafiz Azmath and the other madrasa teachers I met ardently emphasized that they had no concern for having a secular *career*; they wanted,
rather, to express a set of *ethics*. Saleem, another teacher at Madrasa
Arabiya, happily noted that enrollment at the madrasa had increased
significantly in the last several years to over one hundred students, the
majority of whom studied full time at the madrasa. He said to me, "I have
no interest in earning money, gaining the world, or making a name for
myself. This is not my goal. My only goal is that in each home there is one
religious person, who will create an Islamic atmosphere for his family. We
are poor, and we want to die as poor persons." Slouched over on the floor
of the madrasa, wearing his topi and kurta pajama, Hafiz Azmath sum-
marized the principal message they wished to convey to their students:

> My children, this world is full of suffering. The life we get is very
> short. With this brief life, just pay respect to God and to your
> Prophet, live your life as the Prophet told you to. Don't ever worry
> about your food, your health, your family, because whatever hap-
> pens is God's will. The goal of this short life is not to earn money
> but to spend it in worship.

This emphasis away from worldly life supported my observation that
men saw few avenues for material success and claimed little desire for
worldly progress, even as they sought to protect the larger community
and encourage the women in their slum neighborhoods. This emphasis contrasted sharply with the material projects of the women's political
communities.

"Even just with women we have to be modest, so imagine how it must be with men"

Men and women shared the mission of collective responsibility and autonomy, and the relationship between them was generally one of mutual
reinforcement. But it was primarily women, not men, who participated
in all three dimensions of political community. Almost all the women
I spent time with at training centers and Islamic study circles came from
poor families with strict gendered practices. Many left school around the

seventh class, wore burqas, and lived gender-segregated lives. They had different degrees of literacy, ranging from none to modest.

They also revealed a variety of relationships to gendered teachings, segregation, and veiling. I met women who were deeply habituated to wearing the burqa and believed that it maintained a certain order between men and women, an order that ultimately guarded women's safety. Sometimes these same women remarked or joked that they felt resigned to the religious custom. I once asked a few companions in Faiz Nagar the clichéd question of whether they felt hot under the burqa in summer. "Yes," replied Hina. "But what can we do? We're helpless." On another occasion, Hina and her cousins asked me about life as a woman in the United States. Hina mused, "You must feel so sad [*afsos hotha hain*] looking at us." I quickly said no, and that if they were happy, then that was all that mattered. They all nodded and said, "Yes, we're happy." Hina affectionately draped her burqa on me, and her cousin commented, "You should wear it all the time! It looks good on you!"

Then there were those participants and Islamic leaders who actively promoted the burqa and gendered teachings. Some, though not all, belonged to sectarian, reformist Islamic traditions, namely Ahl-e-Hadees. Others participated in some manner in the women's wing of Jama'at-i-Islami Hind (JIH), with its strict teachings. Many of these women, especially leaders, wished to purify Islamic practice of external corruptions (*bida*) such as cultural rituals they argued were Hindu importations into Indian Islam. In this respect, I view them as generally of a reformist tradition.

Women in the centers and Islamic study circles also clearly shared an emphasis on women's comportment and gender segregation. While I heard scores of conversations advocating women's opportunities and education, I also encountered stringent teachings about women's comportment. Some of my companions stressed the importance of not drawing any male attention by, for example, wearing a drop of perfume or wearing anklets or heels whose sounds might attract men. They carefully explained that we must never accidentally run outside the house in a gown while fetching a child. Instead, we must remember to put on a large scarf or our burqas even for such momentary tasks, lest a male neighbor catch sight of us. They actively feared the dangers of mutual desire. As Rehana baji noted, "Even just with other women, we have to be modest, so imagine how it must be with men." These were all applications of the principle of preserving women's virtue that they understood as an obligatory component of their faith.

The social and economic context also encouraged gendered teachings. Hyderabad's steady stream of male migrant labor to Saudi Arabia
and other Gulf countries was among the highest in the country. These
men brought the influence of Wahhabi Islam, and practices like the burqa
and full-time Islamic education, back with them when they returned. This
importation from the Gulf was not unique to Hyderabad, but was perhaps
more visible because of the high numbers of migrant workers.

The temporary migration of men, particularly Muslim men, spoke to
the larger issue of Muslim male unemployment and discrimination in
Hyderabad. The marginalization of men put greater pressure on women
to find income-generating opportunities—but they did so while reinforcing the necessity of the burqa and women-only spaces.

For the many families in which the male head of household was living
abroad on a work contract, wives and mothers-in-law effectively managed
the home. Without their husbands, sons, and brothers, they found ways
to navigate public space alone. Their burqas and women-only spaces provided protection as they did so. Finally, this moment enabled subaltern
Muslim women to inhabit leadership positions both spiritually and in
terms of creating political communities. They ran religious study circles,
worked in girls' madrasas, and participated in various material projects.
All this may still have unfolded in the absence of male migration; however,
migration placed certain pressures on women as well as presented opportunities for them to leave their private spheres.

Political Communities
Seeking Independence Through Community

When I first began talking to elites and middle-class Muslim acquaintances
about my interest in Islam and politics in the city, they almost immediately started talking about Muslim women's education. They raved about
their educational projects, how girls performed better than boys, and the
women's training centers they helped start. The biggest problems they saw
among Muslims—of illiteracy, child labor, and "fundamentalism"—all
came back to the status of women and the need to reduce their isolation.[5]
I learned quickly that women's education and training were focal points
in the politics of Islam. This was not only because I had spent time with
elites. Even walking around Shanthi Colony without any elite or middle-
class contacts, I learned about women's tailoring centers. Anwar told me

of his plans for opening a center attached to Masjid Arabiya. Imam Ghazi, the imam of another mosque in Shanthi Colony, also proudly pointed me to the women's tailoring center attached to the masjid. They hoped, they said, to reduce Muslim women's isolation and "backwardness," build their self-esteem, and in turn uplift the community.

Scores of these women's centers existed throughout the city. They ranged in size and comfort, generally accommodating ten to fifteen old-fashioned sewing machines, a weaving loom, embroidery table, and cutting table. The women, twenty to one hundred at a time, sat hunched over on the floor as they worked by hand. The centers ranged from windowless structures with tin roofs to bright and spacious rooms inside a larger children's school, as in Faiz Nagar.

The participants in these centers were almost all Muslim and came from families with BPL ration card status, or "economically backwards" families as defined by government policy. Nearly all wore the niqab. Most commonly, the women learned textile skills like tailoring and embroidery and, more recently, henna artistry and beautician work. Turning to local Muslim philanthropists and associations was a critical alternative to government self-employment schemes, where my companions insisted they lost all their time and money in the bureaucratic maze of applying for assistance.

Poor women achieved a sense of dignity and accomplishment through gaining these material skills, from sewing to henna application. Nearly every time I visited the training centers, one of the women there excitedly showed me her training booklet, a portfolio of the designs and techniques she was trying to master. With great pride, she would sit me down and show me her practice work—doll-size blouses and petticoats—detailing the types of stitches and embroidery techniques she had used. Over the course of my fieldwork, I pored through countless numbers of these books. More often than not, I left the center with my arms decorated by a woman demonstrating a newly learned henna design.

It is important to acknowledge that women have passed on artisan skills like henna design and embroidery for generations, though men have more visibility in textile work in India. I do not wish to overstate the newness of Muslim women's shared traditional activities. But I do want to emphasize the newness of their expansion and professionalization. And regardless of the content of the skills, women are gathering in public to teach one another and learn.

Material projects like these were thoroughly intertwined with Islamic movements. While middle-class Muslims and elites established many of the women's training centers, religious organizations were also increasingly instituting them, thanks to local donations and remittance money. Participants combined and justified these educational and self-employment training projects with Islamic teachings. Poor subaltern women often brought their religious ideas and practices to these programs, where they encountered the hegemonic ideas of elites.

Islamic teachings and lessons at these centers ranged in frequency from daily to monthly. The Islamic study circle I most frequently attended, in a slum neighborhood of Zohra Bagh, took place in a home down the street from a textile training center. Many of my companions attended their training before the study circle, and then we would walk together to Rehana baji's home in the late afternoon. They always had me sit in the front on a platform with the teachers while the approximately forty women in attendance sat on hard wooden benches and listened for two hours. My companions discussed these Islamic teachings during their textile trainings, and they sometimes discussed their self-employment hopes and prospects during their study circles. Eventually, the study circle group began thinking through the details of starting a revolving loan program.

In the training centers, elites such as Kulsoom apa played a strong role in advocating women's freedoms and material progress, with politicians sometimes tagging along. Because I gained entry to some of these sites through philanthropists, I often found myself invited to ceremonies at women's centers, such as that attended by Inspector Gopal and Mr. Reddy, the Congress Party corporator. The philanthropic board held such ceremonies when a "batch" of women completed six months of training. About forty low-income Muslim women in burqas, as well as a handful of Hindu women, were overjoyed to attend that particular ceremony. I had trouble finding the school, making my way past the water buffaloes sniffing through heaps of trash, the "Bone Setter" shop, "Om Sai Men's Saloon," and dozens of boarded up and blackened apartment buildings before I stumbled onto a small mosque and the ceremony taking place under a colorful cotton canopy. Someone spotted me and immediately called me to the dais to help hand out certificates. At the dais sat several board members, Inspector Gopal, and Mr. Reddy. After making government promises, Mr. Reddy launched into an impassioned speech in which he said: "Before these schemes, our mothers and sisters never even left the house. Today, they are learning to stand on their own." Kulsoom apa then took the microphone: "It is [our] hope that women become finan-cially independent, that they're not stuck inside the home and worried. This doesn't mean taking over your husband or going against him. Your independence will be a great help to your husband, too!" The mix of elite paternalism, which Kulsoom apa represented, and local political compe-tition normalized discourses about the importance of women's financial independence, their freedom to leave the house, and their self-efficacy.

With the backing of elites, my subaltern companions elevated the image of an "independent" woman who had some education and employ-ment. I chose the English word *independent* as a loose translation of the literal Urdu expression meaning "standing on one's own feet"—a phrase I heard repeatedly in relation to these projects. They explicitly acknowl-edged oppression by husbands and mothers-in-law as a primary reason they wished to stand on their own. But this concept of independence must not be understood in terms of individual rights and freedom from others. Indeed, a woman could stand on her feet only *through reliance on other women*, to learn skills and critically, as I will show later, to escape abusive families and marriages.

At the centers I visited, women relied on one another, exchanging tech-nical advice and pushing each other to work harder. In Faiz Nagar, a por-tion of the women earned some income at piecemeal rates for a contractor in Dubai. Each day after arriving, they went to work at the sewing and embroidery machines, encouraging and facilitating one another's train-ing. They also worked collectively on their Urdu or Arabic literacy. Rashida was a lower-middle-class teacher at the training center attached to Masjid Arabiya in Shanthi Colony. For four years, she had taught Urdu and Arabic reading, often combined with Islamic teaching, every day during the wom-en's lunch. Her own story was a mystery to us, as she never married or had children, an atypical background for most local women. Now in her fifties, she dedicated her time entirely to educating other Muslim women. She also sometimes used her small income to buy dinner for the women at the center and for the young madrasa students next door. Women like Rashida were key figures who helped build community through supporting and teaching other women important skills.

Sometimes, when a woman achieved a certain level of skill and inde-pendence, we celebrated her story. In one of the Islamic study circle ses-sions at Zohra Bagh, we discussed the local story of Reena, a young Hindu woman from the slum who converted to Islam against her family's wishes and attended study-circle events from time to time. Apparently, Reena had

secretly wanted to become a nurse, and over many years hid this desire
from her parents, who would have disapproved. Farzana recounted:

> She desperately wanted to work at a hospital. So she prayed to God
> every day. Then one day her sister got very sick, and they went to
> the city hospital for treatment. Reena watched the other doctors
> and admired the Muslim lady doctors. Then she started wearing
> the hijab like them. But she still didn't have the courage to tell her
> parents she wanted to be a nurse. One of the [respected] doctors
> at the hospital said to her father, "Reena is so hard-working, and
> she has a special glow [noor] in her face. Why don't you make her a
> nurse? I think she'd be great." And the father took his advice. Reena
> couldn't believe her prayers were answered—that God placed this
> seed in the doctor's mind. As she learned more about Islam she
> understood that God created us as capable of everything. Reena
> used to go to the women's centers and has learned how to perform
> prayer. When her father decided to support her career, she knew it
> was because of God's will. Masha'Allah [by the grace of God], she is
> independent.

Being a nurse was crucial to Reena's independence and pride. But independence only had meaning in and through community. In this case,
prayer, but also support from her father and a women's religious community, was integral to encouraging Reena's "independence." She became
a nurse through moral community and support. Her success, in turn,
inspired my companions.

As women learned skills or became self-employed from home, they
earned money that alleviated some anxiety about meeting basic needs.
Self-employment, my participants said, provided alternatives to domestic care work or to being "useless" (bekar). The particular industries of
textiles and beauty services seemed to build on a cultural love of femininity and enjoyed an apparently limitless demand. Shaheen, a young
Muslim woman from Zohra Bagh, had graduated from the center. Her
husband lost their savings (1,700 rupees) and Shaheen's few pieces
of gold jewelry to a con man who had promised him a work visa to
Dubai. Her husband at the time sold flowers in a popular city market.
Shaheen's father opposed her going to college, but she said she was
gradually gaining confidence and assertiveness through her work in the

center, and perhaps one day she would be able to assert her desires. But now, she said:

> I make about 1,500 rupees [approximately $35] every month from in-home work. Multiple people come to my door every day with their tailoring needs. And if the customer looks rich, I can charge even more! I used to worry about how to afford food, feed my son and daughter every week. But now I know I can at least feed them, even when my husband can't help.

Shaheen's success was not typical, but it represents the material goal women worked toward. At some welfare centers, the organizers secured bulk demands for garments that provided steady work.

Particularly because the training could lead to some income, most of my companions said their husbands appreciated the welfare centers and supported their efforts. At the same time, leaving the home and attending these centers transformed the women's routines and raised their confidence, threatening the patriarchal order. I did meet some women whose husbands or parents opposed their leaving the house to attend the centers.

Hina was nineteen when I met her, warm, sharp, and full of life. She gained textile skills over several months at the Faiz Nagar center, but eventually her mother and brothers forced her to withdraw. They saw how much she was socializing with others and how "visible" she was on the streets as she walked to and from the center. For a while, I worried that my own presence at the center had also upset and threatened her family. I knew Hina had been talking about me, but was unsure what her family thought about her becoming close to a visiting American and all that I represented. Later, Kulsoom apa managed to convince Hina's family that the centers were safe and positive for young women. Thereafter, Hina attended from time to time, though no longer regularly.

Another woman, Lubna, in her thirties, attended her local center despite her husband's opposition. When I asked if she felt scared taking such a risk, she laughed and looked at me intently with her piercing gray eyes. "I don't care what he says! I keep coming anyway." Like Hina and most other women, she traveled to and from the centers with her female companions. Her friend quipped, "He just wants her to stay home all day, taking his beatings. He thinks that's a better idea!" Lubna continued, "I want to stand on my own, and he's not going to stop me."

Hina and Lubna show how a particular image of women came to life through these training centers. This new model was enacted through a sense of increased independence of movement, socializing, and opportunity, as well as reliance on other women, with whom one commuted every day and shared knowledge of one another's families and marital situations. This type of community building minimized the isolation that nourished the so-called backwardness of poor Muslim women. Most husbands and parents supported the project, though a minority found it threatening.

Islamic organizations also fully supported material projects. Whenever someone doubted the wisdom of women's working, others would circulate Islamic stories that supported women's independence. For example, my companions commonly cited the story of Khadija, the Prophet Muhammed's first wife of twenty-four years until her death. She was an independent businesswoman, several years his senior, and had herself initiated the marriage proposal to Muhammed prior to his religious revelations. Muslims often cite her as an example of an ideal woman.[6]

Even the JIH put its weight behind the new emphasis on women's education and right to work. This came through clearly at the state conference of the women's wing that I attended in 2006. The women's wing of JIH had numerous Islamic campaigns, Quranic classes, women's textile training centers, primary school projects for girls, and scheduled "inspections" of girls' madrasas. The conference displayed many stalls and banners promoting gender segregation and women's veiling—but always attached to the message of women's material progress. One large banner stated: WE USE PARDAH TO COVER OUR BODIES, NOT OUR MINDS. It had a picture of women in niqabs next to an office chair, next to a computer, and with a group of surgeons around an operating table. The banner promoted the idea that Muslim women can be equally educated as men and participate in professional fields, so long as they wear the niqab. In the opening conference speeches, a JIH leader praised the reform efforts of the Prophet Muhammed in his time: "He breathed new life into the role of women. He provided them with a field to work, avenues in which to work. He wanted them to have independence and freedom, a share of inheritance, representation. *In every field of life*, women's importance was acknowledged" (see also Vatuk 2008a, 518).

A good deal of rhetoric during the JIH conference also criticized the West vis-à-vis capitalism and the role of women.[7] I recognized that this criticism held a material purpose beyond rhetorical appeal. For example, another sign, translated into Urdu and Telugu, made the following call: REJECT WESTERNIZATION, REFUSE TO BE A COMMODITY, RESIST

EXPLOITATION, LET'S STRIVE FOR WOMEN'S DIGNITY! JIH and a number of speakers at the conference linked women's apparently low status in the West directly to their commodification. In Islam, they argued, women's (mandated) sexual modesty in public protected them from these unique exploitative tactics of Western capitalism. Again, they sought to tie advocating women's education and public presence with their teachings on veiling, modesty, and gender segregation. Targeting women's material status was clearly central to low-income women's Islamic movements and leadership structures, like the women's wing of JIH. This material component of political communities was self-consciously Islamic, advancing a model of women's material progress and independence distinct from a so-called Western model that my companions equated with sexual exploitation.

These projects I discussed were not merely instrumental in terms of welfare improvement and creating women's skills. They also cultivated a desire to participate in public discussions and practice citizenship. Their political community had a strong material base in education, skills, and literacy, but with a profound acknowledgment that women's independence only developed and took meaning through community bonds.

Employing Shari'a for Women's Rights

Beyond material training and independence, women's political communities in the slums worked to claim women's Islamic rights to divorce and dowry-free marriages. Though my companions engaged with the concept of legal rights, their project was framed around political practice, community, and solidarity. In their legal struggles, they fought for the general principle of women's rightful status in Islam through a community of people to educate one another, accompany women to courts, and negotiate cases with Islamic judges. Their ties were based on trust and mutual accountability. Through collective study and the creation of important interlocutors, women were able to employ shari'a to their benefit, and they preferred this legal avenue over turning to the state.

Women's activities contradict popular images and opinions of shari'a as a set of oppressive, medieval legal injunctions. In a context of heightened communalization and the accusation that Islam is hostile to women, my companions confidently asserted that they enjoyed full rights under Islam. Yet, they confronted these misunderstandings regularly. For example, I attended the citywide press conference for JIH and the Girls Islamic Organization one month before the regional JIH women's conference.

The press conference was an awkward spectacle, with a number of male journalists asking hostile questions of the three burqa-clad women at the dais. As the local president, Mrs. Fayza, spoke about current JIH platform issues, like dissolving women's fashion shows and beauty contests, it was obvious the attending journalists perceived JIH as a symptom of the backwardness of Islam and shari'a. This exchange illustrates the tone of the press conference:

JOURNALIST 1: Will everyone have to be in *pardah* [wearing burqa] at the state conference?

MRS. FAYZA: No, it's whatever one wishes.

MRS. NADIRA: People are giving a bad name to Islam by fixating on the burqa. But we are pleased that more young women are wearing it.

MRS. FAYZA: We're also campaigning against extravagant weddings and gift-giving [*jahez*].

JOURNALIST 2: Don't you think the model *nikah namah* [Islamic marriage contract] needs to change?

MRS. FAYZA: No ...

JOURNALIST 3 [INTERRUPTING]: But this is the modern era! Under what conditions would you change it?

MRS. FAYZA: Shari'a is for all time. It's not supposed to be altered.

This brief exchange at a press conference demonstrates the popular disdain for women who sought to defend shari'a—a disdain that obscured much of the feminist practice and political community these women promoted. In this case, Mrs. Fayza mentioned campaigning against extravagant weddings, a practice that placed enormous financial and emotional pressure on brides and their parents.

Despite all the folk opinions of Islamic law, shari'a is in fact a set of principles rooted in social relations. Historically, and inherently, it has been flexible (O. Roy 1994; Messick 1993). My companions used it especially in their struggle against dowry, the marriage practice of giving gifts in cash or kind to a groom's family. Although the institution of dowry operated primarily among Hindu families and varied across regions, it spread rampantly among the Muslim poor over the last twenty years, evolving into a racket that creates inordinate stress on families and in some cases violent harassment of young brides.[8] The Indian state criminalized dowry in a number of ways beginning in the early 1960s.[9] JIH and other Islamic groups campaigned against it, widely acknowledging that dowry symbolized the devaluation of women and lacked religious justification. Islamic law instead mandates the practice of *mehr*, the promise of a monetary amount to be given from the groom to the bride at a future date.[10]

Among poor Muslim families, the extortion of money and consumer goods from a bride's parents, coupled with the requirement of costly weddings paid for by the bride's family, raised the costs parents associated with having daughters. Especially as Muslim male unemployment increased, marriage became a way for men to access not only dowry but also the potential monetary gain of marrying a woman with some education or earning potential. Though activists and mosque leaders lamented the practice, they argued that families had no choice but to provide a dowry if they wished their daughters to marry. So, parents of daughters saved money where they could, and men took temporary work contracts in Gulf countries to use part of their remittances to fund their sisters' or daughters' dowries.

As Muslim women became increasingly educated, and to a much lesser extent employed, demands for dowry increased rather than diminished. My companions in the self-employment centers often complained to me: "*Baji* [sister], these days they're asking several ounces of gold at minimum! On top of that they want a car and *also* a scooter! The groom doesn't provide anything. In some cases, he never even pays the *mehr*." Sometimes their complaints slipped into requests for money, an awkward incidence I had to manage time and again.

In response to this phenomenon, women's Islamic groups and other Islamic charity organizations campaigned against dowry and against costly weddings. On International Women's Day, the Zohra Bagh community celebrated with great excitement and energy. As usual, I awkwardly sat at a dais with several women leaders as we discussed what the day meant. A well-respected local college professor gave a speech about oppressive institutions for women, including dowry and expensive weddings "in Hyderabad, especially." She emphasized that society must value women as full human beings and not for the roles they must play: bride, daughter-in-law, sister-in-law. Women lose respect in each of these roles, and each is implicated in the dowry system.

Islamic teachers who lectured at the welfare centers and in Islamic study circle sessions addressed the topic of dowry and its incompatibility with Islamic principles. At one study session Rehana baji asked me to participate in a general discussion about the status of poor Muslim women and their religious practice. When we approached the topic of dowry, I timidly confessed that I could not understand why families participated in such a system, led by demands from a groom's family. Rehana baji responded immediately, "Parents are helpless. They don't want their daughters to wait forever to find a husband and then grow old alone." She then reflected for a minute. "But we do have families that are exceptions, who refuse it because they are religious and have fear of God. Farzana's mother didn't ask for dowry from any one of her daughters-in-law." Farzana beamed proudly.

Rehana baji continued and lectured to the forty of us in attendance:

So my sisters, you all must have the courage to say "No!" "I'm not going to pay someone to take my daughter, and I'm not going to demand dowry from anyone!" *Insha Allah* [God willing], little by little, this social evil will disappear, we'll eliminate dowry, and everyone will then *really* be practicing Islam.

One scorching day, Farzana invited me to a girls' madrasa graduation in the Old City. Thankful to see chairs, I found a seat amid the 300 attendees. The students and community, influenced heavily by Ahl-e-Hadees, arranged a number of speeches and end-of-year performances. Among these were morality plays in which students depicted various social problems and sins. A teenage girl walked across the stage, and the crowd grew quiet. She started depicting a woman's rapid disintegration and decision to commit suicide as a result of dowry harassment from her in-laws. Two other girls acted out a scene of the bride's mother and father, already in ill health, seeking a 50,000 rupee loan ($1,000) with interest to pay their daughter's dowry. Wracked with guilt for causing her own parents such anxiety, the young actress declared, "It's better if I just kill myself." We saw her swallow the pills and collapse, after which the curtain closed. A narrator then came in and lectured: "This is how our poor and innocent girls are exploited. God has showed us the evils of giving and taking interest [*riba*]. Interest is never allowed, no matter what you hear. We can find ways of saving ourselves from debt. And dowry is not in Islam. We must pray to God to stay on the straight path."

Through drama, lectures, and religious study sessions, Islamic organizations treated dowry as a grave issue. They employed a legal ethical framework informed by Islam—rather than, say, the state's criminalization of dowry—to undermine the institution and its devaluing of women.

The second legal issue my companions struggled with was divorce. They informed themselves and one another about their Islamic rights to divorce, especially in situations of domestic violence. Among the activists in Zohra Bagh, there seemed a sense of urgency to educate women about their legal Islamic rights, make contacts with lawyers, and spread awareness of the widespread nature of domestic violence. While Muslim men may easily divorce through the Islamic practice of *talaq* (verbal repudiation), Muslim women who desire divorce must secure their husband's agreement. Nonetheless, the religious right of women to initiate a divorce (*khul*) exists, though it requires the forsaking of the *mehr*. *Khul* appears to account for a significant number of Muslim divorce cases, although the circumstances under which these occur remain unclear (Vatuk 2008b).

The study circles took up divorce less pointedly than the anti-dowry campaign, but they increasingly considered the idea of divorce with regard to domestic violence. The Zohra Bagh study circle was connected not only to a training center but also to a group of lower-middle-class activists. Hafeeza baji ran a women's madrasa in the same family home where the textile training center was located. Well-versed in Islamic law, she received phone calls at all hours from women seeking counseling for their desperate marital crises and situations of domestic violence. She and her group of activists, related to Nasr with the civil rights association, told me the story of Noorjahan, a woman they assisted in securing a divorce through an Islamic judge (*qazi*).

Noorjahan had been abused and victimized for fifteen years by her husband and in-laws. "If she was five minutes late in coming home, they would beat her. It got much worse when it turned out she couldn't have children." When Noorjahan made contact with Hafeeza baji and the activists with whom she worked, they walked her through the Islamic court and developed a relationship with the *qazi*.[11] She was able to initiate her divorce despite her husband's lack of consent. Noorjahan later remarried, but in an ironic twist, her ex-husband turned to a civil court hoping to overturn the *qazi*'s decision.[12]

According to Hafeeza baji and other interviewees, civil divorce trials involve a drawn-out and humiliating process for women. By establishing consistent relationships with *qazis*, my companions bypassed civil law, which they saw as disadvantageous to women. According to them, civil courthouses are full of poor, semi-literate women with complicated family problems. These women are often uneducated in the rights they might secure more quickly through Islamic law. As word of local cases like Noorjahan's circulated through the slum community, women learned how to claim divorce rights and they learned that Hafeeza baji and her close group of activists were a source of support in the neighborhood. These women developed a strong reputation as local friends and anchors in poor women's legal struggles.

In this respect, legal efforts helped create a political community that protected women going through dangerous transitions and fought to secure rights or legal reform. Legal empowerment was realized and *practiced* through conversation, performance, and mediation. In short, women exercised legal empowerment in community and with the aid of interlocutors.

Creating Honor Through Skill and Community

Perhaps the most significant component of Islamic movements among poor and subaltern women was their symbolic value. These movements created and circulated honor, as well as a moral community based on trust. My companions in the BPL neighborhoods developed new bonds and a shared commitment to their religious-political space. They achieved this by creating a sense of accountability to one another and to the larger community. This accountability also involved the mutual recognition of alternative forms of honor. Because of the global stigma against many Islamic practices, my companions were painfully aware of the symbolic repercussions of their actions. And when poverty and discrimination excluded them from material and political avenues of success, they subverted their dishonor by valorizing Islamic education and knowledge, in addition to the skills they gained at the training centers.

Why did Islamic education, as an alternative to government education, become so important to political communities? After the 2002 massacre in Gujarat, Muslims felt a strong desire to preserve Muslim identity, in part through education. This was true even in Hyderabad, relatively far from Gujarat. Second, many families experienced government schools as less secular than they purported to be, in the sense that they reinforced Hindu ethnic superiority in various curricula like language and history. Finally, despite robust religious freedoms in India, in a small number of cases teachers harassed students who wore a hijab or burqa. In one notable local case, a school fired an instructor for wearing a burqa. For these reasons, my companions had little faith in public education as a source of truth, learning, or honor.

Instead, in many BPL communities, men and women alike gained honor through religious skills. Like their male family members, Muslim girls and women in Hyderabad increasingly attended madrasas, either full time or part time, and pursued training in *hifz* (Quranic memorization) or *alim* (exegesis) programs. The sense of honor that came from developing expertise in Islam, I argue, was related to a combination of material and religious factors. Among subaltern Muslims, the reality of state retrenchment and extremely limited opportunities for mobility offered little hope for earning respect. I commonly heard poor Muslim women referred to as worthless (*chillar*) or useless (*bekar*). Indeed, my participants in the welfare centers matter-of-factly referred to themselves as *bekar*.[13] Those with some madrasa education were far from useless in these neighborhoods, though. They possessed the critical skill of being able to teach Arabic and *tafsir* (Quranic explication), usually informally. They might thus earn some income, no matter how meager, but more important, they enjoyed the honor and respect attached to this role. They were among the few individuals equipped to perform the work of spreading Islam (*da'wa*).

In poor Muslim families with multiple children, parents sometimes chose one child to pursue formal Islamic education. Rubina, a divorced woman and domestic worker raising three daughters, proudly announced to me that she decided to send her eldest teenage girl to the *alim* program located in Zohra Bagh. She had dreamed of this for years, since she had not been able to pursue Islamic education for herself. Likewise, Mehraj, another young woman at a training center, proudly told me when her brother started training in *hifz*. "The schools in our neighborhood are no good, so my parents thought, 'Why not send one [child] to become a *hafiz*?' It's a big deal to memorize the Quran. It takes a lot of mental power."

Parents and family members gain great esteem in Islamic education and the mental prowess and moral effort it demands. At a special study circle held in a home down an alleyway near the Zohra Bagh slum community, I sat on the stone floor and listened to a number of young girls reciting prayers and hadith from memorization. Their voices echoed through the cheap sound system. One six-year-old girl so impressed everybody with her memorization that the teacher called out to the nearly seventy-five women in attendance, "Who is this girl's mother?" A poor woman stood up shyly, clutching to her ragged sari, as the crowd congratulated her.

Farzana, who invited me to these events, was immersed in children's Islamic education. She was searching for a new school for her son, who had been attending an English government school. She disliked the co-ed school activities and the white school uniform, a color Muslims tradition-ally associate with mourning. Farzana laughed as she complained about the uniforms. "Well, I know there are some things we just need to toler-ate." Her preteen daughter, training in *hifz*, had already memorized a good portion of the Quran. She sometimes recited or sang at the start of our study session. Facing all of us, with her hair perfectly covered, she sang sweetly from an Urdu poem (*na'at*)[14]:

> My Prophet arrived, amidst darkness and lies
> With his message of truth
> He taught us, "Actions are better than empty faith"
> He couldn't convince others
> So a miracle was necessary—
> With the splitting of the moon
> My Prophet arrived

Farzana, again, beamed with pride.

In addition to the creation and circulation of honor among women, my companions enjoyed the sense of "peace" (*sukoon*) they came to depend on from the Islamic study circle sessions. The Zohra Bagh study circle was a moral community involving a process of trust—in one another and espe-cially in the teachers, who served as interlocutors. As one companion said to the group, "I am anxious until the next study circle, and then I feel at peace. If I miss a session, I feel an emptiness in me." Another said that the study circles were necessary because they helped her experience "fear" (*dar*), to be reminded of life's impermanence. Although it may seem counterintuitive, fear and awe augmented the women's faith and practice. These emotions created a sense of peace and certainty of the desire to live life according to Islamic teachings. As we often discussed, religious faith developed through a combination of love of God and fear of God's power. So, we all had to remind one another of the Prophet's teaching to perform each prayer as though it were our last, with great concentration and purity of intention.

My companions sometimes shared their experiences with external hostility to their religious practice. During one session, Suraya, a woman who lived in a BPL neighborhood, but who was educated in mathemat-ics, grew tearful while discussing the topic of the burqa. In front of the group, she said to me, "Please tell them [in America] that we absolutely

are not oppressed. This is an illusion, a myth, that they've created."
She added:

> When I go to the college, my [non-Muslim] colleagues always tell
> me I should just take it off when I get inside the building. "Why
> not be comfortable?" they say. They tell me they feel bad for me.
> I always have to explain to them that this is my choice. I'm *not* phys-
> ically uncomfortable. *Alhamdulillah* [thanks to God], I don't even
> feel the heat. This is my faith, and this is what makes me happy.
> I really struggle with this. I like my colleagues, and I interact with
> non-Muslims all the time. I believe that they're sincere. But then
> I think to myself, they're not Muslim, and they don't understand.
> They always feel bad for me, but I feel bad for *them*.

We all listened carefully as Suraya's eyes filled with tears. Rehana baji
praised her for having the courage to be steadfast in her practice and setting
an example for non-Muslims. Several women talked about the responsibility to explain themselves to others and the limits of others' understanding.
Farzana said, "It shouldn't be a burden you always have to carry."

"Try your best to explain," said Rehana baji, "but if they can't understand, then just set a good example with your practice. Whenever you feel
upset about this, just pray to God to give guidance [to others]."

The most unusual practice I witnessed during these study sessions
involved the use of supplications (*duas*). Every study session ended with
approximately fifteen minutes of supplications recited by the teacher, usually Farzana. While Muslims customarily ask one another for prayers, the
women turned this into an organized practice during the sessions. The
week before, women would speak to Farzana or hand her a note with a list
of worries. Farzana would then incorporate these into her *duas* the following week. All of us would cup our hands and close our eyes as Farzana's
recitation became increasingly impassioned and high-pitched. The supplications ranged from larger requests to God to grant us paradise to specific
requests for help with everyday problems like joblessness or poor health.
Here is a portion of supplications from one session:

> My dear God, we are sinners, we are self-destructive! You are the
>   forgiver, the merciful!
> Help us live according to your will. In all our homes send us your bless-
>   ings and distance all our worries! Let us understand the difference
>   between halal and haram.

Grant good health to brother Rafi, grant good health to Aunty Wahid.
  Normalize Sister Anjum's blood sugar, grant children to Anwar Sakina.
Reduce Aunty Khatija's knee pain, make Habib interested in school.
Put compassion in Ruqaiya's husband's heart, grant my three sisters
  pious in-laws.
Have mercy on Mrs. Malika's soul, give Fauzia *sabr* [patience]. Let there
  be unity and love between Mustafa and Asma.
Ease Roshan's work abroad, put love in Sharifa's mother-in-law's heart.
  Protect our children, have mercy on our ancestors!
Protect us from the mistakes we make . . .

When I would open my eyes to sneak a peek, I saw tears streaming
down Farzana's face, pointed upward toward the sky. Many of the women
seemed entranced, and indeed, I sometimes felt I was witnessing a sha-
manistic performance. In the end, we usually felt relief and a sense of
closure. Farzana or Rehana baji's ability to channel this type of passion
and emotion while carefully addressing each sister's suffering created a
collective effervescence[15] that marked an important closure to each study
session and seemed to solidify the community. The combination of the
trust required to reveal their experiences and ask for help in the form of
supplication, mutual obligation, and honor constituted the invaluable
symbolic component of women's political community that takes place in
and through their Islamic revival.

THESE SUBALTERN MOVEMENTS in Hyderabad were radically new in that
they took community as their means and end, as opposed to making claims
on the state. Because of this, these movements were a noninstrumental
form of politics. My companions made a conscious decision to engage in
these new politics through their experiences with and distrust of the state.
Neighborhood Muslim communities pulled together to uphold a collective
mission, a tendency originating in a type of secularism that valorized religious community identity. Thanks to elite support and labor remittances
from the Gulf, poor and subaltern Muslims were able to practice sufficient
autonomy to create the institutions that would support their projects. In a
context of state noninterference in religious matters, Muslims could freely
pursue Islamic education and use Islamic law to better the situation of
women. Subaltern politics paid particular attention to the status of women
because Muslim women were largely poor, uneducated, dishonored, and
victims of social problems like dowry harassment.

By advocating for women's status and opportunities, middle-class activists and elites made gender visible from above, and subaltern men and women made it visible from below. In other words, those with power, existing at the top of the status hierarchy among the city's Muslims, spoke publicly about gender and emphasized its importance to the political advancement of Muslims. And those among the poorest Muslims also gave central importance to the plight of low-income Muslim women. Men like Anwar and local imams in Shanthi Colony actively supported women's training centers in the neighborhood. Anwar supported women's self-employment and earnings, even as he preached ascetic living and warned against the logic of profit and the negative influence of money. Likewise, Hafiz Azmath and his fellow teachers wished "to die as poor persons" even as they supported women's material projects. Women's political communities did not threaten the authority of the men in their lives or their neighborhoods. Rather, my companions strongly upheld their gendered practices and belief in the sanctity of women's chastity or modesty. Farzana and Rehani baji spent many hours teaching women in the study circle about the importance of maintaining their modesty. Muslim women, they taught, could attend university and work, so long as they maintained their veiling practice and enough social distance from men.

Strict gender norms coexisted with material, legal, and symbolic projects in support of women. The training centers provided textile skills to many thousands of low-income women. Through these centers, women like Shaheen and Hina enacted a new model of a woman with increased independence, potential to earn money, and the social support of other trusted women. Even Islamic associations like the JIH actively promoted women's work and other material projects. For a few women, like Lubna, their husbands resisted women's leaving the private sphere and socializing with non-family members; but elites like Kulsoom apa were sometimes able to step in and negotiate with families. This illustrates how strengthening relationships within the community underpinned material projects and increased independence. Because these training centers were intertwined with Islamic study in some sites, as in Zohra Bagh, conversations involving women's family situations and rights in shari'a took place both in Islamic study circles and in self-employment training activities. Through meeting and conversing in these settings, women began to practice legal empowerment through community. They educated one another about dowry and domestic violence, and important interlocutors helped secure women's Islamic rights to divorce. Hafeeza baji was one of these interlocutors who made herself available every day of the week. My companions gained awareness that having close interlocutors held more promise than civil law.

Finally, subaltern women subverted their dishonor as poor and *bekar* Muslim women by circulating alternative forms of honor. This symbolic project gave them peace, moral support, and pride in their religious and material skills. While journalists had spoken disparagingly with Mrs. Fayza and Mrs. Nadira of JIH, Mrs. Fayza made her opening speech at the regional JIH conference, crying out passionately to the thousands of poor women: "We should take this opportunity to show the world, show all nations, that Muslim women *don't have* pardah *[veil] over our* minds *[dimagh]! We don't have* pardah *over our* hearts *[dhil]!* With our minds wide open, while living within Islam and obedience to shari'a, we can enter any field in the world!" Creating new forms of honor for themselves and demanding their rights to enter the public sphere, they practiced their right to citizenship.

Amid a domestic and global War on Terror, and generalized hostility toward Muslims, poor and subaltern Muslims in India found ways to avoid the state while working to improve their extreme poverty and exclusion. They did not retreat into the private sphere. Rather, they gathered together and, alongside their Islamic revival, participated in material, legal, and symbolic activities that lay the foundations of civil society. They created skills, relations, and space to protect themselves from the state and from the vagaries and indignities of the market. Women in these political communities emphasized a certain freedom and independence through skills and education, but they enacted this freedom in community with women companions and men allies. Secure in these bonds, they ventured outside their homes and socialized with others in remarkable numbers.

5

Politics of Recognition

FOR A BRIEF period, it became my routine to stop by one of my local *alimentaires* in a bourgeois arrondissement of Lyon for my baguette and banter with Zied, the shop owner. He sat behind the counter all day, making running commentaries about politics, grumbling about the arrogant bourgeois locals, and blaring old Egyptian pop songs from his little radio. Each time I saw him, he complained about French "racists" and their hatred of Islam. A man in a business suit walked in for a bottle of water and newspaper. "But *he's* not a racist! He's one of the good ones!" Zied shook with laughter, pointing at his regular customer, who blushed and nodded at me. "I definitely find it hard to wear the hijab here," I said later. "I know," he said. "My wife," he put his hand to his heart and then lifted it proudly into a fist. "She wears the veil."

Whenever there were no customers, he would lean in and lower his voice, frequently glancing out the door to make sure no one else could hear him. "They keep us [*musulmans*] weak, you know."

"Even though you have so many mosques and so many associations?" I asked.

"But there aren't enough! And we're all divided." He excitedly grabbed two coins and a pencil from his cash register to illustrate. "The government said, 'You here are Algerian' [sliding one coin]; 'you here are Tunisian' [another coin]; and 'you over there are Moroccan' [pencil]. And oh boy, did they *hate* the Algerians!"

Zied had lived in Lyon for over fifty years, having emigrated from Tunisia as a child. I asked him why his family left Tunisia. He answered me sheepishly, "Our neighbor moved to France, and he'd come back and visit, wearing nice suits and carrying packs of Marlboros. Then everyone started scrambling to leave." I met two of Zied's cousins, who also left

Tunisia many years ago. One of them, Aziz, was unemployed and would come by the shop. Though none of them had much money, the cousins had all avoided life in the quartiers. Aziz said that when they arrived, it was not exceptionally difficult to get an apartment in Lyon, and because they were bachelors at the time, they did not have anyone to support. "I knew my kids would get corrupted if we lived in the quartiers. I did my best to avoid it." Zied teased another white customer, dressed in a suit, as he sold him a case of beer. "And voilà, *he's* not a racist! Hey, when are you going to find a job for Aziz?"

Another evening as we were chatting about where to go for the end of Ramadan prayers, Zied introduced me to his cousin Ramzi, a car mechanic. Ramzi was sitting in a van with a hookah and was clearly drunk or high. As Zied tried to convince me that Barack Obama was really a Muslim, Ramzi slurred, "There are *five* holy books, the Torah, the Bible, the Quran. . . . " He tried to count on his fingers. "But Muslims don't know anything, we don't practice. Even me, look at me." His words petered out.

Zied and his entourage were amusing characters, but their stories and relationship to Islam and to bourgeois France spoke volumes about their contradictory experiences and practices of religion, their political attitudes, and the pain from discrimination they carried. I frequently saw such pain and contradictions in Muslim-owned shops. On at least two occasions, the Muslim owner suspected or asked whether I was Muslim, and told me not to purchase certain products because they contained lard. They felt they had to offer these products for sale, even though they were not halal. When I took a taxi to a mosque, the Maghrébi (of North African origin) driver invariably confessed his feelings of guilt over not practicing Islam. When I wore the hijab, I sometimes received attention from Maghrébi strangers. Once in the Vénissieux Metro station, a transport worker approached me and said, "Oh, it's so difficult, your hijab. But it's good, it's good [*ça fait plaisir, ça fait plaisir*]." Because I was often on guard, I was not sure if he was mocking me or speaking seriously.

With or without my hijab, I had numerous encounters with everyday discrimination against Muslims in France. One regrettable incident involved a university woman who came to meet me at my apartment when I was interviewing babysitters for my young son. She wore the headscarf and was of Maghrébi background. My son happened to be crying at the moment, and she spoke sweetly to him, "Oh, I know you're scared of my scarf! It's okay, I'll take it off. Don't cry." I assured her that her scarf was not at all an issue. When I called to let her know that I would not be hiring her (for other reasons), her tone and brief words made it clear that she was accustomed to being rejected, presumably because of her hijab. I had heard from several participants that "under-qualified" was a euphemism for veiled. The three words that I heard countless times across the spectrum with regard to Islam in France were the following: "It's very hard" (*c'est très dur*).

During my longest period of fieldwork, I lived in a neighborhood close to downtown Lyon but adjacent to rue Paul Bert. This neighborhood was full of halal butcheries, Islamic bookstores, and North African shops. During the days, women in djelbabs perused the Islamic bookstore, flyers for Islamic events and organizations covered small bulletin boards outside shops, cars blasted music, and young Maghrébi men eyed the non-hijabi women shopping and running errands. These details constituted the everyday Islamic culture I knew in Lyon: vibrant, full of contradictions, frequently confronted with discrimination, and caught between the pious and the profane.

These details provided the backdrop for what I argue was the centrality of symbolic recognition and recognition claims among broadly middle-class Muslim activists. They faced state obstacles to Islamic institutions, and they intensely felt discrimination and racism that drew them closer to Islam. Some of my second-generation companions struggled to reconcile their simultaneous belonging to Islam, France, and the Maghréb while coping with discrimination. I argue that their politics of recognition included two different kinds of paths and associations—one characterized by working with the state to achieve integration, and another by opposing the state through radical critique. Though the field of middle-class activism was not riven with competition as was that among political and philanthropic Muslim elites in Hyderabad, activists experienced profound disagreements over whether or not to work with the state to achieve recognition. And both groups of middle-class activists were ultimately estranged from Salafists in the quartiers. With a combination of regret over this estrangement and disdain for Salafism as a misinterpretation of Islam, they no longer knew how to connect to their subaltern brothers and sisters in the quartiers—and thus they faced a divide that seemed unbridgeable.

Everyday Obstacles and Discrimination

Two factors provided the context for middle-class recognition politics: the numerous obstacles the state posed to Islamic practice, and middle-class Muslims' personal and collective experiences of discrimination. At a broad institutional level, former President Sarkozy made a special priority of integrating Islam, and the state accepted and facilitated the construction of mosques and the creation of Islamic associations. But at the local level, municipalities delayed and obstructed Islamic projects through various means, and accused Muslims of *communautarisme*.

During my fieldwork, Lyon's Islamic associations were working together to construct France's third private Islamic high school, Al-Kindi. On the eve of its anticipated opening in the fall of 2007, the education department claimed the building violated hygiene and safety codes, and it delayed the school's opening by several months. Alain Morvan, the head of the Academy of Lyon, admitted his opposition to the school for its *communautarisme* and "fundamentalism" (*intégrisme*). President Sarkozy later dismissed him over the controversy.[1]

Among other organizations accused of *communautarisme* was the EMF (Étudiants Musulmans de France), a national student group that helped Muslim students challenge discrimination in their universities. The EMF had strained relations with CROUS (Centre Régional des Oeuvres Universitaires et Scolaires), a national public administration that managed student assistance and awarded grants and housing assignments. The group gradually lost its representation in CROUS, following publicized elections in 2004 in which opponents accused the group of *communautarisme*. Eren, one of the association's leaders whom I interviewed, complained about unwarranted accusations of radicalism, general surveillance, and phone tapping. At the time, the group was busy defending students at one of the city's medical campuses. The administration had confiscated the students' identity cards on account of their looking "foreign."

Even in the absence of direct obstruction or harassment by the state, the press released stories defaming Islamic projects. For example, Le Centre Shâtibî, an Islamic education center in Lyon, came under attack in 2006 when it collaborated with Hani Ramadan, the controversial Swiss imam and brother of writer and philosopher Tariq Ramadan. The press, along with local feminist organizations, galvanized protesters against the "menace of Islamization and shari'a." It was in this context of direct policy interventions and a hostile discursive terrain that middle-class Muslim associations did their work. Some associations and individuals responded with bitterness toward France, while for others, discrimination strengthened their resolve to struggle for justice.

"I am just as French as 'Jacqueline,' even with my religion"

Maryam was in her early thirties, and was born and raised in Lyon. Her father emigrated from Algeria in the 1960s and worked as a janitor for city buses before retiring. I met Maryam through Aisha, at Mosquée Hijra. I was sitting outside with Aisha when we spotted Maryam and her husband, Samir. Samir was highly educated and active at the mosque. He asked Maryam and Aisha if they needed anything for their Islamic study circle later that evening. "See," Aisha turned to me. "Here, men and women work together." "Actually," Maryam laughed, "the men work *for* the women!"

Maryam was devoted to her Islamic practice, prayed five times daily, educated herself through the mosque in Islamic sciences and *tajwid* (Quranic recitation), and facilitated *halakah* (study circle) sessions at her apartment for groups of women. Like most of my companions, she also took her veiling practice very seriously. Once, at a friend's place, we had loosened our hijabs while talking and drinking tea. When the friend's husband suddenly came home, Maryam jumped up from the couch and frantically tried to refasten her hijab, and signaled to me to do the same. "It's absolutely critical to have limits [between men and women]," she said. "When we interact in everyday life, you have to keep some distance. We [Muslims] are conscious of this reality. We know very well that there's a certain kind of relation [of desire] between men and women—it's natural. You don't have to hide yourself or cover your face, but you have to be aware." Compared to Maryam's, my veiling was embarrassingly clumsy, and she would gently fix my hijab here and there. She always appeared elegant, dressed in clothing that perfectly coordinated with her hijab as she sauntered into the mosque.

At work, Maryam was pragmatic with regard to her hijab. She enrolled in a computer training course, but quit when the instructors said she had to take off her scarf if she wished to stay in the class. In her full-time job in office administration, her employers allowed her to wear a bandana, but not a hijab. She said that even this slight accommodation was unlikely to continue much longer because her employers found her headwear annoying. "They think I'm 'showing my religion' in the workplace."

Nearly every woman I met in Maryam's circle had similar experiences. The friend who hosted us for tea was upset that afternoon because she had just learned that neighborhood mothers blocked her from the local babysitting co-op. They said they would not allow her to watch their children if she wore her hijab, and they refused to babysit her daughter. Her husband wanted to help her contest the decision, but I did not know of any woman who succeeded in contesting discrimination against wearing the hijab.

Ismat, a woman of Afro-French background and Maryam's best friend, used to remove her hijab for work even though it caused her great distress. But now she was able to wear her hijab because she worked with predominantly Muslim colleagues. "Not long back, I spoke with a lawyer about [wearing it in the workplace], and he said, 'But it's so hot outside! Why would you want to wear it anyway?' How can I explain to him that this is my faith?" Pursuing legal avenues always seemed to prove futile.

Sometimes, women confronted major setbacks due to discrimination after having achieved substantial success in their education or training. Aisha had studied psychology and hoped to become a psychologist. When she moved with her husband to Paris, she reported back the disappointing news that she could not complete her training because no hospitals or clinics would accept her in her headscarf. She said to me, "We [women] are psychologically exhausted, so tired of being seen as victims."

I asked Maryam at one point if she wanted her young daughter to eventually wear the hijab, and she said yes, that it was extremely important to her. "But I don't really know what we'll do in the future and what will happen with the [headscarf] law. I don't feel good about forcing this conflict onto a young teenager, to make her deal with hostility at school. Maybe we'll just have to hope that she'll choose to wear it once she finishes high school."

Through all the hostility they faced in the workplace, my companions at Mosquée Hijra supported one another through a dense structure of solidarity and friendship. Maryam figured centrally in this structure, and her social circle appeared almost entirely Muslim. For most of my companions, this narrowing of their social life developed toward the end of high school. Maryam felt strongly that she had reconciled the French and Muslim aspects of her identity, but this took time. As a child, she had internalized shame of her parents and of their language. But in the last decade, with the dramatic growth of Islamic organizations, she developed her knowledge and piety, and found peace with her identity. Like many young practicing Muslims, her parents taught her an Islam that was primarily cultural, traditional, and perhaps even contrary to the Islam she currently practiced. As Islamic literature was developed and translated into French, and as Islamic conferences in French became available, she began to understand religious tenets for herself.

As we sat on a bench outside Mosquée Hijra one afternoon, Maryam and Ismat reflected on their experiences. Maryam said:

> It's through these associations that we reconciled our identities, that I learned I can be French and Muslim at the same time. These two things don't have to be contrary.... You know, we're not recognized as French, we're not recognized as Muslims, we're not recognized as Maghrébines, so it's really a lot of work to construct ourselves. But there were people there to guide me through this, to explain to me that I am just as French as *Jacqueline*, even with my religion. I'm lucky that I had people [through the mosque] to explain this to me.

Ismat added:

> The media has mixed up everything—Arab, Muslim, terrorist, it's all the same. In the last ten years we've felt more racism. The French are worried that Islam is growing. Maybe they're not racist, but they're scared. They're just scared.... The problem is that the French want to impose their culture—we have to be French just like them, dress like them, eat like them, that's what they want. We can very *easily* be French—but *with* our religion and culture.... In the future, once we can have a normal politics, act in all types of organizations as Muslims but without any difference, and *really* be considered French, then things will have advanced.

Through mosques and associations, both Ismat and Maryam found a fragile peace with their identity as French Muslims despite the everyday hostilities and obstacles they faced because of their headscarves.

But some questions remained emotionally challenging and unanswered, especially questions about one's mortality and spiritual purpose. Maryam struggled as she contemplated her daughter's future in France, as well as her own eventual passing. "What's most important to me is my religion. Before anything else, I'm Muslim. After that, well, I was born and raised in France, I will certainly die in France, so France counts more in my eyes than Algeria, even though my roots are in Algeria. But I confess that I wouldn't want to be buried here. It's just too hard to respect Islamic rites here [in France]. I'd rather be buried in a Muslim country, maybe in Algeria or Morocco."

Regarding her own search for belonging, Ismat concluded, "Islam is about my existence on earth, it's about what's universal, what is my purpose here in being alive. My identity as French is just about France, my relationship to this country. And I need something greater than my attachment to France or the Maghréb."

"As adults, we go back to what our parents taught us"

Just as for Maryam and Ismat, the situation of Muslims in France resonated personally and emotionally for Hakim. Hakim was born and raised in eastern France, on a farm outside a former mining town. His father left Algeria in 1940 and worked in the steel industry for thirty years, retiring when the plant shut down in 1970. Hakim now worked in Lyon in the field of juvenile justice, advising youth through their court proceedings.

Hakim held several leadership positions and was active with JMF (Jeunes Musulmans de France) and UOIF (Union des Organisations Islamiques de France) for over a decade. He rigorously practiced Islam, combining some elements of Sufi philosophy and periodic fasting as part of a spiritual regime. He believed that the younger generation's interest in Islam stemmed partly from the desire to honor one's immigrant parents.[2] "Our parents tried to tell us something about Islam, and like all kids, we didn't listen. As adults, we go back to what our parents taught us. These kids in the banlieues, for example, they're very interested in learning about Islam now, even if they don't practice it." Hakim's love for his father, who had passed away, motivated some of his thinking and attachments. As part of his grieving process, he traveled around the country raising funds for the local Islamic center on his father's behalf, such that the spiritual rewards would go to his father's soul. "When you do these things [for the greater good of the Muslim community]," he recommended to me, "you should dedicate them to your parents."

Algeria, his parents' birthplace, held a powerful place in Hakim's imagination, though he had visited only twice—once in childhood and later, for his father's burial. Hakim and others spoke with a frank morbidity and sadness whenever we discussed burials, which combined many of the salient issues in the politics of recognition: identity, recognition and approval by the state (for Muslim cemeteries), one's relationship to Islamic rites, the permanence of Islamic structures, and hope that future generations would have the capacity and will to honor Islamic traditions such as cemetery care-taking.[3] Ilyas, an activist who worked closely with older generations of Algerian immigrants, spoke about the "disastrous" situation of Muslims who die with no kin or resources to provide for their burial and the increasing impossibility of repatriating their bodies to the Maghréb. Hakim also described the lack of Muslim cemetery space in France as "catastrophique."

In his desire to hold on to the memory of his parents and to pass on Islamic traditions, Hakim hoped to take his children to Algeria from time to time. But like Maryam, he did not plan to impose his own religious choices upon them. He smiled at the image of his seven-year-old daughter. "She already loves playing with her hair. Maybe she'll never be ready [to wear the hijab]. Ultimately, it'll be her choice. I hope in maybe ten years, French attitudes toward Islam will change. Maybe they'll overturn the [headscarf] law. Or, I'd like to think maybe there'll be an Islamic high school nearby that my kids can attend."

For all my companions, religious rights and institutions were necessary for daily Islamic practice, but they also forced difficult, emotional questions made more salient by the immigrant experience: Will I be able to honor Islamic rites? Where do I wish to be buried? Will my children practice Islam? How do I honor the memory of my parents and grandparents?

"I did everything you wanted and got nothing in return."

I met Khalil at a Ramadan dinner at his cousin's home a couple of days before the Aïd celebration marking the end of the Islamic month of Ramadan. Glancing at the television, his cousin cheerfully announced that New York had lit up the Empire State building for Aïd. We commented that we could not imagine such an event in France. "Never," said Khalil. "They don't care." Khalil had a slightly tougher disposition than Abbas, his activist cousin. Abbas surprised me with his jovial, almost innocent attitude, which contrasted sharply to media depictions of him.[4] Unlike Abbas, Khalil was suspicious of me. But his initial gruffness belied his warm generosity and eagerness to talk about his experiences, which gradually came to shape our conversations.

Khalil was born in France after his father emigrated from Tunisia to work in construction. He spent his childhood in a semi-rural province near Lyon. His father had been a resistance fighter against the French in Tunisia, and this profoundly shaped Khalil's early consciousness. Recently,

Khalil had decided to leave France and move to a Muslim majority country. I could tell he was conflicted about his decision to turn his back on France—something that Abbas refused to do. "There's a saying in France," Khalil explained. " 'We accepted the contract.' I ate pork. I almost married a white woman. I left my religion. I did *everything you wanted* and got nothing in return." He did as much as he could to "integrate," but the discrimination never abated.

In childhood, Khalil and his siblings were the only Maghrébi students in his school. He suffered numerous physical and racial aggressions. Despite being tracked in school toward manual skills, he eventually went to university and studied politics. But after a professor told him that he would never earn money in academic pursuits, Khalil left without his degree. Recently, Khalil gained some success in business, though not without obstacles. For example, he was denied a bank loan because for no clear reason he appeared on a list of high-risk borrowers. But now, he joked, he had transformed into a "capitalist pig" and left the activist world he used to share with Abbas, when they worked with youth in the banlieues in the 1990s.

Khalil's wife was third-generation Maghrébine and shared his interest in greater piety. "People stare at us [because of her hijab] when I'm out with her, just stopping at the corner shop. It makes me so angry, makes me want to start fights with them." I personally observed the discrimination that so frustrated Khalil in my own brief time with him. On one occasion, we were looking for a restaurant for lunch in a tourist quarter. I waited outside while Khalil went in to ask the maître'd for a table. The maître'd seemed unenthused, and when he came outside and saw me in my hijab, he hesitated before telling Khalil the remaining tables were reserved. We said nothing and moved on. As we ate at another restaurant, I asked Khalil if he believed the maître'd. He replied, *"Absolutely not at all.* He saw you in your hijab and then changed his mind."

Khalil's experiences with discrimination drew him closer to religious practice and altered his political attitudes. He survived two dramatic and life-changing events that he attributed to racists. The first event was the death of his older brother when they were teenagers. "My brother was in the apartment, playing his guitar loudly. Some racists came by and started giving him a hard time and eventually pulled a gun." He shook his head and looked away. "My mother, she became crazy after that." He quickly added, "It was good that he died" because the family came to embrace their faith more deeply. When the family took the body back to Tunisia for burial, Khalil's other brother Amin was moved by the Islamic rites and how the local community supported them in their grief. "That's when he turned to Islam and brought it back to the family."

In the second incident, Khalil was shot in the chest at a nightclub when a fight erupted. His friend had wound up in a fight with the club's bouncers and shouted to Khalil for help. Khalil ran to the basement of the club to help his friend, and one of the bouncers suddenly shot him in the chest. The shooting left him permanently injured, ending what had until that point been a highly successful career in boxing. The doctors had nearly pronounced him dead and declared his eventual recovery a miracle. "For some reason, God wanted me to live," he said with a tinge of guilt.

These two crises instigated Khalil's decision to develop his faith, as he described it:

> We each have our own destiny, a life span that is predetermined by God. My brother had to be sacrificed for the family to come back to Islam. I'm always struggling to stay on the right path. There are lots of things I did that I regret, that I can't take back. But my faith is everything I am. If you want to understand me, why I do the things I do, why I think the way I think, then you have to understand my faith.

Turning to Islam for community and for spiritual solace helped Khalil survive major tragedies—tragedies that he believed stemmed from racism.

Relationships to the State

Given the structural barriers erected by the state, the discrimination so commonly experienced, and the emotional significance of recognition politics, groups and individuals followed one of two paths: either working with the state or radically criticizing the state and the agenda of integration.

"I think it's going to get better, I really do"

The decision to work with the state for recognition came from years of experience and first-hand knowledge of the steps required to secure basic institutions such as mosques. These represented hard-earned victories. According to Hakim, attaining cooperative relations with local government was the only way to facilitate Islamic practice. After working many years with the UOIF, his "first love," Hakim campaigned for several years to open a new Islamic center in a small city near Lyon. He proudly showed me the tiles he laid down, with the help of his wife, and the buckets of paint they used on the interior walls—clear indicators of his financial, physical, and emotional investment in the project.

One of the goals Hakim had for the center was to normalize the practice of single, rather than gender-separated, entrances. On the eve of its inauguration, he proudly showed me the single entrance. "I was worried it would cause problems in the [Muslim] community to not have a separate entrance for women," he confessed. "But thankfully it hasn't, and we are setting an example that it's okay to have the same entrance." To materialize his vision, he had summoned all his diplomatic skills to maintain good relations with the municipality, asking his colleagues to let him control the negotiations himself. Without government allies, he remarked, the community might have faced last-minute bureaucratic obstacles, as happened with the Al-Kindi high school, noted earlier. Enthusiastically optimistic about the future of a uniquely French Islam, Hakim's long-term goal was to run for local elections. "In France, Muslims are victims of the law," he explained. "They aren't politically informed or involved. And they don't vote in high numbers, which is why politicians don't care about us." But he was confident in his assertion, "I think it's going to get better, I really do."

The CRCM (Conseil Régional du Culte Musulman) for Rhône Alps, the regional branch of the state-created CFCM, practically specialized in negotiating with municipal administrators. When I started my fieldwork, CRCM's president had finally completed negotiations with the Vénissieux municipality to approve the construction of a mosque catering to the Turkish community. The municipality had obstructed the project for twelve years.

The CRCM and major mosques engaged in a delicate dance with mayoral authorities to assuage public fears of Islam and to ensure cooperation with public events. Each year, for example, a mayoral delegation or deputy visited the Aïd prayer gathering, usually in public gymnasiums, at the end of Ramadan in a show of support.[5] I attended an Aïd prayer, organized by Mosquée Hijra, in a public gym where nearly one thousand worshipers gathered. The mayor of the town, which was adjacent to Lyon, visited at the end of the prayer. He took the microphone and wished us all a happy Aïd, and the organizers from Mosquée Hijra thanked him for his cooperation. Maryam, who worked closely with the mosque and helped organize the prayer, listened attentively.

Relations with the mayor may have demonstrated the mosque community's transparency and cooperation with state authorities, but it accomplished little in terms of improving the conditions of the prayer. We were packed like sardines into the gymnasium, which had terrible acoustics and no carpets. This made the prayer difficult to hear and physically uncomfortable. I found it claustrophobic and nearly fainted at one point during the prayer. I finally got up and tripped and pushed my way outside to get some air. I eyed a table with desserts and some drinks. By the time I reached the table, I saw at least two disheveled women stuffing large bags with handfuls of the North African pastries. I felt embarrassed for them and walked away.

Maryam, however, was excited and optimistic. She had worked hard for the prayer to go smoothly. Maryam held a leadership role at Mosquée Hijra and had been with the mosque since the beginning and through its challenges, from local opposition to its initial construction to the later vandalizing of its façade. Almost every time I saw her, she was busy with some administrative task, registering people for Islamic or Arabic courses, testing their level of Arabic literacy, or answering questions about course content. She helped plan the annual schedule of events at the mosque and make arrangements for the Aïd prayer, including everything from prayer mats to arranging a children's section. That day at the prayer, she busily handed out fliers for the mosque's classes and seminars. For her, committing to the mosque was deeply gratifying, even if it required the work of maintaining cooperative political relations, and even if it still left much to be desired.

"We're simply doing the work of citizenship"

The community of Mosquée Hijra was generally educated and politically engaged. A number of my companions participated in Le Comité 15 Mars, for example, a group that formed after the 2004 banning of the headscarf to protest the law and to support schoolgirls dealing with the law's consequences. Several Friday *qhutbas* (sermons) I heard at the mosque criticized the war in Iraq or urged us to attend street demonstrations for humanitarian causes, especially those related to Palestine, an issue close to the hearts of many in the mosque community. During the 2007 siege of Gaza, the atmosphere at the mosque grew especially tense and the *qhutbas* were especially urgent in terms of encouraging political demonstration. Mosque leaders had become more vocal in their opposition to Islamophobic state discourses throughout the course of my fieldwork. Through the media, they publicly criticized the ruling party's proposal in 2011 to have a national debate on Islam's compatibility with laïcité.

Religious teachings at Mosquée Hijra promoted not only civic engagement but also the need to reconcile Islamic practice with the roles of Muslims as French citizens. One of the last talks I attended there was a lecture by a well-known sheikh titled "Love of God." Hundreds of attendees packed the mosque, and we all sat in silence as the sheikh lectured about whittling Islam down to the basic sentiment of love for God—in a world in which outward religious practice was increasingly difficult. He explained:

> Our Prophet knew that in a materialistic society, people needed to be [spiritually] educated. But when there's too much information, like today, we have to just take what's essential. Love of God is the most efficacious practice. It's not *extremism* but rather, liberation— liberation from one's self. And how do you achieve this? Take the time to contemplate the concept of compassion [rahim, one of the names for Allah], the greatest force that will manifest on the Last Day. Read the Quran, not just with rhythm but also with *heart*. It's fine to understand what's halal and haram [permitted and prohibited], but this doesn't really get at *knowing* God, of love. The great companions [saheba] of the Prophet weren't grand theologians, but they understood the essential.

The sheikh was attuned to the notion of living in a laïque society, avoiding the supposed dangers of "extremism," and feeling confident in one's faith and love of God even when one could not practice the rituals of Islam. His religious discourse, and the general discourse of Mosquée Hijra, accepted the need for integration in the dominant society, as well as the need for recognition by the state and public, which at times demanded the restriction of religion to one's private sphere.[6]

Although organizations like Mosquée Hijra chose to work with the state toward integration and recognition, many members still took a critical view of the French state. As Maryam complained, "The state is always obstructing us. Like CFCM, for example—they [the state] should just let it do its work. They don't facilitate our work but instead discourage us, even though what we do is not all religious or proselytizing. We're simply doing the work of citizenship." She made clear that their work was not a violation of secularism but simply a struggle for religious rights. When France passed the anti-headscarf law, the community felt defeated. "It destabilized us a little, all of our local associations," Ismat said. "We saw that even if we struggled against the law, they passed it anyway. And that really impacted us. We had to wake up to reality. We [Muslims] weren't divided on the issue [as often depicted]. But we realized that it would be difficult to gain respect—that Islam in France is going to remain difficult."

Regarding various state proposals to formalize and expand the training of imams into national universities, Ismat complained, "It's the same colonial habits, of interfering in our affairs, as though we don't know how to organize ourselves or how to train our own imams." Aisha's father worked at the Institut Européen des Sciences Humaines (IESH), which trained imams. She felt that imams needed language training in French, but beyond this, any state assistance would be problematic. "They [IESH] don't receive any support from the state and frankly, if they did, the government would want to have control over the curriculum. Imams should be able to discuss positions on political matters, for example, in reference to the Quran and shari'a, not just what's best for the French state."

Despite his optimism, Hakim also saw their community's work as an uphill battle, as he explained:

> I think in France it's more difficult to be a Muslim than in other countries because of the history between North Africa and France. I just have to hope that things will change. In my twenties, I thought we were going to build another world. Then, you know, there was this recent vote by the French Assembly to pass a law proclaiming the "positive role of colonization." And 19 percent of the deputies voted for it! And a lot of French people agreed with it! When I saw that, I thought, "No, this is impossible, it can't be true." ... When I saw that, I thought, okay, we still have a lot of work to do.

"My parents, my grandparents—they died for this country!"

At the fringes of the field of recognition politics was the Parti des Musulmans de France (PMF), a political party that fielded candidates in a handful of local elections, including Lyon. The PMF remained marginal, given its lack of professionalization, the absence of a "Muslim vote," and the failure of its agenda to resonate among working-class Muslims in the banlieues.[7] Its platform emphasized "anti-*laïcité*," seeking to overturn the headscarf ban, and anti-Zionism. Journalists, scholars, and the representative council of Jewish institutions in France (CRIF) frequently accused the PMF of anti-semitism.[8] Vénissieux was one of the few towns where PMF candidates participated in local elections.

I met Nadir Ben-Abbes the same year he had received just over 1 percent of the vote after a low election turnout and minimal campaigning.[9] Ben-Abbes had lived in France since early childhood; his parents migrated from Algeria. He worked as a bus driver and tramway operator in Lyon. Politically active for over twenty years, he avoided the Communist Party for its staunch atheism and worked instead with the Socialist Party (PS). Eventually the PS, too, seemed anti-religion, and Ben-Abbes felt marginalized.

"My parents, my grandparents—they *died* for this country!" He turned red and grew increasingly upset as he spoke with me. "I say to my kids, 'you are *home*, this is *your* country.' I don't ever want them to feel ashamed [the way we did]. I'm with PMF because Muslims shouldn't feel ashamed to practice their religion or stand up for their rights to organize politically on the basis of their identity."

Ben-Abbes did not come across as a professional politician, and his conspiratorial tangents about the Free Masons did not help his case. Other candidates did not take him seriously. A television documentary on French Islam portrayed him almost mockingly and Vénissieux mayor André Gérin made insulting comments about Ben-Abbes's candidacy. In response, Ben-Abbes protested that other politicians had entire teams of assistants writing their agendas and feeding them lines, something he could never afford. But he believed that a day could arrive when his platform would resonate with voters. He deliberately chose to run in Vénissieux because of the high concentration of Muslims, though he had little success. Focused so heavily on religious recognition, he overlooked the majority of issues most critical to residents in areas like Vénissieux's quartiers.

Ben-Abbes's lack of electoral success also shows how unacceptable were recognition demands like overturning the headscarf ban within the mainstream political system. Even to other politically engaged Muslims such as those in the Mosquée Hijra community, his platform was exceedingly unrealistic. To be taken seriously, he needed not only sharper political skills and professional comportment but also acceptance of the language of integration—something he was unable or unwilling to embrace.

"The real message of Islam is anti-capitalist, anti-communist, anti-everything"

The nearly singular focus on religious recognition, at the cost of economic justice, was the principal point of disagreement within this middle-class field. Some of my companions criticized associations that worked with the state, for two main reasons. First, they viewed the state as more insidious and anti-Muslim than did mainstream associations such as the CRCM or even the UOIF. Second, they believed that in their haste to accept the state's logic of integration, associations that worked with the state had lost sight of a more radical agenda not just for recognition but also for meeting the economic needs of Muslims in the quartiers.

Basem, who was actively involved in the UJM (Union des Jeunes Musulmans), one of Lyon's Islamic youth organizations, remarked of the state: "They don't want to integrate Islam—they just want to control it. They want a 'soft' Islam, and the best way to achieve it is to open schools for the training of imams and then prevent the real message of Islam from being spoken. And the real message of Islam is anti-capitalist, anti-communist, anti-everything, and this is what the state wants to avoid." In Basem's assessment, by working with the state and accepting an agenda such as centralized training of imams, Islamic associations would give up the radical potential of Islam.

Farid, a longtime activist in the city, was disillusioned and frank, when he added:

Alright, I'm going to be a little mean in saying this. But the French state, and maybe even all European states, have never wanted to really integrate Islam and Muslims. Even if there are some humanitarian [*humaniste*] politicians who want Islam to be integrated, the majority aren't interested. Quite simply, they don't want us. . . . I think if the state could just send us all back to our countries of origin, if it wouldn't pose a problem with human rights regimes and things, it would do it. But since it can't, what does it do instead? It just passes laws that are increasingly repressive. . . . Forget about "integration"—even just respecting Muslims is a problem, to stop considering them as terrorists, Islamists, fundamentalists and instead as normal people who just want to live their lives. But politicians and journalists insult us morning, afternoon, and night.

For Farid, working with the state would be nearly impossible. Born and raised in France, Farid maintained a close relationship to rural Algeria, where he often visited his extended family. He chose to have an arranged marriage with Samira, a woman from Algeria who moved to Lyon to join him. For various reasons, he had a strained relationship with his parents. As with many things and people in his life, Farid held his parents to his very high personal and moral standards. "Anyway," he said, "my father's a *kafr*."

"Oh come on, Farid!" Samira stopped him. "You're being really unfair. Does he have faith?"

"Sure," Farid said. "But a Muslim is someone who actually applies Islam in his life, not someone who just claims to believe." Though Farid was exacting, he could not be accused of hypocrisy. He held himself to high standards, devoting his free time to volunteer work, supporting international social justice campaigns, organizing conferences and public demonstrations, and raising funds for Muslim political and humanitarian causes. He remained active from time to time with the Islamic bookstore, Tawhid.

"Tawhid," he said, "is not interested in trying to compromise with the state, shake the hands of politicians, and bow down to them." He lamented what he saw in mainstream associations as obedience to the state, indifference to the quartiers, and depoliticization. For example, with regard to the headscarf ban, he said that though Islamic associations held meetings and demonstrated against the ban, they quickly abandoned the issue after the law was passed. "They washed their hands of the issue and everyone went back to their homes. When the law passed we all cried and said 'this can't be possible.' We had large meetings to discuss the issue, but then everyone returned to their corners, and we never united." He argued vehemently, "If Muslims don't fight for their rights, they will eventually just leave and go back to the Maghréb. It'll become [in France] how it was in Spain—they'll be persecuted and repressed until they're all gone."

Over meals at his apartment, or in conversations we had when I came to visit him at the bookstore, I saw Farid working hard to raise funds or encourage other activists to commit to an event or project. "In our work now for Palestine, people come to our events, shed some tears over Gaza, and then disappear.... There's a growing individualism here in France. But to be a good Muslim—to be a good human—is to be concerned with humanitarianism. I try to be as active as I can, even if it's not much." "Is it this bad in the United States?" he earnestly asked me. "You know, not being able to count on anyone? Everyone in his own corner [*chacun dans son coin*]?" Farid worried not only that Muslims would not adequately struggle for their rights but also that they would succumb to an individualistic, depoliticizing logic.

Despite his disappointments, Farid remained politically active and was close with a handful of activists. He introduced me to Abbas, a prominent and long-time activist with both Muslim associations and secular groups in the Lyon region. Abbas, Farid, and other Muslim activists in Lyon had overlapping affiliations with secular social justice associations like the Forum Social des Quartiers Populaires (FSQP) and DiverCité. Abbas had long focused on socioeconomic problems in the quartiers, police violence, and anti-Muslim hate crimes and discrimination. He had been blacklisted as a fundamentalist for several years. He told me that he made it to the top three of a list of candidates for a teaching post in Lyon, but they dropped his name at the last minute following accusations of fundamentalism (*intégrisme*). Diligently, he rummaged through the piles of papers on his desk to show me the discrimination complaint he filed, though I think we both knew it would not get him anywhere.

Like Farid, Abbas disliked mainstream and media-savvy Islamic associations, specifically for their abandonment of the quartiers. "They've been run over by individualistic values and just want to work for themselves. It's not Islamic. Getting food in everyone's stomachs is the foremost duty of Muslims. The Prophet said, 'He who sleeps on a full stomach while his neighbor goes hungry is not one of us.'" Abbas recounted a story (that I later heard from others as well) about the French interior minister in the early 2000s inviting a group of Muslim leaders to dinner. The meat they served was not halal, and apparently the leaders remained silent. Some ate the dinner while others put aside the meat. He argued that the state deliberately manipulated the situation to test how pliable the leaders would be.

In the 2007 national elections, Abbas supported the candidacy of José Bové, a radical syndicalist and anti-globalization activist who actively supported both the Palestinian cause and justice in the banlieues. Abbas traveled to the training institute for imams at Château-Chinon for electoral discussion and campaigning. After he claimed that all mainstream political parties were the same and bad for Muslims, he was disappointed that students and instructors castigated him and insisted he was mistaken. They disagreed over the value of a far left candidate focused on economic justice.

Abbas faced the challenge of balancing his loyalties to Muslim communities with his overall commitment to social justice that transcended the need for religious recognition. He was disappointed with the lack of distribution politics among middle-class Muslims, noting that the CFCM and UOIF submitted to the state and therefore did not represent "80 percent of Muslims." And he was disappointed with the lack of recognition politics among the secular social justice organizations with whom he worked. Some members of the secular group DiverCité, for example, wished to focus on justice in the banlieues, but had trouble accepting religious Muslims in the banlieues.

The path this group of activists took placed them in a difficult position of needing to carve a two-pronged strategy. First, they sought to protect Islam from outside interventions by radically critiquing the state's proposals around Islam; therefore, they could not align with organizations like the CFCM. For example, Abbas recounted, when the state in 2008 insisted on an imam training program to operate through a Catholic institute in Paris, the CFCM wrote a polite letter to authorities merely expressing why it was problematic for Catholic leaders to supervise Islamic training. Abbas, however, wrote a different letter with stronger language, insisting that the proposal blatantly insulted the Muslim community. He found the CFCM's meekness disappointing. Second, these activists tried to align themselves with the far left in hope of supporting economic justice for working-class residents of the quartiers. This, too, placed them in a difficult position, as demonstrated by Abbas's experience at Château-Chinon, where other Muslims strongly disagreed with this political strategy.

Disconnect from Muslims in the Quartiers

Just as middle-class Muslims had different and conflicting relationships to the state, they were on the whole disconnected from Muslims in the quartiers. This disconnect took place following a period of activism marked by great hope and cross-class organizing. As the economic problems in the banlieues persisted across time, the growth of Salafism in the quartiers reinforced the barrier that developed between middle-class activists and the subaltern.

"In fact, everyone has abandoned them"

I had a taste of the class disconnect and of Abbas's disappointments when I attended a weekend-long administrative meeting of DiverCité in an office in Vaulx-en-Velin, one of Lyon's working-class banlieues. DiverCité was a leftist grass-roots association, founded in the mid-1990s in the Lyon region. Its primary agenda was justice for working-class, foreign, and immigrant residents.

I wore my hijab to the meeting and immediately noticed I was the only one in a headscarf. Everyone was polite, but I still felt like an elephant in the room amid the plumes of cigarette smoke, incessant debate, long monologues, and reflections about the goals and future of the organization. One of the themes that members raised a number of times, apart from budgetary and administrative concerns, was DiverCité's struggle to attract interest in the quartiers. That year, DiverCité members had participated in the creation of a new organization, the Forum Social des Quartiers Populaires (FSQP), a coalition of several associations active on issues of social justice and police violence in the quartiers. The FSQP had just held its first conference, along with a concert, in Saint-Denis, outside of Paris. But residents from the quartiers attended in low numbers. Abbas expressed his disappointment with DiverCité and the FSQP's lack of success in reaching out to residents.

"We should've done a better job, spent more time and effort. If we'd had bigger names at the concert, we may have drawn more young people from the quartiers. We were targeting people in the *cités*, but we didn't fully succeed. We have to realize, too, that some people are paid [agents] to break this up, to make sure our project won't succeed." Abbas urged the group to be careful in its choice of collaborators so as not to marginalize minorities and to avoid elitism. He gave an example of a feminist minister who claimed to support the group. "She was a pseudo-feminist. *Real* feminists aren't racist or Islamophobic. So let's be careful about whom we work with, yeah? Because remember, in the past, we didn't want to accept some individuals who were campaigning against Guantanamo. Some of you said, 'Hey, we don't want to give just anyone a platform who arrives under the pretext of *Muslim victim.*'" Abbas was the only member raising the issue of Islamophobia.[10]

Tension and emotion surrounded the questions of whom DiverCité represented and with whom it should collaborate. How could DiverCité do justice to constituents of different genders, classes, ethnicities, and religions? At some point in the meeting, a black activist from Paris spoke and captured everyone's attention. "A lot of people in the quartiers don't have anyone to speak for them. Our group is probably alienating to women who wear the veil. Abbas would be a good candidate to speak to them. Look, I don't want to be an *'ethnicist,'* but this is reality. For example, I'm probably the best candidate to speak to African immigrants." He tried to defend his ideas against another member, who passionately rejected any "particular-iste" tendencies—in other words, recognition of group differences.

The meeting concluded with comments from a Maghrébi man in his early twenties, a resident of one of the quartiers outside Paris. He said he was an artist and that he looked forward to DiverCité's artistic projects among youth in these neighborhoods. He allowed the meeting to end on an optimistic note with his own enthusiasm, despite all the unanswered questions. I couldn't help but think he was the token "quartier resident." His presence mattered for an organization struggling to reconcile its polit-ical goals with the difficulty it had giving and gaining trust in working-class neighborhoods. The role of Islamic practice in the quartiers and the organization's uncertainty in dealing with religion were very much part of this difficulty.

I mentioned to Ilyas, another long-time member of DiverCité, what I observed at the meeting, since he had left early. He tried to make a more positive case for the association. But he also admitted to me that DiverCité's "hour of glory" had passed and stated that the banlieues now constituted "no man's land." He added:

> It's difficult now to mobilize people in the banlieues. When we go
> to discuss things with them, we realize that it's the same conver-
> sation as before, the same reports! [We have nothing new to offer
> them.] And nothing's changed for them! For everyone, not just for
> Muslims. For the first time we don't know what's going to happen
> tomorrow or what's going on right now. We do know that people
> have moved more toward Islam, and this has become predominant.

But Ilyas also insisted that the problems of the quartiers far surpassed the potential and abilities of Islamic associations—Muslim organizations could not fix the social and economic miseries of the banlieues, even though they had a duty to pursue social justice. He criticized organiza-tions like the UOIF for depoliticizing their missions in favor of pursuing only religious recognition, and he praised DiverCité's pioneering work on immigration, former soldiers, "colonial management of the quartiers," Palestine, and the "criminalization of Islam."[11]

Ilyas reflected a great deal on the hopelessness of many Muslims and residents of the quartiers, telling me, as did several others, that Maghrébins were increasingly seeking ways to leave France. As for his own activism and the future, he mused, "Today's generation isn't interested in politics and associations. But there are other means now, like blogs. There are countless blogs coming out of the banlieues, and that's not a coincidence. It's up to us now to see how we can connect with them through these different means."

"Today," Farid asserted, "no one from these associations can truthfully say, 'I work in the quartier.' In fact, everyone has abandoned them." Groups like DiverCité and the UJM enjoyed a social base in the quartiers in the 1990s, but lost that base in the post-9/11 period. The strength of the UJM in the past was precisely that it was anchored in places like Vénissieux, and local residents respected the organization. "And so the state detested us," affirmed Farid. In the early years, many members of the UJM had come from the quartiers, and they prevented others from "sectarian practices, drugs, and delinquency" while also raising political consciousness. Through social events and activities, families in the quartiers developed trust in UJM leaders. This "richesse" sadly diminished over time as individuals from the older generation left or became preoccupied with their own families. Now, according to Farid, the UJM focused only on youth education, teaching Arabic, and Islam. "The real work to be done is in the quartiers, but it's too hard and no one wants to do it. Back when I was involved, UJM's strength was that we worked with other organizations, but somehow it all dissolved, and now we have to start from scratch. We're not organized and structured enough anymore to really struggle with the state."

One of Farid's friends and fellow activists was Bilal, who had converted to Islam as a young adult and had watched the growing divide between middle-class activists and quartier residents. Like Farid, he expressed great regret over this disconnect. "We've become detached from the very base of the community," he admitted. "It's one of our main preoccupations, but it's just too difficult. We're far from the banlieues for one thing, and we don't feel welcome there anymore."

"Now things are worse than ever, and there's a logical turn to Salafism"

"At some point all the Islamic groups lost their weight to Salafism. We just no longer correspond to their [residents'] reality on the ground," said Farid. Bilal concurred, adding that he thinks the problem is more marked in Lyon, where the growth of Salafism made work in the banlieues even more challenging.

Time and again, my middle-class companions pointed to the growth of Salafism, a strict sectarian reform movement to purify Islam of innovations, as a major reason for the disconnect between their associations and Muslims in the quartiers. They saw Salafism as a major ideological divide in the Muslim community, far above ethnic or other potential divisions, and as a tragically misinformed interpretation of Islam. Some complained about Salafists coming to their mosques and trying to proselytize and correct their prayer. Others complained about the so-called refusal of Salafists to integrate into French society. As I found myself becoming more involved in the community of Salafist women in Les Minguettes, my own experience there did not corroborate these opinions.[12]

Farid never quite approved of my interest in the Salafist mosques. "There's nothing to study there," he said, seemingly irritated. Gesturing with his hands to express tunnel vision, he insisted that many Salafis are narrow-minded and quick to condemn other Muslims as un-Islamic and doomed to hell, sometimes for things as superficial as dress. Farid opposed state legislation such as the ban on the niqab, but he believed that the niqab was at best a grave misinterpretation of Islam and at worst, *bida* (an innovation or corruption of Islam). This echoed the opinions of most of my middle-class companions. Women like Samira (Farid's wife), Maryam, and Ismat took their veiling very seriously, but they did not wear the loose and sober djelbab, worn by many Salafist women; nor did they believe in the piety of the niqab. They practiced a general sense of male–female modesty, but not strict gender separation. And unlike many Salafists, they believed in the importance of political engagement, either working with the state or critiquing it.

"It's a real difference in ideology," Laila noted. "The Salafists have gained influence, and they don't care about the future of Islam in France. They just retreat, and they make their wives stay inside." Laila was an educated woman in her early thirties whom I met through the community at Mosquée Hijra. She felt badly that middle-class Muslims "didn't care" about other Muslims in the quartiers and that they simply found satisfaction in their own families, jobs, and consumer goods. Above all, she said, abandoning the quartiers was un-Islamic.

I commonly encountered this combination of regret and disdain. Maryam said, "They don't feel French because of all the discrimination they faced at school and at work. Fine. But it takes a certain strength of character to be able to say, 'You can close the door on me, but I will keep struggling so that you understand me and understand that I *am* French.'

It takes a certain maturity to be able to say this." The tension over Salafism was personal to Maryam, whose brother had recently joined the movement. Her husband, Samir, had a particularly strained relationship with Maryam's brother. Both Samir and Maryam saw themselves as comfortably Muslim and French, and felt strongly about integrating in French society. "But they [Salafis] want to remain separate from French society. They don't want to integrate," Maryam lamented. "They want to live exactly as the Prophet lived instead of accepting modern life."

In contrast to Maryam and others, a few companions had begun to sympathize with the Salafist movement. Khalil was among them. In Khalil's opinion, Salafism presented the last step before terrorism, even though he agreed that most Salafists consciously avoided politics. "Three generations of Muslims tried and failed to better their conditions," he said. "And now things are worse than ever, and there's a logical turn to Salafism." Khalil, along with Abbas, had worked as a social justice and immigrant rights activist in the banlieues throughout the 1990s. Disillusioned with the "failure" of activism, he finally gave up and refocused his life on a more rigorous Islamic practice. And he came to respect the Salafist movement.

"If you want to know why we act the way we act," he repeated to me, "you need to read more about the colonial experience." Living with fear and resentment of police, who treated them like criminals, Muslims in the quartiers felt perpetually excluded. "When I used to work in the *cités* [working-class housing projects], kids would be stopped by the police. The cliché was that the police would ask you 'Where are you from?' and you'd say 'I'm French.' And the cop would smile as he wrote you up, because in the backs of their minds, both knew that you weren't really French." Fed up with their exclusion from French citizenship, discrimination, and police harassment, reminiscent of memories of family stories about the colonial experience, youth of the *cités* were naturally drawn to a movement so dramatically separated from state and society.

While Khalil had once committed to activism and hope for inclusion and mobility, he now began to sympathize with the need for separation. At dinner at Abbas's home, Khalil and Abbas bickered about the new Islamic high school, Al-Kindi. Abbas refused to support Al-Kindi because he disliked "separatist" tendencies. "We have to work together and include non-Muslims. Why should we settle for separate institutions?" Khalil passionately disagreed, arguing that Muslims could not count on respect from other French citizens, and separate Islamic structures were the best form of protection they could hope for. Indeed, though many of its practices garnered disdain, the Salafist community I observed in the banlieues was acting precisely on this belief.

RETURNING FOR A moment to the historical development of *laïcité* as state intervention in religion, it is clear that the state's attempts to control Islam set the stage for the politics of recognition in Lyon. Because municipalities presented barriers and challenges to establishing Islamic schools and mosques, and meeting other religious needs, Muslim middle-class activists had to focus on obtaining recognition from the state. Forging a positive relationship with the state amid accusations of *communautarisme* required finesse and skillful negotiation. For Hakim, acquiring municipal permissions and cooperative relations were hard-earned victories, the only way for Muslims to stop being victims of the law and hostile municipal governments.

For Hakim, Maryam, and others, working with the state and civic engagement toward recognition were obligatory, though they also wished to limit state control of Islam. Having made peace with their complex belongings to France and to Islam, and their sense of loss as children of immigrants, they worried about obstacles to practicing Islam, especially when thinking about their children's futures. For others like Farid and Abbas, focusing on recognition from the state depoliticized Islamic movements and activism and detracted from a more radical agenda anchored in redistribution. Aligning themselves to some extent with far left politics, they more directly critiqued the state and wished to protect Islam from state interference.

Regardless of their relationship to the state, none of the associations middle-class Muslims were involved in had a base among Muslims in the working-class quartiers. As Bilal lamented, they no longer felt welcome in those neighborhoods, and they found the Salafist movement a profoundly troubling barrier to solidarity. As Ilyas remarked after two decades of activism, the socioeconomic problems of the quartiers surpassed the means and comprehension of Islamic associations. For pious Muslim activists, moreover, the class opposition left them spiritually unfulfilled, illustrating how the material and subjective aspects of recognition politics are deeply connected.

Whereas Hakim remained optimistic about the future of Islam in France and Abbas remained determined to keep struggling, Khalil lost hope and began to understand the appeal of the Salafist movement. As an activist in the 1980s and '90s working with youth in the banlieues, he had hoped to help integrate Muslims into French society, but became disillusioned when he was unsuccessful. His personal experiences with racism and tragedy drew him into the Islamic revival and made him sharply question the possibility of recognition. If his generation failed to dismantle the dominant cultural beliefs about Muslims and end their systemic subordination, then separate institutions were the only hope.

As in Hyderabad, Lyon's Muslim middle-class activists distrusted the state. But they had neither the structural privileges nor the wealth to practice the kind of autonomy and produce the type of cross-class relations seen in Hyderabad. Here, too, calls for a more liberal Islam were superimposed on a class tension that had become entrenched. But unlike in Hyderabad, Islamic identities were experienced as unmovable and irreconcilable, thereby preventing cross-class debate about Islamic practice—a dynamic that was perhaps exacerbated by the Salafi rejection of politics.

6

Antipolitics in the Banlieues of Lyon

CAFÉ PATRON 1: I don't know what I think about the [anti-burqa] proposition. But the women who wear it—they do it only as a provocation!

CAFÉ OWNER: The thing is these women don't have a choice.

PATRON 1: But unfortunately, some women are choosing to wear it even though they're born in this country. They should share some basic qualities with the rest of us. Well, I suppose it's not the worst thing to happen in a relationship [*dans un couple*].

PATRON 2 (MAGHRÉBIN): In my house you are *not* welcome if you wear the burqa! It's not Islam, it's not in the Quran. It's the fault of the government, since these people don't have any work. We have too much state assistance in France, and it's made people not want to work.

PATRON 3: I definitely feel bothered when I see it [burqa].

PARVEZ: I work with some of these women in Vénissieux, and they really believe in wearing it. I don't think it's right to say they're forced into it.

PATRON 3: Maybe some of them. But for others, it's not their choice. It's a question of equality and protecting these women.

CONVERSATION AMONG STRANGERS, Lyon, France, 2009

THIS CONVERSATION STARTED spontaneously at a café in my neighborhood of Guillotière the summer before the passage of the anti-burqa legislation. That summer I found myself in several conversations exactly like this one, with strangers and acquaintances full of disdain and pity for women in burqas. Their sentiments about protecting women juxtaposed starkly and ironically with the realities I saw while spending time with Salafist women in the banlieues.

One day, I was waiting in one of Lyon's banlieues for a bus with two companions, Katia and Amel, who wore a djelbab. Amel was complaining at length about how aggressive strangers had become in criticizing her dress over the last few years.[1] Katia, who did not wear a djelbab, grew impatient with Amel and interjected more than once. "Well, let's focus on the positives, right? There are also many people who are tolerant." Five minutes later, after we boarded the bus, a drunken older man proceeded to harangue Amel. "The other day I saw a woman covering her face," he started. "You know it's banned. Why do you do that?" he asked aggressively and leaned in toward Amel's face. "We're in France, you know. In France! Can you just explain to me why? You're turning yourself into an object!" Katia felt scared and moved away from him. Amel, however, was accustomed to such harassment.

Before that incident, I was walking to a grocery store in Les Minguettes with Caroline, a French *convertie* who wore the djelbab. Her exceptionally petite frame often appeared drowned by her brown djelbab. She stood out in public, but she seemed immune to the many stares she received. We were standing at a pedestrian crossing when I saw two men in a truck pointing at her and laughing. I felt infuriated, but she did not seem to care.

On yet another occasion, I was waiting for the tram with two companions from Mosquée Hasan, Amina and Nasreen, both of whom wore the djelbab. A woman physically pushed Amina as she was about to board. I was confused as to what exactly happened and in disbelief. "You really think it's because of your djelbab?" I asked.

"Absolutely, there's no doubt," Amina responded. "She's just trying to provoke me. They really have hate." She and Nasreen explained that this was simply part of their everyday lives. These were clearly not isolated incidents.

Like these women, Fatima was also used to harassment. Fatima lived with her parents in public housing about three miles from Vénissieux, and by the time I met her, she had extremely limited interaction with non-Muslims on a daily basis. Her sister lived in Les Minguettes, and Fatima visited her nearly every day. Fatima's parents emigrated from Algeria and maintained close ties to the country, traveling back almost every year. Her mother worked from home as a seamstress, and the family also lived on her father's pension. Fatima was one of the only women I knew whose parents were also religious, though her mother never insisted on her daughters' veiling. Fatima had worked for years as a cleaner before working for her brother-in-law's halal food business.

When I first met Fatima, she was slowly increasing her knowledge and study of Islam, regularly attending Mosquée Hasan, reading books on her own, and occasionally using Internet sources when she had a reliable connection. Within a few years, she had developed into a highly skilled teacher in her own right, holding classes in Quranic reading and recitation

in her apartment for a diverse array of women in the neighborhood, ranging from non-Muslim, single teen mothers to older Maghrébine women
studying Arabic for the first time.

Fatima and I rode the Metro and tram together to the mosque in Les
Minguettes until eventually she saved enough money to purchase a car.
She was a terrible and distracted driver, and I often feared for my life when
riding with her, but it was still worth avoiding the stares and sneers from
strangers in the Metro. On a cool spring day, running late to the class at
Mosquée Hasan, we quietly snuck in and found a place on the floor among
nearly a hundred women. Malika, the teacher that day, had already begun
lecturing. "All people, whatever their status . . . among us, no one has per-
fection. We all have need for God," she explained a verse from the Quran.
"When the heart is attached to God, you have submission and humility.
When we are attached to him, there is love. Is this clear for my sisters?
[*Est-ce que c'est clair pour les soeurs?*]"

My Salafi companions in Les Minguettes—Fatima, Amel, Caroline, and
others—exulted in their struggle to deepen their faith and attach themselves to God. They did not care for public acceptance, nor did they seek to
engage the state. Their everyday religious practice was their articulation of
dignity, regardless of the great stigma and discrimination that came with
it. The ostracization they experienced, in addition to the general precarity
they coped with, was part of the backdrop of their antipolitics.

The situation for Salafist men differs only slightly from that of women.
Men had more involvement in their neighborhoods, and they were able to
create parallel economic activities and networks. Women, however, were
largely excluded from economic independence. Marriage within the community was one of only a few available avenues for life security.

In this chapter, I argue that the Islamic revival in the working-class
banlieues was a form of radical antipolitics, in which women attempted to
expand the boundaries of the private sphere, retreat into a decentralized
moral community, and develop serenity by trusting divine will. Antipolitics
emerged as the state regulated women's veiling, defeated Muslim political
activists in working-class neighborhoods, and enlarged its surveillance. In
short, antipolitics was a response to the despair produced by the collapse
of Muslim civil society associations in Lyon's banlieues.

Precarity and Salvation

On a cold November evening in the infamous working-class neighborhood of Les Minguettes outside of Lyon, I paced before the entrance of a

tower-block apartment building, anxiously waiting to be let in for a Quranic course. On the wall was a graffiti drawing of a pistol pointed at President Sarkozy's head. After finally being buzzed in, I made my way upstairs in the dank elevator, holding my breath to avoid the smell of urine. When I stepped out, I was relieved to see Farha, a French-Algerian woman in her mid-thirties. Dressed in her black djelbab, she was warm and cheerful. "*Alhamdulillah* [by the will of God]," she smiled. "You found me!"

I followed Farha to the back room of her apartment where two students, also dressed in djelbabs, sat on the floor reciting a verse from the Quran: "And there will be endlessly flowing water and abundant fruit, of unlimited seasons, and [the virtuous] will be seated on thrones, raised high." Farha, who taught Quranic recitation at her home and at the mosque, raised her arms and smiled at this image of paradise. Caroline and Asiya, the two students, closed their eyes and shook their heads, imagining the bliss that might await them. But Farha reminded them, "Only God knows who will enter paradise. For those who don't enter immediately, there will be 'negotiations.'" Caroline and Asiya murmured worriedly. "If one is close to God, there will be rest, grace, and a garden of delights." Farha made us repeat this multiple times in unison, painstakingly slowly, to refine and perfect our Arabic diction and aid our memorization of the verse.

After two hours, this lesson in *tajwid* ended, and we all went to the kitchen to chat over mint tea and bread. Farha talked about, among other things, the pain (*mal au coeur*) she felt when she saw a young Muslim woman in provocative dress being ogled by men at the bus terminal a few days earlier. She regretted that she did not reproach the woman for her dress and behavior. After a long conversation about these matters and more prayers, Caroline and I walked in isolation to the bus terminal. I stepped over broken glass as a car, blasting rap music, whizzed past.

Traversing my way through banlieue housing projects, from one isolated pocket of religious practice to another, I often carefully kept to myself. I knew that crime rates here were much lower than in American cities, but the lack of commercial and public life made me uneasy (Silverstein and Tetreault 2006; Césari 2005; Simon 1998).[2] I wore the hijab, which I felt both stigmatized me and protected me as I found my way around these neighborhoods. The interactions I witnessed in small mosques and in people's apartments seemed to echo the desolation of Les Minguettes. Far from building potential civil societies, the people I knew were in retreat, practicing forms of Islamic discipline that centered on the individual and her salvation, as opposed to a collective project. Their antipolitics—their turn away from the public—came largely from the precariousness of their lives, work, and in many cases, relationships.

References to precarity appeared routinely in Islamic teachings and discourses, and in everyday conversations at the mosque. Mosquée Ennour, one of the small, housing-project mosques I attended in Les Minguettes, provided a small space where several women I knew would talk, complain, and laugh about their worries. They often interjected these discussions into Quranic teaching sessions. They frequently involved anxieties over immigration status, frustrations with various French bureaucracies, and complaints about the difficulty of finding work or self-employment activities.

In general, there was a certain degree of instability in the religious community because of the precarious nature of immigration status and work. Saara, who had been teaching Arabic for a short period, had to end the class when her legal stay in France expired. I did not realize the class was over until the very last day, when she embarrassedly and abruptly confessed to me that she had to return to Algeria. Sumaiya, an immigrant from Syria, also had a hesitant approach to the future, even in mundane greetings and farewells. Whenever I would say "See you next week," she would reply "Maybe, but who knows? I don't know. I always say *insha Allah* [God willing]." While acknowledging life's uncertainty and invoking the phrase *insha Allah* is a customary part of the Islamic tradition, these sayings had a heightened salience for Sumaiya because of her immigration status and chronic underemployment.

Sumaiya was one of the teachers at Mosquée Ennour in Les Minguettes. She taught Arabic literacy and Quranic memorization and explication. After several months of knowing each other, she invited me to her apartment across the street from Mosquée Ennour. "It's so difficult to cook when you live alone," she said as she hurriedly put together a plate of frozen potatoes, stale bread, and cheese spread. Her two-year-old son was crying as Sumaiya complained to me about her numerous errands that week: going to the pediatrician, the pharmacist, her son's nursery, and her job-training in Lyon; plus job searching, dealing with the bureaucracy of receiving her family assistance checks, taking the bus to buy groceries, and applying and reapplying for citizenship. She had enormous anxiety over her inability to acquire French citizenship. She had submitted several dossiers for citizenship, each time getting rejected due to some bureaucratic requirement.[3]

Sumaiya survived on approximately 300 euros a month. She had worked on and off in Lyon, but was recently laid off from a job as a telephone operator. She was training to become a licensed babysitter, but like other women I knew, she was having difficulty completing the many full-day, state-required classes, which took place in different locations throughout Lyon. She knew that as long as she continued to wear the headscarf, she would have trouble getting hired, and she was exhausted with looking for work. In order to find a job, she decided, she was willing to abandon her veiling practice during the workday.

Sumaiya's mosque persona was cheerful and confident, but as we ate in her apartment that day, she had trouble hiding her anxiety. Much to her embarrassment, she broke down crying. On top of everything, she told me, she was considering divorcing her husband, a Maghrébi man who had been living in another country for eighteen years. He rarely visited her and their son. It was her second marriage.[4] "Please," she urged me, "don't tell anyone at the mosque." She lowered her head into her hands, as the tears welled up and her voice faltered. Sumaiya's solitude and her desire to hide the reality of her life from the others at Mosquée Ennour reflected the overall desolation I found unique to Les Minguettes.[5]

Salafi Men and Women

Communities of Salafi men and women were politically withdrawn, but anti-veiling legislation affected women especially by erecting obstacles to their education and employment. While women retreated into a moral community, Salafi men seemed to have greater access to business opportunities and promoted social reform in their neighborhoods. Men in the quartiers also confronted the risk of finding themselves in prison, which infused the choice of turning to Salafism as an alternative life path with greater significance.

"He's a pragmatic Salafi"

In available public spaces in the banlieues such as Muslim-owned "McSnack shops," Salafist men met, discussed ideas, and watched soccer matches together. Though I often ate lunch at such halal eateries, I was almost always the only woman in sight. A friend mentioned that Salafist men who worked or had small businesses in the banlieues were forced to interact with women in these settings, despite their belief in strict gender segregation. Perhaps as a result, they never made me feel uncomfortable at these eateries.

Yassin, a young man of Algerian origin, spent a good deal of time at these shops, though he did not identify as Salafist. Yassin grew up in a nearby banlieue. His father worked in a factory producing elevator cables, and his mother worked briefly cleaning houses. Yassin was the only one among his several siblings who performed daily prayers and actively strove toward greater piety. He acknowledged that Salafist men had had a social impact in his neighborhood, where they campaigned against drugs, alcohol, and gangs. But he disliked certain elements of the movement and viewed it as a result of economic dislocation. As he explained:

> In a way, since society has excluded them, they've [Salafist men] dug in their heels and said, "We don't need society." This is why there's an attraction to this movement. Our economic situation here is catastrophic! An unemployment rate of 50 percent? Imagine that! We can't even get a job in a fast-food joint, especially if you don't have a diploma. It's worse than it was for our parents. Before, it was hard, but at least they could work in the factory. But today, even those who are looking can't find anything. And if you don't have any qualifications, forget it. Maybe at best you'll find a temporary position, where you might work for three days, then they tell you to come in Saturday night, then maybe on a Monday morning, and that's it. What kind of life is this? Our parents, they worked hard and they didn't earn much, but they were paid every month, and they could manage.

Yassin had been able to attend a local university and find employment, but it was occasional and precarious. I met Yassin through his close childhood friend, Mounir, who also grew up in an HLM building in a banlieue a few miles from Les Minguettes and worked as a janitor in his housing complex. Mounir and I first connected through the website of the Grand Mosquée de Lyon, where I introduced myself as a student looking to know people in the community. He was the only person who responded. The first time we met, we sat at a park bench at the Parc de la Tête d'Or, and I was confused when he asked me several questions about my "identity card." He pulled out his card to show me and asked me if Americans were required to carry theirs all the time. He had an intense curiosity about the United States, where he believed it was easier to be a minority, and asked if I would help him learn English. The last time I saw Mounir, he was unemployed and without even a phone, blacklisted from cellphone companies (presumably due to a billing issue, though it was not clear) for six months. His hair had grown long, and I teased him, "You look like a terrorist, Mounir!"

"Everything's a hassle here," he said with frustration. "I can't get a driver's license, can't open a bank account. I'm thinking seriously of moving to Algeria. I think all of us could live on my father's pension."

Mounir's disaffection from his life in France was colored entirely by the discrimination he experienced and the state's hostility toward Islam. In 2004, the mayor of his town forcibly closed a small mosque that he and his father had attended for many years, with vague promises that a new mosque would be built. "More and more, the mosques in the banlieues are being closed. Everywhere! It's a very big problem. The government just wants one grand mosque for the entire community of Lyon. They think it can be like a church. They don't understand that we pray five times a day, not just once on Sunday." Mounir and Yassin also complained about a prayer space in their banlieue that the community had rented from a Catholic Church association. When the church's lease expired, the association wished to move forward and sell it to the religious group. The mayor tried desperately to obstruct the purchase, but eventually legal assistance from the international Islamic movement, Tablighi Jama'at, enabled the purchase to proceed.

Mounir's particular housing project complex, similar to those in Les Minguettes, was among those notorious for crime and drug activity. According to him, the proselytizing of Tablighi and Salafist Muslims in his complex led to dramatic declines in alcohol abuse and street fights. "Islam has cleaned up all these problems," he proudly exclaimed. "It's a totally different place now, and it's safe." Finding Islam was a turning point for Mounir's friends and probably for him, too. He added:

Most of my friends before were delinquents—alcohol, drugs, stealing—they wound up in prison. After prison they said, "I'm fed up with this!" You're here, you're there, you lose your time, you have no goal in life, you don't know why you're here. Then they ask, "What is this thing, Islam? What is prayer? What is Ramadan?" And they start searching. It's a personal choice. No one imposed it on them. It's clear—I'll say it again—*no one imposed it on them*. I really find it a personal choice, because . . . they want to come back to God, you know.

When I first met Mounir, he was not actively involved in any Islamic group, though he had many Salafist friends. A year later, during a conversation with Yassin, I learned that Mounir had begun to identify as Salafi.

YASSIN: Mounir, for example, he's a Salafist!

PARVEZ: What do you mean? He identifies as one?

YASSIN: Yes and no. He's a pragmatic Salafi, more pragmatic than the others.

PARVEZ: He spends time with me, so I wouldn't have thought . . .

YASSIN: Yes, because he studied a little bit [some college]. He knows some history, and so he's a little more open-minded. I think that's why he's more open.

PARVEZ: And you? You don't identify as a Salafist?

YASSIN: Me? No. . . . I don't bother myself with all that. The important thing is that I practice. I don't want to be attached to any movement.

In the banlieues, many men like Mounir identified as Salafist, but in an ambiguous, loosely defined, and individualist manner. Mounir never directly told me he considered himself Salafist, though he spoke often about the movement and his Salafi friends. This was likely because he knew the degree to which middle-class Muslims despised the Salafist movement.

Mounir and Yassin engaged the Salafist movement in the banlieues from different perspectives, but both acknowledged its social impact. In this respect, Salafism among men in the quartiers appeared to have a more public orientation that contrasted to women's antipolitics. Salafi men were stigmatized and harassed in France, but their practices were not the center of national attention, like Muslim women's veiling practices. Indeed, in Samir Amghar's study of Salafi men, he argues that they experience a sense of power both when they attract respect from Muslim strangers and when they incite fear in non-Muslims (2011, 145). Amghar argues that while Salafi men have withdrawn from the state, they have developed an elective affinity with the economic field. Their growing activities include halal sandwich shops, taxi services, Islamic bookstores, clothing shops, and import-export commerce (94, 208).

"I see two options: get married or leave France"

On the surface, Salafist Islam's most distinguishing feature is its strict adherence to gender segregation and gendered rules that are otherwise subject to an enormous range of interpretation in Islam. For this reason, it was nearly impossible for me to interact with men in Salafist mosque communities, and my women companions never allowed me to meet their male relatives. I once made the ignorant mistake of taking a taxi to a gathering of Salafists for a conference. When others noticed I was alone in a taxi with a male driver, they gave me puzzled and disapproving looks.

One summer afternoon, the women's entrance to Mosquée Hasan was locked, and several of us were stranded outside in unbearable heat. The women refused to use the men's entrance or to simply ask a man to open our door. We stood there waiting in the sun, and one young woman even tried to climb in through a window, to no avail. I nervously watched, worrying that she might tumble over the yards of fabric of her djelbab. As an outsider, it was inappropriate for me to take initiative, and I did not entirely understand the etiquette. Eventually one of the women telephoned her husband to inform him that we were locked out and would need to use the men's entrance. Her husband warned the other men to give us space, and we walked as briskly as we could past the men's section and into our own.

Why were women of this subaltern Salafist community—who for the most part did not grow up with such practices—drawn to this particular structure of gendered piety, like the reformist women in Hyderabad? Above all, according to their understandings, these practices were religious obligations, constituting one component of their faith. But as in Hyderabad, there was also a relationship between class position and the appeal of gendered divisions in religious practice. In a context of high unemployment, poverty, and barriers to education (because of their veiling practices), taking on a traditional domestic role provided some security. Marriage, in addition to being encouraged in Islam more generally and especially among Salafists, represented a practical solution to the impossibility of women's working and wearing the hijab. My religious participants typically believed that pious Muslim men had a religious obligation to provide for their families. I saw several young Salafist women excitedly plan for their semi-arranged marriages with Salafist men, locally or near Paris. Upon solidifying the marriage arrangement, these women started to feel bonded to their future husbands and cared for both physically and spiritually. The moral expectations around gender roles therefore appealed to women of lower-class positions.

Amina was a twenty-nine-year-old woman of Algerian background, born and raised in France. She regularly attended the mosque, but often kept to herself. Amina worried about finding a husband while also growing increasingly depressed with her job search. Because of her heartfelt belief in the benefits of rigorous Islamic practice, she was mortified to admit to me one day that she could not quit her cigarette addiction because of her depression. One Ramadan night at the mosque, she had to slip out to have her cigarette.[6] I found myself in an odd scenario, following her in the dark and rain to find a secret place where she could indulge. We whispered in the dark outside an apartment entrance, she in her black djelbab and with her pack of Marlboros. I found myself spraying her djelbab with a half-bottle of eau-de-toilette to cover up the smell. "What can I say," she said. "I'm depressed. I don't have a job, I'm alone, so I sit around all day and chain-smoke. We all have our own path. But please, don't tell anyone at the mosque." With Amina's financial troubles, she was anxious to marry. If gossip spread that despite appearances, Amina was a chain-smoker, her reputation in the mosque communities would be tarnished and she would have trouble finding a husband.

Yet there was also a shortage of employed, religious men. Amel searched for a marriage partner, but there were few suitable individuals. She also felt strongly that she must feel some emotional and intellectual connection with the man who would be her husband, which even further limited her options. Disappointed with one prospective groom, she confessed to me, "I felt as neutral toward him as I would [toward] a chair." Struggling with the growing suspicion of Muslims and anti-veiling legislation, she said, "The laws are against us. I see two options: get married or leave France."

For some Salafist women dealing with the possibility that they might never marry or have children, the structure of gender-segregated worlds provided an alternative to conjugal families. For others, the world of Salafist women and their teachings was a welcome refuge from troubled marriages or in the aftermath of divorce. One woman I knew, a *convertie*, had married a Maghrébi man who divorced her.[7] She was raising their daughter alone. She began wearing the djelbab, attending the mosque in Les Minguettes, and studiously participating in the classes. The classes at the mosque provided her a community of women who offered moral support and a set of teachings that emphasized trust in God and spiritual strength. Especially after abandonment or divorce, having a space away from men had appeal.

Salafist women in Minguettes created spaces for leadership and the circulation of knowledge. Though the teachers were careful to not construct their individual interpretations of the Quran and hadith, they forged their own relationships to Islam by conducting deep exegesis under women's leadership. One product of strict gender segregation was the protection of women's spaces and the chance to flourish as teachers and students. Upholding the norms of separation in this context played a part in upholding women's spiritual and intellectual development.

Antipolitics
Reconfiguring the Private Sphere

The recent history of state intrusion into Les Minguettes left most residents suspicious of outsiders and jaded. It took me some time to adjust to the daily routine of surveillance. On the bus and at the terminals, the ubiquitous EuroSecurité guards stood right next to me, smiling at me on and off throughout the bus ride and walking right behind me when I exited the bus.[8] Through the painful and arduous process of gaining entry to Les Minguettes as a field site, I learned that residents' suspicious nature developed from years of police surveillance.

Because my many middle-class participants did not have contacts in the quartiers, or none that they would share, I took to walking around the residences until one day, I saw a small café tucked away at the basement level of one of the buildings. I was relieved to sit down and order some coffee. No other residents were there. A teenager behind the counter was watching television and smiling at me, and I realized he knew I was an outsider. Another man, about forty, walked in and started wiping the countertop, periodically watching me. He kept toying with a video-game machine and nervously flipping television channels. After finishing my drink and sharing numerous awkward smiles, I said hello and told them I was from the United States. They immediately looked unhappy—and unhappier still, when I blurted out that I was a student. The older man started angrily shaking his head and waving his hand. He then proceeded to yell at me for several minutes, saying:

> I can't answer any questions for you. How am I supposed to know who you are? Why should I trust you? We are on the news everywhere you look! Everywhere! We're always being watched. There are police at every corner, all around this entire complex. Everyone wants to defame us, show that we're terrorists, search for terrorists. The U.S. is behind this, we know that. You're going to go back there, tell people things, and they'll start making recommendations. Don't

you understand? Recommend things, try to change us. Even if you seem very nice, even if your study is very general, I can't speak to you. You're better off speaking to women, go to the mosque.

When I asked him where the mosque was, he pointed ambiguously in two different directions. I walked out of his café, pretending I did not see the drug deal that unfolded in front of me, and I headed for the bus terminal. I passed two women wearing the hijab on a bench. Though I felt trauma-tized by my experience at the café, I decided to ask them for directions to the mosque. They looked at me suspiciously and then silently pointed to an apartment building. I finally found the concrete building and a big metal door, locked shut, with a small sign for the mosque. There was a posting for Arabic and Quranic courses for women and children. Scrawled on it was a phone number, which I wrote down. Later, when I called the number and inquired about the courses, the woman who answered asked me repeatedly, "Who are you?" I answered her several times but doubted that I had relieved her suspicion. She reluctantly told me to come to the mosque next Tuesday. By attending the prayers and classes at this "basement mosque," I very slowly began to know the small community of women who attended every week. From there, I made contacts with women at the nearby Mosquée Hasan, and my time there formed a signifi-cant part of my research in Minguettes.

My own experiences reflected Les Minguettes' reputation for hostility to researchers and journalists, who on occasion had stones thrown at them by neighborhood youth.[9] The climate of stigmatization led to resentment of those who might treat the neighborhood as a kind of zoo, to be observed and photographed. Early in the fieldwork, I took a walk with Mounir in Vaulx-en-Velin. In a neighborhood of housing projects five minutes from a small mosque, we saw a large spray-painted sign reading DEATH TO AMERICA. When I pulled out my camera to take a picture, Mounir grabbed my hand and stopped me, explaining that I might easily have incited a con-frontation with nearby youth who would suspect us of being journalists, state agents, or researchers. In time, I recognized the distrust of outsiders and the social code of privacy. One resident told me that women in par-ticular distrusted outsiders or researchers, for fear of causing trouble for their husbands and sons.

When I found Farha's study circle, the women were thrilled to include me and to proselytize to me. Yet even these relationships were not without obstacles. Farha's husband twice told me that she was not available when

she was. I had to work hard to convince him that I had received their contact information from his mother, which was true. After weeks of stumbling, Farha and her students accepted me. In the end, they did not care
where I was from because they deeply believed that Islam had a universal-
ity that needed to be distilled from cultural factors and national boundaries.

The suspicion I encountered made perfect sense as I learned more
about the area. Three major incidents defined Les Minguettes in the last
decade. First, the French arrests of two young men who were sent to the
U.S. military detention center in Guantanamo Bay, Cuba, occurred in Les
Minguettes.[10] Second, the police raid of a housing-project mosque accused
of ties to Chechen militants occurred around the same period. Third, the
deportation of Abdelkader Bouziane, who worked in Minguettes, took
place in 2004 as I described in the opening of chapter 1.

When I was conducting research at Mosquée Hasan, several people
outside the mosque community told me that without a doubt, state agents
attended the women's classes on a regular basis. I was initially incredulous
that a spy could lurk among this group of women I was coming to know.
Eventually, when I saw the degree of privacy each woman sought to maintain, this no longer seemed so outrageous. No matter how much we came
to know and like each other, we never truly knew the private details of each
other's lives. There was always an element of uncertainty and mistrust.

This underlying mistrust shaped my initial entry into Les Minguettes
and the general relationships inside the mosque, and it defined residents' relationships to the state and law enforcement.[11] For example,
Sumaiya often complained about raising her son in a neighborhood like
Les Minguettes, where cars were burned on a near-weekly basis. "But you
know, I understand why [Maghrébi youth in the neighborhood] riot," she
reflected. "The police are constantly bothering them. We hear stories all
the time, and I saw it myself." She relayed various local stories of mysterious disappearances and even murders of Maghrébi youth. "You never
know, but I really think—many of us do—that it's the police." The mistrust
expressed by Sumaiya followed the collapse of civil society and heavy state
intrusion into Les Minguettes. In this context, residents placed increased
importance on maintaining and protecting a private sphere.

It was not always like this in Les Minguettes. The neighborhood was
part of the deindustrializing, undesirable urban periphery for decades,
but it also enjoyed a period of intense social activism and flourishing
civic associations during the 1980s and '90s under François Mitterrand's
socialist administration. Ahmed, a longtime resident of Les Minguettes

and former activist, remembered the 1983 march for social justice, which reporters labeled the "Marche des Beurs." "There was so much hope back then," he recalled. "Today, it's all gone. There's nothing." Ahmed's popular Islamic youth association in Vénissieux had once hosted weekly activities including family events, academic tutoring, youth clubs/sports, after-school activities, and training in debate and public speaking.

According to Ahmed, as local youth began feeling politically empow-ered, their presence appeared more threatening to Vénissieux mayor André Gerin. In the aftermath of 9/11, the state attacked this network of Muslim activists and placed them under surveillance, eventually leading to their decline. Like a number of former activists, Ahmed was blacklisted in Lyon as a fundamentalist and potential terrorist, which according to him made it virtually impossible to access many jobs and services. His defense of the two brothers who were sent to Guantanamo led to greater notoriety for him and a public confrontation with Mayor Gérin, who he said pit-ted other Muslims against him. His association collapsed and today, said Ahmed, "I have a family now, kids to support. I can't put my family at risk. For all of us, it became too hard to find work or even have respect. And I'm tired. I can't do it anymore." He mused:

> What did we want when we were younger? To get out of the banlieue. To be *le bon francais, avec la bonne baguette* [a respectable Frenchman with a baguette under his arm]. Now, there are exactly two struc-tures left in Minguettes: the drug dealers and the mosques. And the mosque leaders are totally incompetent and uneducated. They don't have the means to be politically active or organized.

Ahmed's trajectory reflects the decline of Les Minguettes, its civil society structures, and the hopes that bonded Islamic and secular associations. It also shows the precise mechanisms by which the state demoralized and broke apart networks of youth and Muslim leaders, leaving only a drug market and unorganized mosques in their wake.

The state's regulation of mosques and Muslim activists coincided with the banning of the headscarf in schools and growing discourse about the oppression of Muslim women. Conversations in mosques and the practice of covering one's hair were no longer considered private matters. In this context, reconfiguring and expanding the private sphere was a primary desire of antipolitics. The most recent step in eroding the private sphere was the attack on the burqa that began in 2009. As Lynda, a companion from Mosquée Hasan who wore the niqab, stated: "It's starting again."

Given this monitoring of Islamic practices, defending the private sphere was one of the only responses available to poor Salafist communities. Salafist women sought a de-territorialized conception of the private sphere that would allow them to carry the burqa as a private practice of the self into public space.[12] For example, apart from the street and educational institutions, public hospitals became a public space where women tried to negotiate their privacy. Often this meant simply demanding a female doctor, but it sometimes meant requesting some accommodation of their need for modesty in medical exam rooms. When visiting the hospital for asthma treatment, Amel refused to entirely disrobe. The doctor did not want to treat her until, finally, a Maghrébi nurse stepped in and persuaded the doctor to reconsider. There was no such resolution for Asma, a young Afro-French woman who wore the djelbab. Asma cried throughout her medical exam and vowed to not return to the hospital; previously, another doctor had trouble managing Asma's clothing situation and dismissed her as having a psychological problem.

To public authorities and to the state, the presence of the burqa in public space was harmful to the public and to the women because it promoted violence against women, sectarianism, and fundamentalism (Assemblée Nationale 2009). The only domain that the state truly conceded as the private sphere where women had control over their dress was the space of their apartments.

In addition to de-territorializing the private sphere, Salafist women reconfigured the private sphere toward the self and away from the domain of family life. While the state was eager to enter the domain of the Muslim family by insisting that men were coercing women into wearing burqas, Salafist women rejected both the state and men, or any other family members, as their agents of liberation. Their private sphere pertained strictly to their individual relationship to God, and both the state and their families could be expelled from this sphere if they interfered with that relationship.[13]

This conflictual scenario does not pertain to all of the women of Mosquée Hasan, but most of the women I met in Les Minguettes chose to wear the djelbab or the niqab—indeed, sometimes against the wishes of their husbands, parents, or brothers. While public debate on the practice often centered on the question of whether women choose to wear the burqa, many women of Mosquée Hasan were unmarried and/or came from nonreligious families. They were not coerced into the practice by a husband or men in their families.

For some women, others' misconceptions of and disgust toward the practice had painful personal consequences, especially enacted by their own family members. Estranged from her family and unemployed, Amina, for example, lived alone in Vénissieux. Her family did not practice Islam, and her brother was abusive. She had minimal contact with her mother, who once said to her, "You think anyone's going to want to marry you, dressed like that [in a djelbab]?" Though of Muslim origin, her family mocked Amina's religious practice and offered her no material or other support.

Contrary to the popular image, some women asserted their desire to wear the djelbab or niqab against their husband's will. Ahmed, the former activist from Les Minguettes, recounted the story of his good friend: "His wife insists on wearing the burqa, and it's driving him crazy. He finds it completely embarrassing." During a session at Mosquée Hasan, one woman, perhaps in her mid-thirties, broke down crying in front of fifty other students. She had a scarf roughly tied around her hair and was wearing a tight Moroccan robe instead of a djelbab, unusual among the students at Mosquée Hasan. "My husband doesn't want me to wear the hijab. He insults it, constantly criticizes me for wanting to wear it. Others make fun of it, too. And I have a job in the [Vénissieux] city administration. I have to take it off for work. I don't have a choice. I don't know what to do." Unable to reconcile her desire to start a rigorous spiritual and religious practice with her external constraints, she said she was growing increasingly depressed.

Malika, one of the teachers at Mosquée Hasan, was troubled by this story, but insisted that the djelbab (and at least headscarf) is not optional but rather, obligatory. In a sympathetic but firm manner, she shared:

> Remember, the Prophet's companions were always mocked and ostracized. They were even tortured. I can't be the judge of your decisions, but all I can say is that it's not a choice, we can't say no to God. You have to have courage to do what you believe. People laugh at me all the time. They get in my face and ask me aggressively why I do this. Try to explain very simply and directly, in a well-mannered way. But once they get aggressive or mock you, just leave it. Don't engage them. Just turn inward.

She offered to give this particular woman the number of a sheikh in Saudi Arabia who could talk to her husband. In general, women's approach to such strife was to try every possible avenue to reconcile with their husbands. If, ultimately, the husband obstructed his wife's Islamic practice, she would have the right to demand a divorce.

French conversions to Salafist Islam and "born again" experiences also reflected a reconfiguration of the private sphere that was increasingly oriented away from the family (O. Roy 2006). A common explanation for the growth of Salafism is its appeal to the marginalized sons and daughters of immigrants in the declining working-class banlieues (Césari 2002). Having suffered the loss of cultural identity and exclusion by French society, these young men and women are drawn to Salafism for the many ruptures it demands and celebrates—from family ties, street culture, and French (non-Muslim) society (O. Roy 2006). Disaffected youth in working-class banlieues, even those without an immigrant background, do not feel part of any culture or society and welcome the redefinitions that Salafism imposes on one's life. It has been argued that Salafi Islam in France reflects the detachment of ethnicity from Islam (O. Roy 2006, 2004). As Mélissa, one of numerous young French *converties* I met briefly, proclaimed: "I gave up everything. I left my family, everything I knew, when I embraced Islam."

Women in the mosque setting explicitly discussed this detachment of Islam from ethnicity. At Mosquée Hasan, Malika once had the following exchange with her students:

STUDENT 1: What about a person who's Arab, Muslim, but doesn't pray or anything? But he fasts during Ramadan. Will he go to hell or heaven?

MALIKA: Nobody can say who goes to heaven or hell. But he doesn't believe? He doesn't have faith?

STUDENT 1: No . . .

MALIKA: Then he's a *kafr*. There are Muslims with weak faith, and those who simply don't believe. If he doesn't believe in God, he's a *kafr*. It doesn't matter if you're Arab, or if your name is Muhammed or Abdullah.

STUDENT 2: At another mosque I go to, the imam said that we shouldn't label people who were born Muslim as *kafrs*.

MALIKA: Right now in France, unfortunately, you just do as you want, regardless of *sunnah* [the way of the Prophet]. If he believes but also sins, well, we have no right at all to call him a *kafr*. But you think that a nonbelieving Arab is more Muslim than a practicing Muslim whose family was Catholic or atheist? I don't believe that at all.

In this discussion, Malika made clear her position that one's ethnic status had nothing to do with being a "believer." What mattered was the state of one's faith. In her courses, Malika often reminded her students not to take for granted their status as Muslims simply because they were born into Arab or Maghrébi families. This idea distinguishes the Salafist movement from "folk" Islam and from middle-class discourses that take a more ambiguous approach to the question of defining who is Muslim (O. Roy 2006, 2004).

Another way to understand this phenomenon is through the notion of reconfiguring the private sphere. For Salafists, the status of being Muslim is not linked to embracing a public or extended family but instead to an inward orientation and state of faith, which is inherently private. Families may stand in the way of one's private relationship to God. Thus, the defense and expansion of the private sphere against an intrusive and paternalistic state is crucial to antipolitics. But here, women are engaged in an antipolitics against both the power of the state and sometimes, their families.

Retreating to a Moral Community

The women I knew in Les Minguettes were effectively barred from secondary education and employment, and subjected to social ostracization. Poor Salafist women retreated into the "lairs" (Konrád 1984, 203) of a semi-organized, private community to find moral support and refuge from the politicization of their practice and from conflicts with the men in their lives. Though many women I met shared close emotional bonds with their Salafist husbands, there was also tension between men and women at Mosquée Hasan. The regular presence of numerous women at the mosque, alongside the deliberate separation of men and women, produced problems from time to time. For example, when men did repair work on the mosque's façade outside the women's entrance, members felt a mutual annoyance that the others had transgressed their gendered boundaries. According to Ahmed, a few men at the mosque resented the women's active organization and leadership.

In some situations, women appeared more competent to teach Islam than the male imams. Sumaiya sometimes snickered or shook her head during the Friday *qhutbas* at Mosquée Ennour. I recall one *qhutba* that seemed replete with dubious information. The imam lectured, "It's very important to choose a good wife, because this will influence the behavior of your children. First, you have to clean yourself ... and pray before you sleep with your wife. If you do so, God will give you good children." Sumaiya looked at me and smiled knowingly.[14] Eventually, she stopped attending the mosque for a period. She told me politely, "I really didn't like the imam. I don't think he always knew what he was saying."

Although the women had some conflicts with men and seemed isolated from much of society, their regular meetings at the mosque represented an attempt to build a supportive community, especially in light of the marginalization they usually faced. The ethos of religious practice at both Mosquée Ennour and Hasan reflected this tension and sense of urgency. During prayers, for example, women obsessively focused on standing close together, shoulder to shoulder. At times, I was nearly knocked over as women grabbed my arms, pulling me closer. I got the impression of a community huddling together to protect itself. "There can't be any space between us [as per the Prophet's teachings]," I was told. "If we stay close together, the devil can't get past us." This sense of protection coexisted with the fundamental uncertainty and mistrust among the women in Les Minguettes. Though they lacked complete openness and trust, women nevertheless facilitated one another's spiritual path, shared teachings and ideas about Islam, and empathized with each other over their stigma as Salafist women.

The tendency toward refuge and support sometimes manifested in the phenomenon of possession by *jinns*. One Sunday, Yasmine, a young woman who regularly attended Mosquée Hasan, suddenly started speaking gibberish and shaking. This soon turned into screaming, weeping, tearing her clothes, and foaming at the mouth. We were all extremely frightened. Malika grabbed Yasmine and held her tightly. She loudly recited Ayat-ul-Kursi, an important verse and prayer in the Quran commonly used for protection and blessings. Some Muslims believe its recitation has the power to alter certain circumstances and diminish danger. With Malika firmly holding her, Yasmine calmed down. Malika explained that evil spirits exist, though we do not know exactly why, and emphasized that we all had to sit closer together and surround Yasmine to protect her. We moved closer, forming a tight circle on the floor.

The next week, Amel collapsed backward onto my lap and was quivering and weeping. Even after we all worked to calm her, she continued to moan and fall over for the next two hours. The teachers repeatedly explained:

> This sister is very sick. Just as God created humans, he also created a parallel race of spirits that we can't see. They come here precisely to scare us, to stop you from coming here. But *insha Allah* [God willing], you will continue coming to the classes. Don't have fear of this sister, just pray for her.

I gently broached the subject with Nasreen, who had some training in exorcism and Islamic healing (*roqaya*). "How do we know [Amel] doesn't just have some illness in her head?"

"No, no, that's not Amel who's moaning and shaking, it's the *jinn*. Amel isn't actually like this in everyday life. But look what courage she has to keep coming here. I had a friend who was coming to the classes last year when she got possessed. She got so frightened and couldn't handle it. She left and never came back."

My own bias was to consider these episodes as a physical release, a channeling of personal stress into a more religiously acceptable form that attracted attention and sympathy. But whatever the reality, these episodes tightened the community, as the teachers encouraged us all to keep coming to the mosque and to sit closer together.

While my companions gave and received moral and religious support, they were unable to share material support. Because of their djelbabs, Salafist women in Les Minguettes faced economic and social ostracization. Few French employers hired women who wore the hijab, let alone the djelbab. Especially for unmarried women, the reality of unemployment was an everyday obstacle and source of stress. Most of my unmarried companions searched for work as domestic workers, one of the few jobs in which employers might allow them to wear their hijabs or djelbabs.

After she was laid off by the telephone company where she worked, Amina knew that she would be able to subsist on her unemployment benefits for only a few months. After that, if she did not find a new job, she would have to manage on welfare assistance of 450 euros per month, and her rent was 250 euros. As the deadline approached, her worries increased. "But then I remember that God is guiding me and I shouldn't have fear. Malika always tells us not to worry, to trust God. That's what I'm trying to do. It always feels good to hear her say that." Like several other women,

Amina depended on the moral support and weekly routine of coming to Mosquée Hasan. When classes were occasionally canceled, she felt exceptionally disappointed.

The economic exclusion Salafist women experienced related to their estrangement from the education system. A number of young women I met at Mosquée Hasan dropped out of high school when the 2004 law against the headscarf in public schools was passed. While taking the Metro after class, soon after we had met for the first time, I had a conversation with Fatima, who dropped out of high school after her first year. We spoke softly in each other's ears as two pariahs well attuned to others' perceptions of us:

PARVEZ: I hate being stared at like this. Do you find it difficult?

FATIMA: Yes, of course. But I don't even see it anymore. I don't feel bad anymore. This is really something beginners feel. In the beginning I used to see it, they thought I was weird or crazy. Then I realized that it's them. They're the ones that are crazy, that have a problem.

PARVEZ: Was it your decision to drop out of school, or your parents'?

FATIMA: It was me. I got tired of taking [the scarf] on and off [at the entrance to school], and I started feeling really uncomfortable. I explained to my mom that I didn't want to go anymore. She was disappointed, but she understood. You know there's been a crisis here over the last five years [over this issue]. So I just dropped out. I fell out of touch with the world of school and students. But I actually started working as a housecleaner with a bureau [in the banlieue], and I don't have to take off my hijab. I know how things work now, and I can navigate the world of work. My life is full. I have free time, but I stay busy with my Islamic study.

At twenty-two, Fatima had already gone through years of personal struggle over her decisions and gradual turn toward a rigorous Islamic practice. She took some pride in earning money as a housecleaner, before later working for her brother-in-law. But even this created distress, as she complained that the other women with whom she shared her duties were rude to her. "One of them is a Maghrébine [of North African origin and a nonpracticing Muslim]. Sometimes they're the worst. She sneers at me while we work. I try to ignore her. I'm trying to transfer to something where I can just work alone, in peace." Fatima balanced her alienation from French society with her study of Islam. The courses at Mosquée Hasan provided consistent structure and meaning to her. "Twice a week is good, twice a week is okay," she mumbled to herself as we drove to her apartment: two sessions were just enough to carry her through each week.

For Fatima and her older sister, Lynda, who also quit high school, their intensive study of Islam was an important and satisfying replacement for secular education, but they would have liked to have finished high school or pursued a university education if their religious practice was tolerated. During one of the classes at Mosquée Hasan where the teacher discussed the compatibility of scientific knowledge with Islam, a student asked to what degree it was acceptable to pursue science and higher studies in the absence of the larger goal of promoting Islam. The teacher gave an ambig-uous response, saying "only God knows [the relationship between worldly knowledge and spiritual advancement]." She then reminded us, "But we all know, that for us [in France], it's not even an option."

Lynda was upset with the French attitude toward Muslims. Having cho-sen to wear the niqab, she was later directly impacted by the banning of the burqa. A week after I met her, one of the local banks in Les Minguettes put up a sign on the door with an image of a woman in a niqab with an "X" through it. Lynda remarked: "I was expecting this. But what's most upset-ting is that it's other Muslims who are doing this. They're sell-outs. I hate the fact that they're the ones who represent us [to the state], who speak for us. Actually, they don't represent us [in the banlieues] at all." Lynda was criticizing the few Muslim associations and institutions like the Paris Mosque (Grand Mosquée de Paris) that announced their support for the commission to debate the burqa.

Both Lynda and Fatima remembered clearly the attacks on the hijab when the 2004 headscarf law was debated. When the debate on the burqa started in the summer of 2009, I asked Lynda what she would do if a ban went into effect. "I'm going to get out of here. My husband and I are looking into getting a house in Algeria. We can't take it here in France anymore. I spent a year in Egypt a few years ago and was so much happier being in a Muslim country."

Over time, I lost track of the number of people, both men and women, who claimed they were exhausted with their stigma and would be happier in a Muslim society. As Fatima said, "Ultimately, we have to move back to a Muslim country. You see the way people look at us and hate us. Why put up with that?" When I asked her if she would miss France, she reflected for a moment.

"Yes, I'll miss the euro," she said. "But then I don't need much in life to be happy." She laughed, "Our parents left Algeria for France, and thirty years later, their kids want to leave France for Algeria."

While many Salafist Muslims found ways to move to places like Egypt or Yemen, at least temporarily, for others, such migration was not realistic. As Fatima admitted, adjusting to a poor country like Algeria might prove too difficult despite the poverty and marginality they experienced in France. When Fatima left to spend the month of Ramadan in Algeria, she contacted me every few days to inquire about the group and the classes at Mosquée Hasan, which she sorely missed. Fatima and others depended on the teachings that were central to this moral community and, I argue, to the public disengagement and autonomous refuge that defined their antipolitics.

Achieving Serenity in a "life of suffering"

In the many months of women's classes I participated in at Mosquée Hasan, some of the major themes were patience (*sabr*) in the face of suffering and how to find happiness in a life defined intrinsically as *la vie musibah* (a combination of French and Arabic for "the life of suffering"). This focus on life's impermanence and the fact of suffering was unique to the Salafist community in the poorer mosques, even though mortality and salvation are important and prominent theological themes in Islam more generally. With the absence of strong Islamic civil societies in the banlieues, major obstacles to economic stability, and disintegrating families, the mosque's continual messages of *sabr* and serenity spoke directly to the bleak situations faced by many of the women. For Salafist women, developing serenity through trust in divine will was key to augmenting one's faith. This practice served to alleviate anxieties and regrets. "Everything is in God's hands," Malika said. "Once you accept this, apply this, you stop living in the domain of the imagination [imaginary fears]. Then you can sleep in tranquility [*tu peux dormir tranquil*]," she added in a lulling tone.

To achieve perfect faith, she taught, we had to continually work to reform our hearts.[15] In doing so, we privileged our private and inner states. Indeed, teachers often emphasized the private and personal nature of one's faith: it was considered prohibited to boast about one's Islamic practice such as fasting and charity, or to assume that one had purity of heart. Wearing the djelbab was viewed as obligatory, but no guarantee of one's inner state of faith. Contrary to local stereotypes of Salafists as obsessed with outward practice and vesture, Malika said to me, "Look, I never judge anyone for their practice. I don't know why others think we're obsessed with the djelbab. It's only one practice. You can have the perfect outward practice but have no faith and vice versa."

The ultimate goal of reforming and "nourishing" one's heart (*nourrir ton coeur*), attempted through prayer and practice, was feeling love of God. This was the key to complete faith as a Muslim. The feeling of love is a nebulous concept, and my companions frequently asked questions about what it meant. The teachers emphasized that it is never a simple matter of outward practice but, rather, a state of heart that one achieves or with which one might be blessed. Deep compassion, for example, exists in the heart and is an important religious virtue that reflects love of God. But no one really knows the state of one's own heart, or that of others. Dalel, one of the teachers at Mosquée Hasan, repeatedly told the story of a Jewish woman who was a prostitute, living at the time of the Prophet Muhammed. As recounted in the sayings (hadith) of the Prophet, this woman offered a bowl of water to a sick dog one day, although she was suffering from thirst. According to the Prophet, all her sins were forgiven based on this one act of compassion. "But," Dalel was quick to remind us,

> Not everyone glorifies God through compassion in the heart, as she did, though she didn't know it. It's a function of what's in the heart of each individual. Everyone is particular. To be forgiven for a grand sin like adultery, for example, you have to regret [*tawba*] and commit good acts. But both regret and good acts are weak, if they are weak in your heart.

We often discussed what it meant to have regret. Teachers emphasized that God only accepts regret when it is sincere. Specific practices, prayers, and reforms in one's daily life could demonstrate regret, yet it is only when one really feels the remorse that God might forgive the sin.

Students frequently asked, "How does one go about reforming one's heart?" The ambiguous answer reflected a mix of physical practice, good acts, and prayer—specifically, supplications to ask God to strengthen one's faith. Indeed, in some moments, we explored physical practice in great detail and with a sense of anxiety. But the women clearly acknowledged that excessive detail about comportment could also be negative. Dalel one day fielded numerous specific questions about the act of physical prostration in asking for forgiveness. Finally, she dismissed the questions: "Look, above all, in prayer you should be full of happiness. It's something primordial. My sisters, be careful about getting so caught up in details that you forget what's in fact primordial."

In addition to good acts and prayer, one's heart is strengthened through the enactment of *sabr* (patience) and trust in divine will in the face of life's adversities and, ultimately, the fact of mortality. In Malika's words,

> To not accept the fact of death, to actually blame God, is sinful and ignorant. It's like taking the characteristics of nonbelievers inside of us. The act of lamentation is a contradiction of *sabr*. The word *sabr* derives from the word for "imprisoning." Imagine, if something tragic occurs, you can lose control and act crazy, throw yourself on the ground. Imagine instead that you draw your arms toward you, turn inward, and "imprison" or enclose that part of you, and stay calm. *Sabr* is like a medicine that is bitter but delivers sweetness and serenity. Especially in our Arab countries, when someone dies, you see women tearing their clothes and screaming, "Woe is me!" To hit yourself, tear your clothes, is not permitted. Only God gives life, and only God can take it.

The achievement of patience and the "imprisoning" of grief was part of maintaining one's dignity, which extended to all situations of suffering.

Through trial, one is challenged to enact patience and achieve a stronger state of heart. One sister asked Malika, "What if I think God tests me more than I deserve to be tested? I didn't sin that much after all."

Malika responded, "We don't have the right to proclaim ourselves or anyone else as sinners or non-sinners. God tests the state of our hearts, and that's all. Why do we suffer maladies? The Prophet said, 'To test our hearts.' And why? 'To elevate our rewards.' Despite the agony, the recompense will be even greater."

Faridah, a French *convertie*, asked, "But how do you practice patience? How can I make it work?"

"For example, through language," Malika responded. "Don't ever complain and lament your situation. Make supplications, ask God continually to open your heart and help you develop patience."

The idea of never complaining fit a larger pattern of teachings around speech and social interaction. Specifically, discussion of the Prophet's teachings raised questions about a number of sinful behaviors, including gossip, probing personal questions, questions or comments designed to embarrass someone, lies, and spreading information one was unsure about. "In general," said Dalel, "It's not good to talk too much. If I talk a lot, about anything and everything, I forget all remembrance of God."

It was not until I processed this message about speech and social behavior that I better understood the culture of this mosque community. What many perceive as unsociability among burqa-clad women is, in fact, women's work to incorporate these messages into their comportment, with the goal of attaining *sabr* and dignity. Maintaining a degree of privacy and silence was essential to their relationship to God. While this was true to their teachings, it is also difficult to disentangle from their fear of surveillance and lack of social trust.

With many of the mosque teachings centering on *sabr* in the face of adversity, even tragedy, Malika asked whether it is possible to attain joy in *la vie musibah*. She devoted much of her sessions to addressing this question, employing the writings of Sheikh Sa'di from a small booklet entitled *Les Clefs pour une vie heureuse* (Keys to a Happy Life). She lectured:

> It *is* possible to find happiness in this life of suffering [*musibah*]. In sadness and misfortune, what is the path of [Muslim] believers? That when there is joy, you *recognize* it, you feel it in your heart. Only real believers recognize that these blessings come from God, that we have our eyes and ears, we can eat and drink. We can hope for other things in this life, but it is obligatory to be satisfied with everything that God gives us, even misfortunes, even grand catastrophes.
>
> My father, in Algeria, he's an old man and poor. But he's serene. You see smiles on the faces of all these poor old people in our countries [Maghréb]. Not here in France. The more riches they attain, the more they are full of worries. For all humans, it's innate to seek the way of peace. But we have the aid of God and faith. We recognize joy, and that it comes from God. This is the main difference between believers and nonbelievers [*kafrs*].

According to Malika and other teachers, it is only through love of God and patience that one might attain happiness (*la vie heureuse*) and embody the state of being Muslim. For my companions, this was particularly meaningful, given the multitude of obstacles in their lives. Malika had a school-aged daughter who was mentally and physically disabled. I sometimes saw her around Les Minguettes in a cheap wheelchair, and several of us would affectionately help her with schoolwork when she came to the mosque. Malika's own background thus made her lectures on serenity and faith more compelling.

Malika and other teachers such as Leila and Dalel addressed the importance of living in the present moment, forgetting the past, and not worrying about the future. This emphasis spoke to the anxieties of the women in their classes. Malika reminded us that we cannot control our life paths and must continually practice a type of discipline to have the serenity that comes from faith in God. Malika explained:

> You have to always work on yourself. If your heart has peace, then anguish and sadness disappear. You don't have work, you're worried about the future, your retirement, what'll you do when you're sixty? Or you don't have children, a husband, and worry about who'll take care of you when you're old. But we can't know the future. Only God knows. No one else can access this. An individual can't do anything to intervene other than work on herself. And we don't even know— we could die before any of these situations present themselves. So don't waste time worrying about what you may never confront.

To achieve serenity, it was important to let go of past grievances and fear. Fear was often presented as a temptation of the devil, intended to lead one away from faith in God and the present moment and toward sickness. She continued:

> [What does it mean] to forget unpleasant things from the past? It doesn't mean to be amnesiac. To be human means we're constituted by our past. You can't forget but you don't want sadness to resurface. You have to make an effort in your heart, make an effort to close the door, struggle against the sadness when it tries to resurface.

Struggling against sadness and working on one's "heart" was part of preparing for the month of Ramadan, when one concentrates on spiritual practice. In the weeks preceding Ramadan, discussions at the mosque turned to preparing ourselves for a spiritual regimen of fasting, prayer,

and strengthening faith. Malika emphasized the importance to this process of letting go of fear:

> Faith is an act of the heart, so don't let it fall into the domain of
> imagination. As soon as an individual falls into the domain of illu-
> sion, he's going to fall into nervous depression and sickness of the
> heart. Generally, the origins of our fears have no reason. How many
> people, in their minds, imagine problems? A mother doesn't culti-
> vate her child's fear of darkness but tries to get him to understand
> that it's imaginary. You sleep alone at night, you hear a noise, and
> your imagination runs wild. Or the fear of losing your child is so
> strong that you're too anxious at the park. You worry he'll disappear
> when in fact, he's right there at your side.
>
> This type of fear brings anguish, sickness, in some cases hypo-
> chondria. If you trust in God, all sickness of the heart and body can
> disappear. There'll be a sense of peace in your chest and a joy that's
> indescribable. God is the creator of the sun, the moon, the earth—
> and so I place my faith in [him] instead of all else. This is sufficient.

This particular lecture demonstrates the utmost importance placed on
one's individual relationship with God. When Malika discussed trusting
God above all else, she explicitly referred to other systems of belief, other
people, technologies, and the state.

My companions in the women's courses at Mosquée Hasan were working to achieve a state of perfect faith (*la foi complète*) that revolved around
their ability to attain serenity and conquer their fears. Given the uncertainty
about their futures regarding marriage and employment, aggression from
strangers, police harassment, and a state that viewed them simultaneously
as criminals and as victims, fear presented a constant dark cloud that they
had to work to sequester or eliminate. The only way to combat fear, they
taught, is through faith. Antipolitics thus had both a spiritual and a material component. It aimed to counter fear by solidifying faith in God *and* by
consciously focusing only on the physical moment, rather than dwelling
on the past or anticipating what comes next and what may never occur.

ANTIPOLITICS WAS A logical response for subaltern minorities who were
managing state regulation of their everyday practice and who were disconnected from middle-class Muslims and their politics. It followed
the fractures and weakening of the immigrant rights movement in the

banlieues of the 1980s and '90s, and the demise of activist networks in the post-9/11 years. As urban management became more repressive, and the class bifurcation among Muslims widened, the Salafist movement gained appeal and offered solace to young women and men facing unemployment, precarity, or the prospect of years in prison. The retreat from the state and from politics altogether is not the same as apolitical apathy. Rather, it was a conscious decision. My companions knew what they stood to gain and what they might lose by participating in instrumental politics. Ahmed decided he could not risk his family's safety by continuing his activism.

One of the results of both the state's assimilationist interventions and the class disconnect in Lyon, in contrast to Hyderabad, is that issues of gender in the community were invisible. Women turned their backs to the intense spotlight the state shined on them as vulnerable victims in need of protection, so as to carry on with their gendered practices, sometimes even in opposition to their husbands or parents. Amina thus lived alone, estranged from her mother and anxious to find a husband in the Salafist community. Amel proclaimed she had only two choices as a Salafist woman—either to marry or to emigrate. Salafist men, for their part, focused on economic activities to secure their means for survival and support their families. For Mounir, the movement positively impacted his quartier and perhaps helped keep him away from petty crime and prison.

For both men and women in Les Minguettes, state surveillance of mosques and police raids meant that defending the private sphere was the most important project for them to undertake. The women of Mosquée Hasan carved out a space and established a set of activities to protect their faith. Their most important relationship was their private, individual relationship to God—a relationship on which their ethnic or cultural backgrounds and families had no bearing. They also strove toward forming a moral community, for refuge from their ostracization and marginality. The teachers encouraged all of us to stay together, especially when Yasmine and Amel became possessed by *jinns* that same summer when the burqa debate started.

As much as my companions relished the moral community, a lack of social trust permeated the local culture. Sumaiya had not told anyone of her imploding marriage, while Amina had not revealed to anyone her anxieties or her cigarette addiction. With the many worries and fears the women carried, the third component of antipolitics focused on serenity in *la vie musibah*. Women listened and discussed with rigor and enthusiasm how to free themselves of anxiety and regret by striving continuously toward love of God and perfect faith. On this topic, Malika's compelling lectures kept many women firmly committed to the mosque, encouraging them to embrace a "respect for the present" and to "push the state out of [their] nightmares, so as to be afraid of it less."[16]

As France's war on terror expanded following the *Charlie Hebdo* and Bataclan attacks, Muslims in the quartiers continued to abandon the public sphere to the state. The opposite of political communities, their Islamic revival was a retreat into the private sphere, in both a literal and a metaphorical sense. It was anything but an attempt to Islamize the state or willfully alter the public sphere. Antipolitics allowed for self-preservation, as it rejected all attempts to engage the state or participate in a system that marginalizes faith.[17] At the same time, state surveillance that fueled a larger distrust, and the class estrangement within the Muslim community, made a noninstrumental politics appear foreign and out of reach.

7

Conclusion

DEMOCRACY, FEMINISM, AND THE WAR ON TERROR

OVER THE LAST decade, the issues addressed in this book have not sub-sided. France elected eleven mayoral candidates from the right-wing Front National, while India reelected the Hindu nationalist BJP as its ruling party in 2014. The 2015 *Charlie Hebdo* and Bataclan murders reinvigorated debates about the "problem" of Islam and of integrating minority youth in Europe, as the Mumbai bombings in 2008 and 2011 raised worries about the radicalization of Indian Muslims. Adding to the tensions, ISIS and Al Qaeda have expressed their intents to attract specifically Muslims in South Asia and Europe to their networks. More globally, since the Arab Uprisings, pundits increasingly refer to Salafis as "populist puritans" and dangerous fundamentalists with a universally "warped vision of a new order" (R. Wright 2012). The politicization of Islam remains in full force in every direction, even as academics have weighed in to correct the misper-ceptions of Islam that undergird a growing racialization of Muslims.[1]

This book began by describing the backdrop of the global War on Terror and state surveillance in France and India that made ordinary Muslims suspect. I asked, given the disproportionate poverty, unemploy-ment, and discrimination they experience, how do Muslims, as denigrated minorities, make claims on the secular state and attempt to improve their situations? How does active participation in Islamic revival movements overlap with these claims and efforts? These are not questions typically posed within the conventional framing of Islam, which instead assumes that Islamic movements seek to Islamize the state or promote Islamic law, and in the final analysis, that Islam is simply not compatible with democracy. The conventional view asks how we might "win the hearts and minds" of Muslims and engender a liberal reformation.[2] All four cases I presented in Hyderabad and Lyon challenge this conventional view. Far from Islamizing the state, the communities I studied were making basic political claims along an axis of redistribution and recognition, and were striving to practice some autonomy from the state that politicized them, whether by retreating into private life or by building their own political communities. These communities are arguably at the heart of democratic practice.

By participating in religious communities across two cities and across class, I captured some of the diversity of beliefs and practices among Muslims, highlighting how misguided it is to point to theological teachings as the explanation for their politics, as well-known theoretical approaches have done. While conducting global ethnography, I saw that citing globalization as the explanation for Islamic movements across the global North and South also fails to reveal much about their nature or conditions for their emergence. Theories arguing that globalization have produced inequalities and cultural crises of identity for Muslims obscure the active role of the state in politicizing Islam and creating the conditions under which movements emerge and to which they respond.

This book also departed from scholarship that insists Islamic revivals constitute forms of politics because of the way pious practice alters people's subjectivity. Analytically distinguishing between movements that take the state as their object and those that take community as their object, this book demonstrated that not all politics are the same. In the case of Lyon's urban periphery, the pious women I knew had such little desire or ability to impact the public or the state, or even to practice citizenship and build communities of trust and reciprocity, that it is deeply problematic to depict their religious revival as politics in any form. In sum, these various approaches to Islamic movements take for granted the extent to which the secular state has politicized Islam.

How have Muslim communities responded to top-down politicization? What conditions explain the type of politics they developed in the contemporary, post-9/11, neoliberal period? To summarize, under France's militant form of secularism that seeks to control religion while eliminating it from public space and institutions, the politics directed at the state are recognition politics focused on religious liberties and symbolic recognition of Muslim identity. Because laïcité in France selectively erected obstacles to collective worship in mosques and Islamic schools, veiling in public, and requirements like halal food, Islamic associations had to struggle for state recognition of their religious needs and equal respect more broadly. The historical stigmatization of religion and the elevation of a universal conception of citizenship hindered organizing along religious lines, so that eventually those in the working-class banlieues were left without ties to middle-class Muslims, and the immigrant rights movement they built weakened and fractured. State surveillance further severed cross-class ties and compelled Salafists in the quartiers to retreat into the private sphere.

Under the conditions of India's flexible secularism that facilitated religious practice, state-directed politics aimed for economic redistribution. Because Indian composite nationalism rested on the notion of communities and community rights, it ignored the gross class and caste inequalities within religious communities. For this reason, relatively secure in their religious liberties, Islamic associations and Muslim elites struggled for reservations, public goods, and social welfare projects. A pluralist model of secularism that valorized religious community, coupled with a long history of patronage, encouraged stronger cross-class attachments among Muslims and a relationship based on paternalism. Inflows of remittance money and competition among Muslim elites on the terrain of distribution led to political protections for subaltern Muslims and material support for their community politics, in which they were able to practice some autonomy from the state and construct their own civil societies.

With these findings, this book made three theoretical interventions. First, the contradictions of secularism determine the nature of minority religious movements. Secularism in both countries defined the conditions of equality and citizenship. In France, the state claimed neutrality but then proceeded to treat people of Muslim origin as unequal citizens, decisions rooted in complex histories of imperial ambition. When Muslims made claims in the name of their community, or complained of discrimination, they were accused of *communautarisme* that violated secularism. In India, the state claimed it would facilitate equality for all religious communities, but here, too, Muslims who tried to mobilize against discrimination in jobs or welfare were accused of communalism. These fundamentally contradictory tendencies generated the politics of Islamic revival as one effect.

Second, Muslim class relations influence the agendas and political potentiality of Islamic movements. The capacity of minority middle classes and elites to provide networks, organizations, and resources to working-class Muslims sets the grounds for their political mobilization. Where they had deep connections to the poor, as in Hyderabad, middle-class Muslims emphasized redistribution. Cross-class relations also nourished greater conversation around gender relations and debates within the Islamic tradition, if only because of greater commingling of interpretations and practices. In Lyon, middle-class Muslims had concerns for the poor and spoke of the importance of redistribution, but were unable to effectively mobilize toward this goal in part because of the class division.

Third, distinguishing between an instrumental concept of politics that takes the state as its object and a noninstrumental politics that takes community as the means and end gives greater precision to the analysis of Islamic revival movements. This distinction also highlights the limited potential of a movement of antipolitics and the transformative potential of noninstrumental politics. This intervention does not tie subject formation to the state, nor does it adopt the view of the state. Instead, it reflects the practices and desires of the religious men and women I came to know.

Political Effects and Potentialities

I have argued that the politics of Islamic revival fall into categories of either instrumental or noninstrumental politics. This section explores critiques and potentialities of the four movements, with attention to their nature as either instrumental or noninstrumental.

What is the transformative potential of redistributive politics among Muslims in Hyderabad? To begin, much of the literature assumes that religious movements and class movements are antithetical, and the former cannot support political or economic transformation. Such transformation, after all, requires a secular orientation.[3] Thus, scholars tend to criticize religiously identified political parties like the MIM and policies such as reservations for minorities as identity politics. Some have even argued that reservations agendas in India have undermined redistribution and deradicalized social movements (Basu 2012; Mehta 2004). Clientelism, some argue, is not the same as a popular democratic movement. At worst, it may reduce the autonomy of subaltern groups because their desperation for basic material needs leaves their democratic rights at the mercy of brokers and diminishes both the responsibilities and the capacities of the state (Heller 2000, 512; Fox 1994). At best, "it seems, in a sense, to buy women off with very modest resources; but insofar as it does bring them into public spaces and help them to acquire a greater sense of their own agency, it contributes to their becoming citizens, rather than just denizens of the city" (Harriss 2007, 2720–21).

The growth of religious associations that work with the poor raises similar concerns.[4] Some argue that associations do not really represent the urban poor, or that skills, schools, and other welfare benefits described in chapter 3 may have importance, but also lead to entrenched hierarchies dominated by the middle class and elites—who in turn partake in cultural disciplining that echoes the colonial era (Harriss 2007; Wyatt 2005).

These serious concerns might lower hopes for Hyderabad's middle-class politics.[5] But as I tried to show, Muslim middle-class activists and elites directed their energies almost entirely toward serving the needs of the poor, with the right to education as their primary object. In some key low-income pockets I observed, such as Zohra Bagh, activists provided welfare in a clientelistic fashion, but they also encouraged subaltern mobilization and political consciousness. It therefore lies within the realm of possibility that Hyderabad is in the very early stages of the type of transition seen in the Indian state of Kerala, marked by decreased poverty, subaltern mobilization, and increased state accountability owing to intense electoral competition. The issue of state accountability is both critical and complex. On the one hand, accountability in Hyderabad may have declined with an expansive philanthropic network, rather than the state's providing essential services to the Muslim urban poor. On the other hand, robust political party competition, driven by both electoral and paternal redistribution, has forced the state to acknowledge the importance of welfare services like health and education.

Compared to the Communist Party in Kerala, neither the MIM nor the Muslim philanthropic community was entrenched in broader coalitions of the urban poor that would provide wider hegemony. Recently, however, both groups have sought to expand their scope and appeal to both Muslims and Dalits, with the MIM explicitly aiming for this expansion.[6] Further, like the Communist Party, redistributive politics in Hyderabad focus on health, gender, and education. Overall, I argue that redistribution and religious identity claims are not antithetical, especially in a context of state retrenchment from social welfare. Only time will tell whether redistribution politics in Hyderabad will eventually lead to greater justice for the poor.

Likewise, with the politics of recognition in France, the long-term results remain to be seen. As individuals like Hakim believe, Islam is en route to "finding its place" in France, developing institutionalized relations with the state, achieving normalization, and gaining acceptance in everyday life. In the last five years especially, middle-class Islamic associations, including those presented in chapter 5, are increasingly speaking out in self-defense against Islamophobia and anti-Muslim violence (alongside denouncing terrorism). Perhaps only after Islamic organizations more firmly embed themselves in French associational life and feel empowered to defend the community might a class-based political imaginary be redis-covered. But as long as Islam and Muslims remain under attack, fueling recognition politics among the middle class and antipolitics in the banli-eues, it remains uncertain or unlikely that Muslims can bridge the class divide toward a more transformative movement for social justice.

AS MIDDLE-CLASS REDISTRIBUTION and recognition politics focus on claims on the state, they constitute ordinary politics that can potentially achieve important rights and material concessions. But my subaltern participants simply rejected the goal of making claims on the state. In the Indian case, their movement was a noninstrumental form of politics focused on community as a means and end, rather than an instrumental form aimed at the state. To consider the implications of community poli-tics, it is worth reflecting here on the principles at stake between these two different concepts of politics.

In the Arendtian framework, political energy directed at the state only substitutes for true action, replacing it instead with the "logic of rules and standards" (see Markell 2010, 61; Arendt 1963, 29–33). Such logic obstructs people's will to practically engage in activities, and their ability to understand their activities and political communities as something fun-damentally inaugural, with radical potential. In sum, it leads to political apathy and weakening of the public realm. The ultimate threat to partici-patory democracy, for Arendt, is the lack of spontaneous action and lack of responsiveness to events—in a sense, a loss of perceived agency that in extreme form could overtake whole groups of citizens and pave the path for totalitarian domination (Markell 2010, 79). Struggling with the state for civil rights, for example, may be critical (Arato and Cohen 2010, 167). But relying on the state bureaucracy as a form of politics only lengthens its tentacles, allowing it to reach into all spheres of life, including those once considered private and intimate (Calhoun 1997, 234; Arendt 1958, 33). Thus, the stakes involved in community politics are simultaneously pro-tection of a private sphere and public realm, the latter of which is the only potential site of participatory democracy. For my subaltern companions in Hyderabad, their Islamic revival had much more at stake than concessions from the state.

I argued in chapter 4 that poor women in Hyderabad were building the foundations of civil society through their material, legal, and symbolic projects. But here, too, questions linger about the long-term effects and transformative potential of these projects. For example, what are the implications of encouraging women's self-employment rather than advocating for structural change? Some scholars criticize self-employment and Grameen Bank-style programs as neoliberalism masquerading as feminism (Karim 2011). Ananya Roy (2010) has argued that microfinance is a case of subprime lending with links to imperialism and new frontiers for capital. There appears an uncomfortable overlap between the World Bank's vision, as well as older colonial charity efforts focused on women, and grass-roots organizing for women's education and skills. In light of this, one could read the case of Hyderabad with cynical caution. But I think doing so would overlook the important gains Muslim women have made amid severe poverty and isolation. The projects in Hyderabad were not imposed by foreign NGOs to placate subaltern communities or to enforce individualistic behaviors and support for capitalism. They were, instead, based fundamentally in community relations, where members shared a religious, ethical framework.

Compared to political communities among Hyderabad's subaltern Muslims, what are the effects and consequences of antipolitics in Lyon's urban periphery? Foremost, antipolitics enables self-protection and preservation of faith. It provides a moral and spiritual refuge for women who learn and teach Arabic literacy and religious exegesis, and who explore numerous issues of ethical significance in their individual lives. Teachers like Dalel and Malika developed crucial intellectual and religious leadership roles. As in Hyderabad, they did not establish their own interpretations of texts but, nonetheless, they learned to rigorously engage and comprehend the principles they believed they must follow. They were in no way passive absorbents of Islamic teachings. At the same time their antipolitics was far removed from the material and legal projects evident in the women's political communities in Hyderabad, and antipolitics did not fortify the community as an end in itself. Although my Salafi companions offered one another moral support, they held on tightly to their personal privacy. The trust and openness that flowed through Hyderabad's political communities was absent in Les Minguettes. Together, these factors sharply limit the political potentiality of the pious transformations that occur in the Islamic revival in Lyon's banlieues. Antipolitics has shunned both instrumental politics and efforts to protect a public realm.

Feminist Struggle

These political effects (or lack thereof) have direct consequences for the potential of feminist struggle. Women's practices, as seen in chapters 3 and 5, lay at the core of a cultural class struggle among Muslims. Clearly, it is women's practices—indeed, their bodies—that embarrass the middle-class, represent a propensity toward terrorism, and define the nation as liberal-secular. This does not mean that women want to make a political statement or draw more attention to their lives, which are already under international scrutiny, but simply, that they are politicized from various directions. But tensions among Muslims of different classes over gender entail particular consequences for gender justice and feminism.

In Lyon, recognition politics rendered gender invisible, having the opposite effect of the French state, which made gender hyper visible. While state and public discourses judge and lament the status of Muslim women, I observed very little discussion or debate about gender inequality or feminism among my companions. The middle-class women I knew enjoyed collaborative relationships with their brothers at the mosque and actively participated with men in Islamic associations. They were far busier managing employment discrimination than in discussing issues of gender or feminism within their communities. The working-class Salafist women lived in gender-segregated worlds, without the space for, or perhaps relevance of, feminist agendas. Working-class Salafi men struggled to earn a living or maintain small businesses to provide for a future family while promoting piety in their housing projects. Men and women together upheld strict gender roles and patriarchal authority as an alternative to the crisis-ridden families of their neighborhoods (Amghar 2011, 136–37).

The invisibility of gender was not only a reaction to the French state. In Hyderabad, state hostility to Muslim gendered practices existed alongside feminist goals and discussions within Muslim communities. Gender was visible from above, as the Hindu right criticized gender relations among Muslims, while other state politicians highlighted the importance of women's upliftment. It was also visible from below, as subaltern men and women spoke openly about the need for women's education and welfare. Thus, in Lyon, the absence of cross-class dialogue, in addition to the state's hostility, accounts for gender's invisibility and the seemingly limited potential for feminist movements. It is ironic that policies in the name of *laïcité* express concern for women, but curtail avenues for feminism among minority women.

While antipolitics and the struggle for religious recognition in Lyon reinforced normative masculinity and femininity to some extent, the case of Hyderabad is more unusual in that redistribution and political communities unsettled traditional gender roles. In India, despite the politicization of Muslim women, Indian composite nationalism and noninterference allowed for cross-class relations and political mobilization. Women organized around personal law to seek divorce or advocate against dowry, an act made possible because the Indian state never demanded or controlled Muslim representative institutions. Upper-middle-class women in Hyderabad actively participated in redistributive politics as leaders and volunteers, drawing attention to the conditions of low-income women. Low-income men and women supported a mission of collective responsibility and autonomy, even as subaltern men were excluded from the material benefits of political community. Instead, they sought temporary employment in Gulf countries, a path riddled with uncertainty, and sometimes abuse and criminality based on anecdotes I accumulated over years. An open question is whether low-income men will continue to support their wives' and daughters' earning potential and bargaining power—or whether their own exclusion from economic empowerment will backfire.

As to my poorest companions, the more I saw subaltern, burqa-clad women organizing themselves and pondering their futures, the more certain I became that women's building and practicing of political community is a form of feminist practice. This need not be qualified or considered a paradox, as scholars have generally done.[7] Some have even argued that there can be no such thing as an Islamic feminism because of the supposed contradictions between gendered practices and feminist ideals (Moghissi 2008, 1999; Winter 2001; Shahidian 1999). In arguing that women's political community is a form of feminist practice, I draw broadly on the notions of a nascent fourth-wave feminism focused on democratic politics (Steinmetz 2009; Wrye 2009) and specifically, on the idea of feminism as a "practice of freedom" (Zerilli 2005) wherein women form new political associations with others.[8] It might seem unusual to portray this case as feminist struggle, when the women supported the principles of Islamic law and did not seek legal reform or rights from the state. Nor did their subjective desires include Western conceptions of liberation. As Linda Zerilli quotes from the 1987 publication of the Italian manifesto *Sexual Difference*: "A freedom that, paradoxically, demands no vindication of the rights of women, no equal rights under the law, but only a full, political and personal accountability to women, is as startlingly a radical notion as any that has emerged in Western thought" (2005, 93).

This is not to deny the importance of constitutionally guaranteed rights but, rather, to explore the possibility that developing female interlocutors and the creativity of something like political community may be as or more critical to freedom than the granting of equal rights. Accordingly, this book has tried to shift the focus from veiling and its signification of gendered norms and the types of rights that religious women do or do not desire and instead to emphasize simply the creation of political community—that is arguably a prerequisite to the exercise of rights but, more importantly, an end in itself. Over the course of my research, the question of why women willingly took up the burqa in such great numbers became far less interesting and fruitful when compared to the issues that mattered the most in the women's lives: their access to education and employment, their capacity to feed their children, and their ability to participate in a world outside their private, individual selves. As these issues came to the fore, the supposed paradox of sectarian Muslim women practicing feminism began to unravel.

But the question of women's veiling, like the question of what drives the Islamic revival, continues to dominate public and intellectual attention. The quest to explain religiosity has driven both cultural and structural approaches to Islam, and to some extent has left its traces in this book. If the theoretical proposition that religion rises in response to anomie and suffering bears some truth (Geertz 1973; Berger 1967), then we might easily predict Islamic revivals in many parts of the world with rising inequality and numerous forms of degradation. But like Clifford Geertz (1973) wrote of the malaise caused by the obsession with definitions of religion, I believe a political and intellectual malaise has taken hold, caused by an obsessive search for explanations for increased Islamic religiosity.[9] In the hope of escaping this malaise, I tried to place this book in deep conversation with other issues, including class relations, feminism, and the nature of secular democracies.

Class, Democracy, and the War on Terror

Islamic revival movements and the political forms they can take are not monolithic. This book tried to show how and why they differ and ultimately, what these movements imply about broader potentialities for social justice and transformation and feminist struggle. One of the aims of this book was to destabilize the dominant frames that homogenize Muslims and obscure the importance of class. Many of the women and men I presented would be widely seen as sectarian fundamentalists. But such an assessment fails to accurately reflect the complexity of their relationships to their faith and religious texts. And it completely dismisses their relationships to their social and political worlds. I tried to show how the very notion of sectarian fundamentalists is a political construction that categorizes and stigmatizes poor and marginalized groups.

Judging religious practices such as veiling is a form of symbolic violence. These judgments are essentially arbitrary and are imposed upon subaltern Muslims from outside and from above. We tend to think of these judgments as ideological or religious differences, but I have argued instead that we might consider them as differences of class. They "enter into the very constitution of social (class) relations and can serve as instruments of domination . . . they constitute *stakes* in the contention between classes and class fractions, as between other social collectives" (Wacquant 1993, 131). Such judging is powerful in that it solidifies a social order, ultimately enforced by the state, in which both Muslims and non-Muslims take for granted an association between "backwardness" or "fundamentalism" and "the burqa." The classification scheme of liberal versus fundamentalist Islam has legitimacy *because* those of higher social and economic status impose it.

What does all this mean for the War on Terror?[10] First, it means that the struggle to "win the hearts and minds" of Muslims masks the reality of class domination. Second, it means that some of the highest ideals of democracy are enacted in places we might not expect, such as in the slums of Hyderabad, more freely than in the birthplace of modern democracy. Indeed, one of the dangers of political theories about plural democracies is that they emphasize liberal subjectivity over democracy—and thereby reinforce symbolic violence while overlooking political communities in unexpected places.[11] Third, if democratic practice can blossom in deeply religious spaces, an approach to Muslim communities that suppresses religion with the goal of preventing terrorism is thoroughly misguided. In the aftermath of the Bataclan massacre, France rushed to shut down a number of mosques, targeting especially Salafist mosques and leaders. As Olivier Roy (2015) has argued, this strategy misses the point, because ISIS recruits among nonpracticing young people. The young people who are most vulnerable to terrorist recruitment crave meaning, and closing mosques cuts them off from a major venue where they might find it.

It remains unclear what will come from such measures related to the War on Terror, or from the immense pressure the French state exerts on communities like those in Les Minguettes. In the meanwhile, it is almost certain that current legislation will keep Salafist women locked in domestic spaces and further estranged from French society.[12] While I have painted a much brighter picture of politics in Hyderabad, we know that the Hindu political right has made anti-Muslim discourse and violence more acceptable in everyday life. Hyderabad's political landscape may be unique in many ways, but it still demonstrates the vital importance of strong civil societies and parties that can fight back in defense of the marginalized. Community solidarity and trust are the keys to, at minimum, self-preservation and, most optimistically, to the potential for flourishing that lies in a noninstrumental vision of politics.

Between the "Logic of Logic" and the "Logic of God"

The research for this book was informed by the ideal of reflexive ethnography and the extended case method: I relied on dialogue with participants and observations across space and time that revealed connections between processes of everyday religious revival and macro-level forces of state and economy. I used these dialogues and observations to extend theories about the politicization of religious practice.

My presence as a researcher was an intervention in the field. It created effects, both positive and negative, and allowed me to learn about my participants' social worlds through the dynamics of our interactions (Burawoy 2009). Because every ethnographic encounter (and researcher) is unique, it would be difficult to exactly replicate this study. Nor are the arguments presented in this book generalizable across minority Muslim societies. Instead, *Politicizing Islam* offered a theoretical claim about types of secularism and the role of ethnic minority class relations that others might consider and reconstruct in other urban and national contexts.

In this appendix, I describe how I gained access to my field sites, focusing on the impact of my social position, the state surveillance that haunted the research and my participants, and the interventions I made in the field. The extended case method is attuned to the effects of power, some of which are revealed in this discussion: for example, the domination I exerted through my nationality and class position in Hyderabad and in both sites through my higher education; the excluding or silencing of other voices such as those of poor and subaltern Muslims who felt oppressed by Islamic revival and sectarian movements or those of marginalized men with a different sort of interaction with the state.[1] With these power effects in mind, I reflect here on the depth and nature of the bonds I developed, the different experiences of veiling across the two cases, and the moral dilemmas I faced over faith and epistemology. I describe the personal transformation that unfolded as I tried to find peace in the tension between the academic's "logic of logic" and the "logic of God," which structured the lives and sensibilities of my participants.

My interviews and relationships in the field came about primarily through snowball sampling. Before traveling to India, I sent emails to a few associations and Urdu editorial offices, and most responded. I connected with the Islamic Academy for Comparative Religion and Students Islamic Organization, which led me to the women's branch of the Jama'at-i-Islami Hind. Through this method, I also met Nasr, who introduced me to his sisters and the Zohra Bagh Islamic study circle. I tried the same technique with France, sending emails to associations before arriving. I received only two responses; one did not lead anywhere, and the other eventually led me to Mounir. These initial electronic forays foreshadowed much about these field sites: the trust and openness of Hyderabad and the caution and mistrust of Lyon.

I started fieldwork in 2005 in Hyderabad, where I moved into a flat in the New City. The building was on an affluent street that overlooked the Shanthi Colony slum. From my balcony, I could see the dusty streets, stray animals, and slumlike housing. A tall, thick wall separated the slum from my street. Rahman was one of the auto-rickshaw drivers always parked in front of my building. Among his band of rickshaw drivers, he was obviously the friendliest and most talkative. I began hiring him for my transport on a regular basis, and he became a de facto assistant. Rahman benefited from regular employment owing to my daily outings, and I sometimes paid him to run minor errands. When I explained my research project, he offered to introduce me to people in Shanthi Colony, beginning with Anwar. He said Anwar was an important figure in the neighborhood and would know enough about religious and political life to be of help to me. So he drove me to Anwar's small stone house, and we knocked on the door.

Anwar trusted Rahman's judgment, but he was suspicious of me—not so much because I was American as because my religiosity was weak. He worried I would get things wrong and convey inaccurate things about Islam. More fundamentally, I think he feared the consequences of my doing this work for professional gain. He encouraged me to prioritize faith and piety over writing a book. "They [Americans] are going to say to you, 'If you follow the Quran, you're just going to stay in the mosque, and you won't earn the world.' May Allah help us. Our greatest downfall is feeling inferior to them. Don't listen to them," he warned me. But despite his warnings and concerns, he was also intrigued and curious about the research, and he ended up being generous with his time. Through him, I came to know his mosque and madrasa staff.

Anwar, Rahman, and the families and individuals they introduced me to in Shanthi Colony likely felt they couldn't refuse to talk to me because of the gross class difference between us. They had much potentially to gain by welcoming an educated

American and perhaps, in their eyes, too much to lose by refusing me. Eventually, Anwar learned that, indeed, I had connections to the city's Muslim elite.

After a few months of knowing each other, Anwar asked me to help him establish a women's training center in the neighborhood, as the madrasa happened to have extra physical space. His daughter had seen my photo in a local Urdu newspaper from an event at one of Mr. Haq's schools. At that point, I had already connected with Mr. Haq, other elites, and their schools, thanks to a family connection. I was nervous to bring this up with Mr. Haq, but when I mentioned it to his assistant, Kulsoom apa, she thought it was perfectly reasonable, especially since the physical facility already existed. I was surprised that only a few months later Mr. Haq gave his financial support, and the center opened. Hundreds of women from the neighborhood immediately expressed their interest in joining. Today, Anwar and I are tied to one another through this women's institution and share a mutual respect, though I am sure he still has concerns about my religiosity.

Although it was profoundly meaningful to me to have made a positive contribution to the neighborhood, my association with philanthropists rigidly fixed the kinds of relationships I would have with poor residents. They treated me with a combination of respect, fear, and manipulation, effectively laying to rest any illusions I might have harbored about being a fly on the wall to observe their everyday lives. The same scenario applied to all the relationships I developed through the women's training centers in poor and slum neighborhoods. On the one hand, middle class and elite activists helped me gain access to poor residents; on the other hand, I represented the power and status that poor residents envied and feared, and that they knew perfectly well was arbitrary.[2]

It was both impossible and socially unacceptable to hide or minimize the wealth and status disparities between poor families and myself. For this reason, it made sense to my poor companions that I lived in a decent flat in the New City and commuted into BPL (below poverty line) neighborhoods by car or auto-rickshaw. In these particular Muslim areas, it may have actually been disrespectful for someone of my class position to move into poor or makeshift housing without running water. The choice of where to live had both methodological consequences—I could not live as they lived nor experience the daily conditions they experienced (the sine qua non of participant observation)—and moral effects for the researcher and participants.

Not long after the opening of the Shanthi Colony women's center in April 2006, I flew straight to Paris without a single contact. As luck would have it, it happened to be the same week as the UOIF (Union des Organisations Islamiques de France) annual conference in Le Bourget, about twenty kilometers from Paris. The conference draws about 150,000 Muslims from around the country. Having seen a flyer for it in a halal shop, I diligently attended the conference over a couple of days, listening to panels and lectures, strolling around the bazaar, and stopping at the many booths. At one particular booth I had a conversation with two association activists, one of whom was Hakim. The other had a fiancée in Lyon who was attached to the Mosquée

Hijra community. When I went to Lyon and found an apartment, I called his fiancée and through her met several middle-class activists and association members, like Maryam and Farid, connected to Mosquée Hijra and Tawhid. They all welcomed me warmly.

I asked people how I might study an Islamic association or mosque community, or simply meet people, in one of Lyon's outer banlieues. Few had contacts there, and those who did found it a strange request. In any case, I made no progress, though eventually in 2009, Farid gave me Ahmed's number, who reluctantly agreed to an interview. In retrospect, I was projecting my research experience in Hyderabad, where Islamic associations were firmly connected to poor Muslim communities and welfare programs, onto my field site in Lyon. I incorrectly assumed I would easily meet religious people in one of the working-class quartiers. Nothing was further from the truth. As I described in chapter 6, I wandered around Vénissieux until I made my way into Mosquée Ennour and from there, Mosquée Hasan.[3] This early hurdle captivated my attention, illuminating dynamics that later took center stage in my analysis.

Before accessing these mosques in Vénissieux, I attended a large mosque in Saint Fons, an adjacent town. There I met a young Maghrébine woman, dressed in a black djelbab. She was affectionate with me because she saw that I was new. We talked for a while, and I told her who I was and what I was doing. She agreed to chat with me the following Friday at the mosque. I expressed my gratitude. She kissed me on the cheek and said, "But of course, you are my sister [*vous êtes ma soeur*]!" But when I showed up that Friday, she pretended that she did not know me and seemed to have no recollection of our conversation. Even worse, she deliberately kept her distance and practically ran from the mosque after the prayer was over. I felt confused, then guilty and horrified when I realized she must have thought I was a spy.

At one point, in my desperation and increasing worry that I would never gain access in the banlieues, I posted a flyer at the Vénissieux Metro station and another fifty in housing-complex mailboxes in Les Minguettes, advertising for a paid research assistant. I received only one phone call from a young man who agreed to meet. When I showed up in Les Minguettes at our agreed place and time, he was nowhere to be seen. These few early experiences in 2006 of scaring people away and being castigated (see chapter 6) fueled a growing paranoia and awkwardness in presenting myself that I perhaps never overcame, even long after stumbling into Mosquée Ennour in 2006. If it had been my own country or native language, I might have spoken with more confidence. But as events unfolded in France, despite the longevity of my relationships and my facility with the culture and language, the paranoia never abated.

Unlike in Hyderabad, I had no clear status advantage I could wield in Lyon, and my American nationality was an enormous liability, especially in the post-9/11 era of U.S. President George Bush. But my subjects also had an orientalist fascination with Indian culture, so my South Asian background proved my biggest asset. "Ah, *l'Inde!*

J'adore le Bollywood! (Oh, India! I *adore* Bollywood!)." Even among Salafist women, India's exoticness helped suspend their suspicion and crack open the door.

Also unlike in Hyderabad, my companions in the banlieues were perplexed by why I mostly lived downtown or why I chose to surround myself with "racists" and nonbelievers. In the beginning I had no idea how to seek housing in the quartiers. By the time I had invitations from people to live with them in Les Minguettes and would have felt comfortable doing so, I had a small child and was reluctant to confront the challenges of living with him in the housing projects, such as broken elevators and poor plumbing. I also feared exposing him to violence.[4]

But this led to uncomfortable moments. Asma, a young black Salafi woman, once came to my apartment while I was living in Lyon's tourist quarter for a few months. To my surprise, she had never once visited the area despite having lived her whole life in the municipal region. "Be careful!" she warned me repeatedly. "Downtown Lyon is full of racists. There are lots of 'skinheads' there." I tried to assure her, unconvincingly, that it was fine. When she came to meet me there, she was practically terrified as we walked up the cobblestone alleys. "Next time, Zehra," she said, "just call me and come stay in our apartment."

Though some companions may have preferred I live in the banlieues, for others it would have seemed bizarre. Sumaiya, for example, detested Les Minguettes, especially as a mother on her own. She likely would have found it disturbing had I moved there, knowing I had the money to live elsewhere.

Navigating the Language

Apart from managing differences across class and nation, I also had to navigate different languages. Cross-language research and the acts of translation are not merely technical matters but in fact constitute the production of meaning.[5] I was constantly, often automatically, searching for equivalent English words. In doing so, I was making judgments about the cultural meaning of various words.

For fieldwork and interviews in Hyderabad, I spoke in the local dialect of Urdu (Deccani Urdu), with the exception of interaction with a few elites and educated association leaders who communicated with me in English. I recorded official interviews as well as public speeches, amplified *qhutbas*, and religious lectures at events and study circles. Because some speeches and lessons used a pure form of Urdu that is today less commonly spoken in everyday settings, I used assistance in transcribing and translating these.

Throughout the research in Hyderabad, I took nightly field notes in English, which means I was often automatically translating ideas and conversations from Urdu into English. Some meaning and cultural nuance were lost in the process. In France, I wrote nightly field notes in a mixture of English and French. Again, my recollection of some conversations was based on translations done in the moment. All the fieldwork and interviews occurred only in French, as nearly none of my interviewees or companions spoke English. My less educated companions used a good deal of slang (*l'argot*) that I tried to understand through context or sometimes asking people to repeat themselves. I noticed that they sometimes eliminated the slang for my benefit. They also injected a handful of Arabic words into the conversation that I eventually learned. In religious learning settings, in both cities, I read, wrote, and recited in classical Arabic alongside others.

In all three languages, I had a clear accent and made mistakes that immediately placed me as foreign. In neither Urdu nor French did I have a particularly educated manner of speaking. This raised suspicion, intrigue, amusement, and endearment, sometimes all at once. The most absurd example was from a conversation with Asma in Les Minguettes.

I felt embarrassed that I was not fasting that day in Ramadan. She asked me, "Do you not have enough iron [in your blood] [*Tu n'as pas manque de fer*]?" But in my latent paranoia of disappointing my companions with my weak religiosity, I heard, "Aren't you scared of hellfire [*Tu n'as pas peur d'enfer*]?" We then proceeded to have a rather strange conversation until she realized my confusion and clarified her question.   .

Phasing out the Interviews and Ditching the Recorder

No matter the language, I realized early on that requesting interviews was tense and awkward in both field sites. The mere presence of my small digital recorder had repercussions. If I wished to really develop rapport, I had to put it away. Eventually, I phased out the interviews, which freed me to concentrate on my relationships.[6] Scholars have pointed out the limitations of interviews vis-à-vis participant observation toward the goal of understanding social action and behavior because of the evident discrepancy between what people say in an interview situation and what they do (Jerolmack and Khan 2014). Above all, what interviews reveal are the views that people are willing to communicate in that particular interview context (Dean and Whyte 1958).

As an American researcher and woman, seeking to interview Muslims who were under various forms of surveillance was not an ideal approach. For the interviews I did conduct, some interviewees agreed to recording while others refused in both research sites. In Vénissieux, mosque teachers explicitly requested attendees to not record lectures, even though teachers deliberately started every lesson by announcing that the mosque was "completely open and everyone is welcome."

The art of crafting good interview questions on this topic was challenging because of the clichéd nature of questions about Islam. I could tell my subjects were annoyed and exhausted by having to defend or describe their views, especially related to gender. They seemed to have rote answers, or their facial expressions shifted negatively as soon as the clichéd questions came tumbling out of my mouth. I also sensed that those of more marginalized positions felt pressure to sound articulate because they were being recorded, and for this, I felt guilty. I recall Mounir's wanting to hold the recorder, fumbling with it and holding it too closely to his mouth.

Some individuals were quite simply terrified. Rahman introduced me to Suraj bhai, who worked in a small photography studio next to Masjid Arabia. When Rahman scheduled an informal interview with him and brought me into his studio, Suraj bhai sat on the opposite side of the room, with one leg practically out the door, and spoke inaudibly. His first question was, "Where are you taking me?" Confused, I explained I was simply doing a project for school and wanted to talk with people about their lives and Islam. We painfully got through an interview, but as soon as I turned off the recorder, his disposition changed. He relaxed and had more to say about his life and opinions. This effect of recording commonly occurs in ethnography, but the surveillance of Muslims exacerbated it well beyond the norm.[7]

On Fridays, men attending the Friday prayer dominated the street, and police heavily patrolled the area. Some days, the area looked militarized, such as during President George W. Bush's 2006 visit to Hyderabad. Protectively, Suraj bhai insisted I sit in his studio on Fridays, away from the chaos, to hear the *qhutbas* from the loudspeaker and watch happenings on the street. I didn't again scare him with a recorder or trouble him with structured questions, even after we had built some trust. Eventually, we became close enough that when I would forget to come or did not have time to visit, Suraj bhai would ask if I was upset with him [*naaraaz tho nahin hai?*].

Gender and Its Intersections

Managing gender relations in a tradition that values or requires some degree of gender separation was something I learned to do early on. Though I found strict separation an unpleasant challenge of the fieldwork, over time I started to view it as simply an extreme solution—even a logical conclusion—to the types of romantic jealousies and relationship troubles normal in any heteronormative and secular liberal community.

The gendered dynamic emerged organically on a case-by-case basis, so I cannot generalize about people's willingness or unwillingness to interact across gender. I did find that women were just as likely to enforce gender separation as men. And I did understand from the beginning that I could not do sustained participant observation in all-male spaces such as madrasa classrooms, men's sections of the mosque, or among Salafi men.

Some individuals adhered strictly to religious teachings that forbid unrelated men and women from spending time with one another in private. In two cases, in Hyderabad, they asked me directly to bring my spouse or another male relative with me, which I was able to do on these occasions. In Lyon, one male companion seemed to prefer that I be accompanied, but he never directly required a relative. I sensed a mutual uncertainty in these cases, where it was not clear if they thought *I* would be more comfortable with a male relative or if they themselves felt uncomfortable having to interact in private with an unrelated woman. Sometimes, we could avoid the issue by meeting in their homes with their wives. Thus, I came to know Anwar's wife and children, as well as Hakim and Abbas's families.

The effects of gender differed across my cases according to how it interacted with other facts of my social position, as theories of intersectionality would predict. For example, in Hyderabad, though I could not worship in the men's mosques or join predominantly men's groups and activities, I could spend time with low-income men like Suraj bhai or Rahman because our class difference made it more socially acceptable. In other words, as an educated American I was somehow entitled to any "service" or assistance, even at the so-called cost of poor men's masculinity. Again, in Lyon, class did not play this mediating role. I could not walk into the field wielding any obvious power vis-à-vis my subjects, men or women.

In both cases, however, the gender segregation, and I believe some extent of traditional male chivalry in these communities, prevented me from seeing the more violent side of everyday life in the slums or working-class housing projects. Much of this would have been police violence and illegal business activity. I only heard of these things second-hand from my women companions, such as the fatal stabbing of one young woman's older brother in Faiz Nagar or the tax evasion by one Salafi man in Lyon.

My gender obviously set the boundaries of the fieldwork. It also made me vulnerable to moral judgments that many ethnographers face. In long-term ethnographic research, subjects sometimes perceive the ethnographer as a bit of a freak—they wonder why someone would leave behind his or her community and family for months on end to learn about another society.[8] This is likely exacerbated for women and even more so in traditions that place utmost value on family and children. Subjects are more likely to ask, "Why isn't she home with her children?" Or, "Why doesn't she have children?" At different points, depending on my situation, I had to answer both these questions. At the same time, my subjects' reactions to my research as a woman far from home combined slight disapproval with pride. Both men and women said they were proud to see a woman of Muslim origin pursuing higher education. Amel even asked me to speak with home-schooled girls in Vénissieux because they had so little exposure to highly educated women. My unusual presence was clearly an intervention in communities currently grappling with the value of and possibilities for women's education.

Bringing on Surveillance?

For whatever positive interventions the fieldwork made, they hardly outweighed the concern that my presence may have led to greater surveillance of certain individuals. In Hyderabad, while I heard frequently about surveillance and police abuses, I never suspected that I had been followed. So, as I discussed in chapter 3, when the police questioned me and presented knowledge about my whereabouts and student status, as I tried to secure an exit visa, I was surprised and frightened. They were not interested in me but in Nasr. During a confusing conversation, I nervously tried to protect him, and they begrudgingly let me go when I invoked the name of a relative who was powerful in the business community. When I got home later, I held my breath as I opened the door, worried they may have destroyed my computer. But everything was where I had left it.

Things were not so straightforward in Lyon. I couldn't escape the watchful eyes of random people or security guards, and I believed, like everyone else, that spies attended the mosque. But I never knew for sure. With the sense of increased racism after the burqa ban and foiled attacks on the mosque, the unease only grew over time.

In the aftermath of the *Charlie Hedbo* killings, things got worse. Hate crimes against Muslims increased, as did virulent public discourse against Islam. In June 2015, a man considered to have ties with Lyon's Salafist community beheaded his boss in a factory in a town south of Lyon. When I visited that year, I felt more scared than ever of public aggression. Fatima's sister was busy making arrangements to leave France for Saudi Arabia to try a new life. Amel, who said a man on the street motioned three times that he would kill her if he could, was scared and distraught. She stopped frequenting the public library, which used to be one of her pastimes. On the eve of finishing my book manuscript, I became increasingly uneasy about the whole research project. Selfishly, I looked for some reassurance in a painful conversation with Amel. In a downtown shopping mall, we sat face to face.

PARVEZ: Do you think maybe it was a bad idea [for me] to study Islam in France?
AMEL: There are too many obstacles here to learning. I don't think France is a good place to do research, no.
PARVEZ: No, I don't mean for myself. I mean that sometimes, I worry I shouldn't have studied Minguettes. I never wanted to cause any problems for [people at the mosque] or do anything that could harm the community.
AMEL: Well, we have nothing to hide. What you saw was the truth.
PARVEZ: It's true, [her] classes are all open . . .
AMEL: There are already spies in the mosque. I'm sure [she] has a file.
PARVEZ: Yeah.
AMEL: Zehra, since you write about us, don't you realize you've probably been followed too? I'm sure you have been.
PARVEZ: I always thought it was possible, but I don't know. I haven't had problems yet.
AMEL: The thing is, if someone has influence in the community, they want to stop them. [She] has too much influence now.

As we looked at each other knowingly, I felt ashamed that maybe in Amel's mind, my work could have brought on more surveillance of her by way of affiliation, though she said she thought she already had a file because of other contacts. Her brother wanted her to be more careful about with whom she associated, and I felt myself implicated among the individuals who concerned her brother. Our conversation gave me little peace about the effects of my research on residents or the sense of paranoia I carried over years.

It did, however, reinforce my understanding that stigma and fear are contagious and can make you feel crazy.[9] Which one of us had been stained and why? Amel or myself? Had she caught the fear from me or I from her? Was that shopping mall security guard focused on us, or was he just doing his job? As far as I know, police had not interrogated Amel. But she carried a strong fear of surveillance and intervention. As she recounted several local stories of discrimination, disappearances, and threats from social services of taking away children, she stopped and asked me, "Do I sound crazy to you?" "No, I believe you!" I assured her. "But . . . it's unbelievable [*mais . . . c'est incroyable*]."

It is important to point out that my own presence as an outsider and sympathetic researcher could have encouraged Amel to confide, complain, and tell me the specific story she wanted to convey. In this way, any ethnographic writing produces a particular narrative (Geertz 1973). It might leave out the mundane activities that structure and color everyday life, like caring for nieces and nephews, cooking meals, taking naps, and watching YouTube videos. At the same time, in spending as much time as possible with people in their own social context, I can say confidently that they live in a world colored by fear, insecurity, and insularity. This does not, however, mean that they lack great joy and love in their daily lives, activities, and relationships.

BONDING, VEILING, AND BELIEVING

Together, the realities of state surveillance and social position presented me indirectly with the issues that most plagued me—the depth of the relationships on which the ethnography depended and questions of faith and epistemology.

Developing Bonds

In the attempt to see what their subjects see and to understand their perspectives, ethnographers are sometimes accused of losing all objectivity, or "going native." This is a jarring accusation when one has worked hard to get inside a social world— entering the emotional lives of participants and developing close bonds. If ethnography at its best takes the researcher to the point of thinking and feeling as their subjects do (Desmond 2014, 561), it effectively requires trust, generosity, sympathy, a level of emotional depth, and perhaps attachment on all sides. But when these personal attachments started to feel more important than the intellectual project, I knew it was time to stop the ethnography. This was not about preserving objectivity but about allowing myself to feel comfortable writing about the relationships I developed.

I anxiously pondered the nature of these relationships and whether or not they would yield ethnographic depth. Because of the comparative design and multiple locations, the study sacrificed some depth in favor of breadth. This was not always an analytic strategy, but sometimes resulted from my subjects' real constraints and my own weaknesses. There were many moments when I wanted to (or did) run from the combination of responsibility and intimacy that any deep relationship requires.[10] And the precariousness of some people's lives made it difficult to maintain contact. I tried hard to maintain my relationships with Mounir and Sumaiya in the banlieues over the years, but with all of their job and housing instabilities, I eventually lost touch with both of them.

Most disturbing was the impact of my social position in Hyderabad. My relationships with very poor families suffered an interminable power dynamic based on our material and status inequality. I had an obligation to repay Rahman for his time and help, but this became fraught when I met his family in Shanthi Colony. His wife saw me as a wealthy benefactor, not understanding that I was only a student. She asked me repeatedly for money for their daughters and eventually for a daughter's wedding. She also asked me to help him purchase his own auto-rickshaw. He felt embarrassed by this, and I could tell he received daily pressure from her to ask me.

As I sat on the floor in the women's training centers, women of all ages overwhelmed me with stories of their poverty, family tragedies or violence, and despair. Over time I became hardened to these stories, even mistrusting a few of them as performances. Probably over a hundred different people directly asked me for money. When I asked Kulsoom apa how I should handle this, she laughed and shrugged, "They think everyone's a donor." This gulf between us, I believe, limited the emotional depth I could achieve or even ethically seek. What kind of bond could I share with someone for whom the cost of my cappuccino meant the difference between enrolling their child in school and sending him out to labor?

Still, in Faiz Nagar I became "close" with Hina and her cousins. But Hina's relatives began repeatedly asking me for money for her future dowry. I received letters in the mail from her and her cousins, but I suspected that someone else had written them. This tarnished the relationship and left me with an unfulfilled sense of responsibility for her welfare when I later had to cut off contact. Discouraged by this power imbalance, I did not know what to make of our friendship.

Eventually, I think the true moments of trust and attachment occurred through the power of a universal emotion—in this particular case, heartbreak.[11] At the same time that her sister-in-law harassed me for dowry money, Hina sought my help in facilitating a clandestine romantic relationship with Zain, a twenty-year-old fruit seller in the Old City. Like various other ethnographers who suddenly found themselves very useful, I had a mobile phone and access to a car (Rabinow 2007). Hina increasingly relied on me for advice, and I understood the stakes of her relationship. This was her chance to have a "love marriage" instead of an arranged marriage with a stranger, but she could have found herself in grave trouble if her family found out.

Sadly, her brother discovered the relationship, threatened to assault Zain, and forced Hina to end their communication. She asked me to mediate as she begged Zain to wait for her. I did what I could, but I also pushed back when I thought she was being unreasonable. Zain refused to wait, saying angrily to me on the phone, "If she doesn't have the courage to stand up to her [fundamentalist] family, there's nothing I can do. Her mother needs to know that Hina *wants* to marry me. Fareen *baji* [sister], I'm 110 percent committed to her, but I'm trying to make it, make some career for myself in business. I can't get caught up with [backward] people, threatening me, trying to ruin my life." Meekly clutching my phone, Hina said goodbye to him, and her face fell. I sat quietly with her while she looked down at her hands and tried to suppress her anger and sorrow.

For a moment, the power of these emotions bridged the enormous gap between us, of nationality, class, and status. In empathically witnessing her heartbreak, some things became clear: her degree of helplessness with regard to her family and the shame of their "backward fundamentalism" before men like Zain. Moments like this were like breakthroughs in the ethnography. They required me to go against the principle that the "informant is always right," and they fed on the emotional vulnerability of my subjects, which always felt ethically fraught.[12]

In Vénissieux, I could not rely on my subjects' emotions. People were guarded and slow to reveal much about themselves, let alone their pain, and almost nobody asked anything of me. It bothered me that I could not learn as much as I would have liked about companions like Fatima or Asma. The bonds here seemed more mysterious and delicate.[13] Until I better understood the context of surveillance and tasted the fear myself, this left me continually confounded as I wished for confessional stories.

I remembered a question from Renato Rosaldo's "Grief and a Headhunter's Rage" (1989/1993, 167): "Do people always in fact describe most thickly what matters most to them?" The answer in Vénissieux was a clear no. Whatever depth or closeness I forged, I finally realized, was not through language but in moments of religious practice and maybe more specifically, in Quranic recitation. Recitation, the mosque teachers emphasized, constituted a "higher" and transformative activity. As I wrote one day in my field notes:

> Sometimes I feel so distant from [my companions]. But I feel connected precisely through the recitation. It's a slow process, start and stop. Fatima stops us. "All in one breath," she commands. "Find the sound further back in your mouth." We start again, heads down, struggling to recall the verses. As each sister recites, I wait, hanging on to each letter to see if she'll make it. She closes her eyes and enters her zone. We each want the other to succeed. We all smile when she's done. "*Masha Allah*" [As God has willed], says Fatima.

The more I latched on to the physical practice of Quranic recitation, the more I forged a deeper bond that allowed me to understand their social worlds better than through conversations, personal revelations, or obvious emotional expression. Those moments of recitation collectively transformed us.

This critical aspect of the fieldwork demonstrates the advantages of a "carnal sociology," learning through the body—and, I argue, spirit—to illuminate a social world. But I never gained "virtuosity," and barely achieved competence, as some ethnographers aimed to achieve, such as Mahmood in Islamic pious practice (2005) or Wacquant in boxing (2004a). Intensive training in piety or recitation as a bodily craft would likely have taken me down a different theoretical path, one that anthropologists of Islam have widely pursued, to explore pious subjectivity as a form of ethical and political practice (Fernando 2015; Jouili 2015; Wedeen 2008; Mahmood 2005). To perceive something like the influence of class relations or the role of social mistrust, I had to step away from religious training.

Wearing the Hijab

Because of the importance of the hijab in the communities I studied, I could never really step away from bodily religious practice. Veiling posed pragmatic issues in the methodology and moral dilemmas that became my principal struggle.

Raised in a Muslim family, I had the knowledge, skills, and sensibilities to conduct participant observation in these communities. I knew how to read Arabic, perform obligatory prayers, and fast; and wearing different forms of head coverings was neither exotic nor frightening. My large extended family includes the full range of Islamic traditions and practice, from the rigors of Salafi-style reformism to the ecstasy of Sufi-inspired poetry. My family also crosses sectarian divides, a rare phenomenon, so I grew up attending the annual passionate Shia mourning rituals. This drew criticism and lecturing from individuals like Anwar and Khalil. If I had emphasized my Shia background, I would truly have been an outsider in these Sunni communities.

Though I had just enough knowledge and experience of Islamic practice to participate, I felt extraordinarily clumsy—a sentiment painfully familiar to many ethnographers. For example, I could never correctly say, "barak'Allah oufik." In the communities I knew, people used this Arabic expression (May God's blessings be with you) in place of "Thank you." But I always said either "merci" in Lyon or a mispronounced version of "barak'Allah." Both elicited a short stare and silence, as people perhaps wondered why I missed such a basic expression.

Throughout the fieldwork, I conformed to different moral orders, compartmentalizing various facets of myself. I could do this because of my background in Islam and because I was habituated to living as a minority in predominantly white, Christian-origin societies. But compartmentalizing often brought various tensions to a head, in particular, in wearing the hijab.

I wore the hijab because from a pragmatic standpoint, it made sense to do as my companions did to ease the pains of ethnographic entrée. Wearing it set the contours of the research in important ways. If I did not wear it, women would still

have welcomed me in their spaces, but some may have made me an object of pros-
elytization. I cannot know for sure, but reasonably, this would have heavily influenced my conversations and relationships. In both cities, I did not wish for people
to perceive me as yet another researcher judging women for their veiling. The hijab
also shaped the ethnography by limiting my circle in Les Minguettes to practicing Muslims and mostly women. This was only one "subculture" in the neighborhood, and it cut me off from others.[14] As I mentioned, men from the banlieues like
Mounir or Ahmed would likely never have exposed me to anything impious, such
as the drug trade.

At the beginning of my fieldwork in Hyderabad, I draped a light orni over my
head, barely covering some of my hair. Middle-class women commonly dressed in
this style, but I stood out sorely in the streets of Shanthi Colony. There was little
I could do to hide my Western foreignness and class location. My somewhat lighter
skin tone, haircut, and even the way I walked drew people's attention in these neighborhoods and in particular, drew street beggars. This sometimes snowballed to the
point where my presence created a spectacle. Anwar cheerfully lectured to me about
the benefits of the niqab around the same time as I began despising how much
I stood out in Shanthi Colony. I decided to buy a niqab, timidly began wearing it, and
found that I enjoyed the freedom it afforded me from looks and stares. Sometimes,
though, a handbag or a ring would give me away.

As he drove me around in his auto-rickshaw, Rahman found it strange that someone of my class position would wear a niqab, a practice he associated with poor
women. I wore the niqab sometimes, but not always, among my companions in Faiz
Nagar who loved that I dressed like them. In other poor women's centers, I wore a
hijab or only lightly draped a scarf. Some women told me that the niqab protected
them from inhaling some of the toxic vehicle fumes that pollute the city and encouraged me to wear it at least for that reason. When out with philanthropists or wealthier women, I followed their lead and usually did not cover my hair at all.

This inconsistency and flexibility never quite struck me as morally problematic
in India. With very few exceptions, no one challenged me on this, either. Because my
family is of Indian origin, it also happened to be the approach to veiling in which
I was raised: the hijab is a matter of individual faith—but it is also a *social* practice
whose effects and enactment depend on context.

In France, such inconsistency or flexibility was rare. So I wore a hijab through
almost all the fieldwork in Lyon, though I did not wear the djelbab. This made
me stand out at Mosquée Hasan, but the djelbab signaled a commitment to veiling and to the Salafi community that I clearly lacked. It would have felt dishon-
est. I also could not manage the stigma and isolation that wearing the djelbab in
France can entail.

The French women I knew who wore the djelbab could not take for granted
their right to do so; they wore it while facing extreme stigma, job discrimination,
and social ostracization. Though some women may have initially begun wearing

the djelbab simply to signal their belonging to the Salafi community, they used these struggles actively to develop their courage and faith. How could I be so careless about my choice to wear the hijab? This threw me into crisis as I worried that I was being unfaithful, in the many meanings of the term. My carelessness troubled me immensely because I feared it betrayed my companions. Whenever someone asked if I wore it all the time, I told the truth, appealing to my own family background and experiences in India. But it was rare that anyone asked about my relationship to either the hijab or to faith. I realized through the religious teachings that these were considered deeply private matters. The extent of my faith in God, my doubts, and my sins were not really for anyone to know, question, or judge. Eventually, I came to peace with the complexity of the position I occupied as a participant observer.

But the stigma remained unbearable. I dreaded riding the Metro, which I had to do, eventually learning to avert people's gazes and busying myself with a book. Because Metro rides were so uncomfortable, several companions wanted badly to learn to drive and to own a car, though the fees for driving schools were prohibitive. I myself succumbed and briefly dabbled with learning to drive a manual-shift car. When I quickly burned out the clutch, I finally resigned myself to the Metro.

I always felt better when other veiled women were in the same Metro car, and I observed some interesting interactions. Once I saw a young white man approach a group of sisters in the Vénissieux station and begin a conversation with a woman wearing the sitar, a full covering that hides even the eyes (an exceptionally rare practice). He was interrogating her about various matters over the course of the ride, but doing so amusingly, also asking her for spiritual advice. I sat fascinated as she gestured with her gloved arms and explained to him that he might, in fact, be possessed by a *jinni*. He was receptive to the possibility.

The moral dilemma I felt over the hijab was the edge of an abyss of reflection I had to do about the research project and its epistemology and the nature of faith. Why was I capable of inhabiting such different moral systems? What did this mean about integrity and faith? My Salafi companions, at least in France and perhaps India too, wondered the same. They quietly expressed disapproval of my living among and spending time with non-Muslims, not because of any dislike but because they thought I would find it too difficult to augment my faith and practice Islam. In a way, they were right. Fasting, prayer, and practicing gender segregation are not easy without companionship and community support. Sometimes I was surprised by how little Fatima, for example, knew about the dominant culture. She had little awareness and knowledge of events like Easter and Bastille Day. Perhaps she found it annoying that these events impacted my life in any way. Sometimes we had more frank discussions. We talked once about music, and how she, like some Muslims of the Salafi tradition, stopped listening to music because of its impious effects. I told her I could never give up music because it was too dear to me. She understood, though she sent me some literature on the topic a few months later.

Possibilities for Faith

Even more than the hijab and other practices like fasting or giving up music, the dilemma that most heavily weighed on my conscience was the simple fact of doing research for my own professional gain. Sometimes it seemed ethically corrupt to dabble in religious life for the sake of a career endeavor. Ethnographers have written about the guilt they feel about leaving the field and returning to their comfortable lives in academia. In this case, I felt guilt over returning to a life structured almost exclusively by worldly and secular values. Professional gain was a motivation that my most pious subjects did not understand, or perhaps, fully respect. My subjects were either too polite to directly challenge my life choices or felt they could not critique something as prestigious as a doctoral degree. Though I sought to explain my research or the process of writing a thesis, they were far more interested in my religious practice or education.[15]

For me, this ran up against the meaning of informed consent. Some ethnographers encourage participant observers to continually reinforce informed consent when participants may very well forget that a researcher lurks in their midst (see Zavisca 2007). But reminding participants can be awkward and discomforting. As Philippe Bourgois (1990) wrote, "If we recited to our informants their rights to privacy and informed consent—like police officers arresting a suspect—every time we spoke with them, we would make terrible fieldworkers" (52). In my case, reminding people not only had an air of the police but also reminded them of the disappointing fact that my motivations were in the end, worldly.

Of course, the research had the "warrants" (Katz 1997) that drive a number of ethnographies and that some participants valued: it sought greater understanding of morally condemned groups of people, and it was documenting new forms of social life and politics amid a global religious revival. At the same time, as Michael Burawoy wrote:

> On whomever's side we are, managers or workers, white or black, men or women, we are automatically implicated in relations of domination.... Our mission may be noble—broadening social movements, promoting social justice, challenging the horizons of everyday life—but there is no escaping the elementary divergence between intellectuals, no matter how organic, and the interests of the declared constituency. (2009, 57)

I faced this tension between the genuineness of piety and the work of academia throughout the fieldwork. When I turned to my analysis, I had a parallel struggle: to confront my "intellectualist bias," in Bourdieu's terms—the "logic of logic"—or my tendency to view the world "as a spectacle" that I must interpret through an academic lens (Wacquant 1992, 39). The intellectualist bias obscures the practical logic that informs how subjects act and feel and live meaningful lives—in this case, their embodied knowledge about Islamic practice and their investment in acts of worship from recitation to fasting. For them, the logic of practice was merely a reflection of God's requirements. But I was constantly confronted by the "collective scientific unconscious" (Wacquant 1992, 40) that molded the way I approached religious practice as a coherent sociological phenomenon. This meant reflecting on not only the political and intellectual construction of "Muslims" but also on the Western construction of religion and the realm of faith as neatly distinct from the realm of science.[16] Where my subjects saw the work of God, what was it that I was seeing?[17]

IN HIS SOCIOLOGICAL study of music, Max Weber wrote, "Without the tensions motivated by the irrationality of melody, no modern music could exist." For Weber, it was precisely the tension between rationalization and the non-rational that opens up the possibilities for beauty in music (see Swidler 1922/1993, xvi), and rationalization "can never completely devour" our "melodic needs" (Weber 1958, 9–10; see Swidler 1922/1993, xvi). Only toward the end of my fieldwork could I hear the irrational melodies. I started taking immense pleasure and meaning in Arabic recitation, appreciating the breath and poetry, and savoring the sound of a single letter. I felt a deep joy and peacefulness every time I heard Malika say, "Everything is in God's hands." As Farzana pleaded with God, tears streaming down her face, with utter humility and surrender in her voice, I felt alive. I had not achieved any mastery or any solid state of faith. What I felt was an openness to the perceptual possibilities. This was the ultimate irony: sitting among a group of "fundamentalists," I learned not the truth of anything but the potential to feel something different.

Through moments like these, fieldwork transforms participant observers, whether temporarily or permanently. It also compels them to view themselves and their societies differently. In my struggles with veiling, I was struck by my own vanity, my need for approval from the dominant culture. Back home in the United States, I noticed sharply the deep-seated dislike of religious people among liberal colleagues, students, and friends. I found this so ubiquitous and casually expressed that I gradually started avoiding discussions about my work. At best, I would compartmentalize to get through the conversation. Above all, this fieldwork left me with a troubled and unsettled questioning of what it means to have integrity in one's actions and what it feels like to do something with conviction. Perhaps in some cases, as I learned, the deepest scars and agonies of fieldwork are also the greatest gifts.

Interviews

Apart from participant observation, I conducted a total of 39 semi-structured interviews lasting at least one hour each. All were recorded and transcribed except in those few cases, in both sites, in which my interviewees asked that I not record them. As explained in appendix A, I conducted these interviews only during the earlier phases of fieldwork. All interviews in France were in French; in India they were in Urdu and in English. All interview translations were my own.

France	India
Activists with organizations or mosques: 11	Activists with Islamic/ welfare organizations: 6
Organizations included *Étudiants Musulmans de France, Jeunes Musulmans de France, Union des Jeunes Musulmans, Union des Organizations Islamiques de France, Tawhid/le Centre Shâtibi, DiverCité*	Organizations included *Students Islamic Organization, Islamic Academy for Comparative Religions, Jamia Nizamia University, Jam'at-i-Islami Hind, Confederation of Voluntary Associations*
Vénissieux city administrator: 1	Muslim politicians: 2
Residents of the quartiers: 3	Muslim philanthropists: 3
	Madrasa teachers: 3
	Mosque leaders: 4
	Slum residents: 6

Notes

CHAPTER 1

1. "Le méchant imam de Vénissieux," *Ligue des droits de l'homme (LDH)-Toulon.* May 2004, http://ldh-toulon.net/Le-mechant-imam-de-Venissieux.html.
2. J. Paloulian, "Kamel Kabtane: L'affaire Bouziane témoigne d'une belle hypocrisie," *Le Progrès*, mercredi 28 avril 2004, 2.
3. Debarshi Dasgupta, Smruti Koppikar, and Snigdha Hasan, "The Mirror Explodes," *Outlook*, July 19, 2010, www.outlookindia.com/magazine/story/the-mirror-explodes/266145. Estimates of the number killed by police range from four to nine.
4. Muslims in France do not generally employ the term "burqa." The legislation that passed banned the niqab, a facial covering. See French Assembly Hearings (2009).
5. Statistics from India are from the 2011 Government of India census (Ministry of Home Affairs 2011). The government of France does not collect data on religion or ethnicity. Scholars and different research institutes have offered various estimates based on immigration status. The estimate of 4.1 million comes from a study of 22,000 residents conducted in 2008–9 under the direction of Patrick Simon. See Simon and Tiberj (2013).
6. The term "subaltern" derives from Gramsci (1971) and refers to classes that lack political voice and representation. In the early 1980s, scholars developed the Subaltern Studies project to interrogate the silencing of non-elites in the writing of South Asian history (Chaturvedi 2012). I use the term to describe stigmatized Muslims living below poverty levels. They lack political voice and are not considered equal citizens. The contemporary usage of "subaltern" resonates specifically within the South Asian context. In the French context, my low-income participants are members of the dislocated, postcolonial working class, although literature ubiquitously refers to such members as "immigrants."

7. Muslims made both recognition and redistributive claims in both cities. But the middle-class Islamic organizations presented in this book clearly had one dominant agenda in each city. The organizations also all measured success in the field as either achieving some sort of recognition from the state (Lyon) or accomplishing a form of redistribution (Hyderabad), even though they had disagreements and debates over particular issues. I gathered this information inductively, by interviewing members and observing the major parties in the middle-class field of Islamic associations in each city and through participant observation conducted in mosque or Islamic study activities among the middle class and elites.

8. I saw nearly no evidence that these fractures were based on the different ethnic origins among French Muslims, as is sometimes argued (Warner and Wenner 2006).

9. See "Mapping the Global Muslim Population," *The Pew Forum on Religion and Public Life*, October 2009. See also Kuru (2009, 18). Compared to majority Muslim countries, the political potential of minority Muslim activists is limited to the domain of civil society and to certain types of policy demands, as opposed to state takeover. Piety movements are extremely unlikely to translate into capturing the state. This makes fears over shari'a implementation unfounded. But there is nonetheless a spectrum of movements where Muslims are minorities. There exist religious revivalist movements, those that self-consciously engage with the state to acquire legal rights, and fringe militant groups that violently target the state based on transnational connections and agendas.

10. Statistics on hate crimes in the European Union are extremely hard to locate. Advocacy organizations have called for member states to adequately track hate crimes, but France has not supplied any numbers to the OSCE human rights office reporting on these matters. Official numbers from the Ministry of Interior reflect crimes reported to authorities and likely understate the true number. Some estimate that less than 20 percent of victims report anti-Muslim crimes because of distrust of police. The Collectif Contre Islamophobie en France (CCIF) compiles and investigates incidents directly from victims. Its numbers are over twice those reported by the ministry. In 2012, the ministry reported 201 acts, while CCIF reported 469. CCIF reported 691 acts in 2013 and 764 in 2014. Acts range from physical assaults to mosque vandalism to harassment involving pig remains. See Matthieu Goar, "Comment mesure-t-on l'islamophobie en France?," *Le Monde*, January 28, 2014.

　　According to the definition put forth by the Center for Race and Gender at the University of California, Berkeley,

> Islamophobia is a contrived fear or prejudice fomented by the existing Eurocentric and Orientalist global power structure. It is directed at a perceived or real Muslim threat through the maintenance and extension of existing disparities in economic, political, social and cultural relations, while rationalizing

the necessity to deploy violence as a tool to achieve "civilizational rehab" of the target communities (Muslim or otherwise). Islamophobia reintroduces and reaffirms a global racial structure through which resource distribution disparities are maintained and extended.

Available at http://crg.berkeley.edu/content/islamophobia/defining-islamophobia.

11. For example, in the 2005–9 World Values Survey Wave 5, 50 percent of Indian respondents agreed that religion was "very important" in their lives, compared to 13 percent of French respondents.

12. In November 2008, members of the Pakistan-based Lashkar-e-Taiba attacked a railway station, hotels, cafes, and theaters in Mumbai, killing about 165 people. In November 2015, the Islamic State of Iraq and the Levant claimed responsibility for the attacks in Paris at the Bataclan theatre, cafes, and restaurants that killed 130 people.

13. The fear of *communautarisme* stems from a larger discomfort with identity politics, seen as an unfortunate import from the United States (Bouvet 2007).

14. See P. Williams, "Hindu–Muslim Relations and the 'War on Terror,'" in *A Companion to the Anthropology of India*, ed. I. Clark-Decès (Oxford: Wiley-Blackwell, 2011).

15. Venel (2004, 9). Jennifer Fredette (2014, 121) writes, "It is important to end the stereotype that all Muslims are immigrants, but it would be an analytical mistake to ignore the immigration question when considering Muslims in France."

16. A key distinction between the two cases is the absence or presence of a welfare state. One might argue that France's provision of subsidized housing, health and unemployment benefits, and retirement pensions would dramatically shape minority politics. These provisions certainly mitigate the reality of low wages and unemployment; however, my French working-class participants nonetheless expressed anxieties over their lack of economic security.

17. In Michèle Lamont's interviews with white native French workers in the banlieues of Paris, respondents revealed strong negative attitudes toward North Africans based on cultural incompatibility rooted in religion, poor work ethic, inability to assimilate, and overuse of public resources. "Immigration and the Salience of Racial Boundaries among French Workers," in *Race in France: Interdisciplinary Perspectives on the Politics of Difference*, ed. Herrick Chapman and Laura L. Frader (New York: Bergahn, 2004), 141–61. See Etienne Balibar, "Is there a 'Neo-Racism?'" on the idea of a cultural racism, or a "racism without race," in *Race, Nation, Class: Ambiguous Identities*, ed. Etienne Balibar and Immanuel Wallerstein (London: Verso, 1991), 17–28. See also Amiraux and Simon (2006) on how the social sciences have contributed to the denial of the effects of race in France.

18. Figures from INSEE (Institut national de la statistique et des études économiques) (2013) reveal that the Lyon agglomeration is 13 percent immigrant, over half of whom are estimated to be of Muslim origin based on country of birth. I include

the countries Algeria, Morocco, Tunisia, Senegal, Mali, Comoros, Guinea, Mauritania, Turkey, and Pakistan. This figure excludes all those of Muslim origin born in France. See INSEE, RP2013 exploitation principale, for Unité urbaine de Lyon.

19. I use the French term "quartiers" to refer to poor neighborhoods officially designated as either *zones urbaines sensibles* (ZUS) or *zones franches urbaines* (ZFU), sensitive and tax-free zones, respectively. Generally, these are designated as priority zones for urban development owing to unemployment and other indicators. As of 2011, there are 751 ZUS in France, of which 100 neighborhoods are ZFU, with relatively higher concentrations of precarity and degraded infrastructure. The quartiers I refer to in the Lyon area are all designated as ZFU. See Pan Ké Shon (2011, 2). The generic term "quartier" otherwise refers simply to neighborhood.

20. See "Estimations de population par quartier," INSEE, no. 8212350. Statistics were revised in March 2011. The proportion of those holding a foreign nationality, regardless of birth country, is 23 percent. When including those classified as "immigrés," or those born abroad to foreign parents and residing in France, regardless of nationality, the total is 40 percent of the population.

21. Its origins as a movement are debated, with some citing eighteenth-century Arabians and others citing nineteenth-century intellectuals in Egypt. It is also internally debated as to which Islamic groups, schools of thought, and practices may be considered Salafist. Salafism has historically been a pietist and apolitical movement, after some involvement in state politics in the late nineteenth and early twentieth centuries (Stemmann 2006). See Euben and Zaman (2009) and Hourani (1962/1983).

22. See Adraoui (2009).

23. The increased participation of women in Islamic revival movements has been documented in a number of places (Deeb 2006; Mahmood 2005), though far less so where Muslims are minorities.

24. Telengana was formed in 2014 after a long struggle for statehood. See Kingshuk Nag, *Battleground Telengana: Chronicle of an Agitation* (New Delhi: HarperCollins, 2011).

25. Poor residents of Hyderabad's Old City, and especially certain neighborhoods within the Old City, are stigmatized. But there are also wealthy families who inherited palatial homes in some sections of the Old City and for whom there is no stigma attached to their place of residence.

26. Ahl-e-Hadees in India, as one can glean from national news and from the group's website, explicitly condemns terrorism and denigration of non-Muslim religions, and supports the idea of "moderation."

27. For some, implicit in this question is a resistance to the state and media's imposition of Muslim identity onto individuals and groups regardless of their diverse beliefs and behaviors; see Brouard and Tiberj (2011).

28. Survey measures can also signify different things. For example, mosque attendance might indicate emotional or community belonging, rather than religiosity. It also may have more to do with mere accessibility of mosques. Polls in France show an increasing tendency to self-identify as Muslim and claim to have faith, although low levels of practice (but higher than Catholics) (Laurence and Vaisse 2006, 75–83). This might indicate various things—for example, respondents feeling like they *should* have faith or not practicing because they lack community and institutional support. Or perhaps it has no real explanation.

29. Césari (2013).

30. See also Kirsch (2004), Wuthnow (1987), Needham (1972), and Bellah (1970).

31. Jeanette S. Jouili's (2015) ethnographic study of Muslim women in France and Germany demonstrates how pious women struggle to fine-tune Islam as a tradition while living in societies that demand secular sensibilities.

32. From a theological perspective, the basic definition of a Muslim is someone who believes in one god and the status of Muhammed as a messenger. In the Quran there is also the idea of "people of the book," whereby all members of the Abrahamic religions are considered believers. The Quran further states that there were other prophets throughout history who are not mentioned in the book.

33. Following José Casanova (2009), I approach secularism as both an ideology and a modern statecraft principle. What determines the type of secularism a state pursues is the relation between state separation from religion and state regulation of religion in everyday life. This relation in turn has implications for democracy.

34. Laborde argues that laïcité is closest to the liberal philosophy of toleration (2002: 168) and does not inherently justify legislation that would curtail religious freedoms (2010: 5). For a history of laïcité, see Poulat (2003) and Baubérot (2000).

35. Literature on the subject of African American poverty and segregation is useful for understanding why elites matter. It points to middle-class financial support for community institutions that provide social infrastructure, positive effect on property values, and successful role modeling (Pattillo 1999; Wilson 1987). It also shows how middle-class flight leads to the spatial isolation of the poor, reduced job access, and greater exposure to violence. Perhaps most critically, minority elites and middle classes serve as a "buffer" between the poor and white middle class and the impact of joblessness (Pattillo 1999; Wilson 1987, 56). Not everyone agrees with this positive assessment. Some emphasize that the black middle class pursues its own material interests, displacing the poor (Hyra 2008). Others argue that associational life supported by the middle class may provide things like safe zones for children, but ultimately, the fate of the poor depends on larger structural forces (Venkatesh 2000; Stack 1974). At the same time, minority middle classes and elites can draw the attention of politicians and

policymakers, and in this way have a definite impact (Taub, Taylor, and Dunham 1984; Crenson 1983).

36. To take only one example, in 2014, comedian and political commentator Bill Maher invited atheist author Sam Harris to his show and agreed with him that Islam is "the mother lode of bad ideas." Maher has widely condemned liberals for failing to denounce Islam (Beinart 2014).

37. The term "fundamentalism" originated in early twentieth-century American Protestantism. It is therefore problematic to apply the concept to non-Christian religions, though sociologists of religion have tried to provide analytical definition to the term and argue for its universal applicability (Riesebrodt 2000).

38. Mehdi Hasan, "What the Jihadists Who Bought 'Islam for Dummies' on Amazon Tell Us about Radicalization," *New Statesman*, August 20, 2014, www.newstatesman.com/religion/2014/08/what-jihadists-who-bought-islam-dummies-amazon-tell-us-about-radicalisation.

39. These efforts often come from liberal standpoints in the hope of clarifying misunderstandings about Islam. However, in translating Islamic teachings into familiar terms, they fail to point out that we lack many of the concepts and language to understand the faith on the basis of its own terms and history—for example, the concept of "belief" does not directly exist in Arabic (Asad 2013). Put differently, some liberal efforts to learn about Islam fail to understand Islam as a discursive tradition, wherein practices and interpretations shift in the dynamic historical course of striving for what Muslims perceive as correct practice (Asad 2009).

40. The division of Islamists into moderates and radicals is employed in different ways. For example, Suhaila Haji (2002) uses the terms to distinguish between those Islamists who support equal minority rights within an Islamic state (moderates) and those who would curtail them (radicals). On "jihadis," while a small number of scholars use the term for historically specific cases, the American think tank RAND initiated its use to categorize various contemporary movements, described in a 2000 publication defining "jihad" as a "religious offensive" and "unlimited war against the West." See Sedgwick (2015).

41. Such approaches ultimately reflect the question "How do we liberalize Muslims?" Because they do not deeply interrogate their categorizations, this scholarship reflects a way of thinking about Islamic revival that is a priori politicized and elevates liberal ideals such as voting—and/or ignores the equally violent history of liberalism.

42. For a comprehensive analysis of philanthropic giving, the symbolic value it holds for philanthropists, and its relationship to neoliberal capitalism, see Morvaridi (2015).

43. I leave aside the theoretical question of whether material redistribution can, in fact, be detached from the need for recognition. The question of to what

extent recognition and redistribution are irreducible is explored in an exchange between Nancy Fraser and Axel Honneth (2003). In her article, Iris Young (1997, 147–60) critiques Fraser's dichotomy in part for overlooking the ways in which recognition can be a means to redistribution. See also Wacquant (2004b, 11).

44. Fraser (2003, 7) notes that redistribution has both a philosophical reference, to liberal theories of justice, and a political reference, to types of claims that political actors and social movements make. She does not always specify these claims but states they demand "a more just distribution of resources and wealth."

45. Piliavsky (2014).

46. I use "trust" here in a concrete sense, rather than abstract or generalized, of "shared affective aspects of [a] social world" that exists among a community of individuals (Seligman 1992, 16). While trust may not be essential to civil society, many have argued that it accounts for the strength of civil society (Nannestad 2008; Putnam 2000). Where a degree of social trust exists, the needs for predictability and "moral clarity" are better met (Fine 2007, 7).

47. While I liken the movement to the seeds of civil society, it also overlaps with prefigurative politics, coined by Carl Boggs (1977) and embraced in anarchist writing. Prefigurative politics acts out the ideal social relations, ethics, and democratic participation of a future community, rather than trying to gain concessions from the state. See Graeber (2013). In reading the description of community politics, other concepts may come to mind, like subaltern counterpublic (Fraser 1997), political society (Chatterjee 2004), or Max Weber's charismatic communities. Each of these in some way shares an element of intentionally seeking political power vis-à-vis the state, which does not resonate with the movements in Hyderabad.

48. In her ethnography of young Muslims conducted in the Paris region, Mayanthi Fernando refers to her interlocutors' claims not as rights to recognition but as "the right to indifference" (2014, 77–85). Although I use the term "recognition" in Nancy Fraser's sense of a claim for justice, my findings support Fernando's argument that Muslims are simply seeking equal rights to citizenship.

49. Fraser (2000).

50. The definition of "piety" is ambiguous. The term implies virtue, devotion, and fidelity. Although it generally connotes a devotion to religious virtue and godliness, these are not necessarily conditions for piety. As a philosophical problem, the definition of "piety" is explored in Plato's *Euthyphro*. In this book, I use the term occasionally to refer broadly to a commitment to a virtuous life, but otherwise use "religiosity" in reference to commitment to Islamic practice specifically.

51. The debate on justice versus self-realization as two unrelated objectives overlooks the effects of the type of class dynamic I present. For example, Nancy Fraser writes in response to her interlocutors, "Recognition should be considered a matter of justice, not self-realization" (1998, 38).

52. Addressing a different set of questions, Paul Lichterman (1996) features the issue of self-fulfillment as he explores the relationship between American individualism and the practice of making political commitments.

53. As Eickelman and Piscatori (1996/2004, 21) note, part of what makes "Muslim politics" distinctive are notions of social justice and community solidarity, among other issues that are important in the Islamic tradition.

54. This is not to deny the Muslim feminist movement that has existed in Lyon since its beginning in the mid-1990s. See a conversation between activists Zahra Ali and Saïda Kada, "Antiracisme et antisexisme: itinéraire d'une femme musulmane engagée en France," in Ali (2012, 187–201).

55. As Connolly (1974/1983) and Warren (1999, 209) argue, there are normative stakes involved in defining politics, which makes any conception of politics "essentially contestable."

56. Arendt (1958).

57. See Göle (2002) for a discussion of the relationship between Islam, subjectivity, and public space. See Wedeen (2008) on everyday life as political performativity in the construction of Yemeni nationhood. Tuğal (2009) argues that everyday piety is political because hegemony, which links society to the state, is constituted through everyday life. This is compatible, Tuğal writes, with Bourdieu's analysis of the embodiment of principles of division. See also Bayat (2010, 251) and Hirschkind (2006).

58. In Saba Mahmood's (2005, 37) ethnography of Egyptian women's participation in the Islamic revival, participants do not seek institution of Islamic law or direct engagement with the state. They in fact accuse Islamists of corrupting Islam by trying to include it under the domain of the state (52, 119). This is also the case with Tablighi Jama'at, the largest transnational Islamic movement, founded in India, which deliberately shuns politics (Metcalf 2002).

59. Eickelman and Piscatori (1996/2004, 20) state that "Muslim politics," like all politics, involve struggle over the extent of state control of everyday life.

60. See Gille and Riain (2002).

61. The exceptions to this are the names of well-known politicians, educational centers, and large mosques, like the Mecca Masjid and the Grande Mosquée de Lyon. I did not alter the names of neighborhoods in Lyon because it is not possible to present the analysis while sufficiently de-identifying them.

62. I have not changed the name of Tawhid, as it is a well-known local institution that appears in other scholarly work.

63. Paul Rabinow (2007, 153) writes, "The present somewhat nasty connotations of the word do apply at times, but so does its older root sense 'to give form to, to be the formative principle of, to animate.' . . . The informant gives external forms to his own experiences, by presenting them to meet the anthropologist's questions, to the extent that he can interpret them." Writing largely of the discipline of anthropology, John Van Maanen (1988/2011, 95) noted: "In what is rapidly

becoming something of an in-group term in fieldwork circles, both informants and fieldworkers are 'interlocutors' in cultural studies and are therefore jointly engaged in making sense of the enterprise." Precisely because it appears a rather in-group term, however, I also avoid the term "interlocutor."

64. Almost none of my participants in either France or India wore a sitar, which covers the eyes. The niqab is a facial covering, excluding the eyes. The hijab is a headscarf that covers all the hair and neck. In this book I generally employ the terms that my participants employed. In France, none of my participants used the term "burqa," even though national debates employed the term. They used the term "djelbab," a loose body covering that typically does not include a niqab. In India, Muslims commonly used the term "burqa" to refer to a full body covering that typically included a niqab. When describing political discourses more broadly, I sometimes use the term "burqa" to refer to full body coverings that may or may not include the niqab. Most public discourses do not make distinctions among veiling practices.

65. The class structure among Muslims in both cities is undoubtedly more complex than appears in this book. Among my middle-class companions in Lyon, several struggled for low-skilled and temporary jobs despite their education. Further, I saw and heard of Salafi men in Vénissieux who operated small businesses, sometimes also employing female family members (Amghar 2011). I did not learn enough to think of this as a parallel economy, but my sense was that the combination of pensions from retirees of the older generation and small local business provided financial stability to some families in poor neighborhoods. Further research would help give a more precise picture of class differences among Muslims (including converts) and in turn, of what class position implies here. It is possible that the salient factor driving life chances and political consciousness in Lyon is neighborhood. In Hyderabad, the range of potential class positions among Muslims was immense. Therefore, any category necessarily encompasses gradations. Among families in BPL neighborhoods, some had access to a few modern consumer goods and unstable sources of income. Others lived in makeshift housing with insufficient food and income, and others worked in street begging.

66. Roy and AlSayyad (2004, 4) write that new religious groups in the Middle East may be occupied in the provision of urban services but differ from traditional forms of populism because they "evade any form of politicization." Davis and Robinson (2012) present three cases of orthodox religious associations, including Egypt's Muslim Brotherhood, who bypass the state and focus on civil society.

67. Asking "Why do they hate us?" was first made popular by Bernard Lewis (1990). Calls for a reformation have come from various figures, from journalist Thomas Friedman to Somali-born, former Dutch politician Ayaan Hirsi Ali. For an analysis of how change in Muslim societies compares to the idea of reformation, see Browers and Kurzman (2004). For a nuanced discussion on Muslim leaders in Europe, though still highlighting the question of liberalism, see Klausen (2005).

CHAPTER 2

1. See Madani (2005).

2. Although the main concern was eliminating the power of the Church, *laïcité* also emerged out of discrimination and violence against Protestants and Jews. Thus, *laïcité* was also driven by concern for equality. In the years leading to the passage of the 1905 law, the Dreyfus Affair marked one of the main events that heightened liberal motivation to secularize the state; see Joskowicz (2014), Leff (2006), and Birnbaum (1996).

3. After the Revolution, *laïcité* went through two major periods of regression: the early nineteenth-century Restoration and the Vichy regime.

4. Alsace-Moselle refers to the region of northeastern France that was part of Germany from 1871 to 1919. Because *laïcité* was encoded before the territory reverted to French rule, the French laws of secularism do not apply there.

5. See Frajerman (2007), Balibar (2004), and Tombs (1996, 16–17 and 139–40).

6. Baubérot (1990: 46; cited in Davidson 2012, 30n75) argues that Judaism was forced to fit Catholic organizational patterns in the early 1800s.

7. While various scholars have pointed out the contradictions of *laïcité*, it is important to clarify different strains of this argument vis-à-vis Islam. The confusion stems from the inconsistency of state policies. On the one hand, it is said that *laïcité* is rigid and unjust because it has justified oppressive legislation and obstructed the free establishment of Islamic institutions. On the other hand, the state has exclusively funded Islamic institutions in particular times and places for the purpose of exercising control over its postcolonial subjects. In these cases, the state abandons the principles of *laïcité* as it sees fit.

8. Naomi Davidson (2012) argues that this over-attribution was the basis of racializing North Africans, such that religion in France is the equivalent of race in other countries.

9. The first phase of emigration was based on temporary labor recruitment of single men, who lived in dormitory-style housing (SONACOTRA *foyers*) constructed in the 1950s specifically for North African workers (de Barros 2005, 29). This shifted gradually to a second phase based on filling jobs rejected by French workers, family emigration and reunification, and the diminishing viability of returning to Algeria. In the 1960s, facilitated by a series of post-Independence Accords, the Algerian population in France increased two and a half times (Sayad 1984, 86).

10. Algerian-born residents continue to represent the greatest numbers of immigrants in France (Borrel 2006), and the specific history of colonial Algeria in many ways defined France's relation to Islam (see Davidson 2012; Silverstein 2004). But it is important to note that many French Muslims come from various parts of North and sub-Saharan Africa, as well as Turkey and parts of Asia.

11. In the words of Abdelmalek Sayad (1991, 61), "when work disappears, the result is the immigrant's 'death,' his negation, or 'non-existence.'"

12. The term was intended to reflect their simultaneous belonging to and alienation from French and Arab cultures, but was actually created by journalists and political pundits.

13. "Arabes de service" is a slang term that connotes token minority individuals who are patronized and exoticized. Used in conversation, it sometimes refers to one who would enact the stereotype in exchange for status or position.

14. Joppke and Torpey (2013, 11–12) see this as evidence that Europe has successfully integrated Islam at institutional levels and therefore, "religious discrimination against Islam cannot be the reason for deficient integration in Europe."

15. See Maussen (2007) on the subject of mosque construction.

16. The Quranic verse that has been the basis for women's required modesty and veiling is verse 31 from Surat al-Nisa. Saba Mahmood (2005, 100–104) provides a view into debates over the interpretation of this verse based on her ethnography of pious women's mosque movements in Cairo.

17. For a recent analysis of European headscarf debates, their development, significations about national identity, and gendered implications, see Korteweg and Yurdakul (2014).

18. Conseil d'Etat, 27 juin 2008, Mme Machbour, no. 286798.

19. See Hajjat (2010) for an analysis of the French state's use of Islam to determine citizenship eligibility.

20. While the majority of surveyed Muslims in France agreed that they "feel French," the percentage is significantly smaller than among non-Muslims. Maxwell and Bleich (2014) argue that immigrant integration rather than religiosity accounts for this variation. They observed similar trends among Christian immigrants.

21. Reported by Antoine Blua (2013).

22. The summer of 1973 saw a wave of racist attacks against Maghrébins, leading to eleven separate murders of Algerians in Marseille and the death of four Algerians in the bombing of the Algerian consulate months later; see Gastaut (1993).

23. For example, see Davidson (2012, 178–82) and Kepel (1991) on the role of such requests in the series of rent strikes in the state-funded SONACOTRA worker dormitories in the 1970s. SONACOTRA was created in 1956; most housing compounds were erected in the 1960s. A consequence of the war, it aimed to eradicate the shantytowns around Paris. It provided transitional and subsidized housing for French-born families, as well as some student housing. After 1962, it officially catered to all foreign workers. See Bernardot (2008), Simon (1998), and Topalov (1987).

24. In some cases, they are pushed to use the language of freedom and choice because there is no discursive room for them to articulate the religious ethics so central to their selves (Fernando 2015).

25. Voting participation by Maghrébins is also 15–20 points lower than among native Europeans. Based on original analysis of the 2004 European and regional elections, Rahsaan Maxwell (2010, 437) argues that group differences in voting

are statistically significant but are mostly explained by neighborhood effect. At the same time, it can be argued that Maghrébi minorities are more vulnerable to the effects of spatial segregation because of their fewer opportunities to organize along ethnic lines.

26. See Tévanian (2005) for an analysis of how journalists and so-called experts constructed the veil as a social problem.

27. Other efforts include turning to the private sector. For example, BNP Paribas, one of the largest banks in the world and headquartered in Paris, started Projet Banlieues in 2006. As of 2015, it had partnered with 320 French associations to support employment training, education, and social programs in "sensitive" neighborhoods (ZUS). It also promoted microcredit in France and other countries around the world. See www.bnpparibas.com/fondation-bnp-paribas/solidarite/projet-banlieues and "BNP Paribas supports Microcredit Week," June 2, 2008, http://usa.bnpparibas/en/2008/06/02/bnp-paribas-supports-microcredit-week/.

28. Frank Foley (2015) demonstrates that France has imposed a more draconian regime of counterterror operations than the UK because France has greater consensus about the willingness to sacrifice liberties and a legal system that allows for far-reaching measures. Foley argues that the more restrained British approach has likely prevented an exacerbation of terrorist threats. See also Bigo et al. (2013) for surveillance measures across five EU member states, including France.

29. Hamidi (2009).

30. See Hajjat (2014).

31. *Le Gone du Châaba* (*Shantytown Kid*) is a memoir by Azouz Begag (1986/2007), who became a government minister in 2005. He reflects on his youth as an Algerian in Lyon and his early years in a *bidonville* (shantytown) outside of the downtown.

32. Neither Hindu nor Muslim rulers enjoyed divine right or ultimate religious authority no matter their claims to spiritual authority (Hintze 1997; Heesterman 1985). See Fazal (2015, 61–62) on ulema in medieval India.

33. Specifically, Articles 25–30 of the Indian Constitution guarantee various forms of freedom of religion and are in tension with Article 44, which promotes a uniform civil code (Madan 1993).

34. Fazal (2015, 88) cites census figures from the state of Uttar Pradesh in years 1911, 1921, and 1931.

35. See Gayer and Jaffrelot (2012, 314–16) for fuller discussion of these factors.

36. Shyamlal Yadav, "Seat of Contention," *India Today*. May 30, 2005, http://india-today.intoday.in/story/aligarh-muslim-university-50percent-quota-for-muslims-creates-a-storm/1/193559.html.

37. For a comprehensive account of the political causes of anti-minority violence in India since independence, see Basu (2015).

38. Some Islamic organizations, like Jamiatul Ulema-e-Hind, participated in writing the Indian Constitution and enjoyed broad legitimacy. Its leaders were graduates of Darul Uloom Deoband, a madrasa founded in 1867 in Uttar Pradesh. Deoband's leaders advocated Hindu-Muslim unity in the anti-colonial struggle and a separation of the realm of religion from state (Ahmad 2009, 19–21). Other major Islamic groups include Jama'at-i-Islami Hind (JIH), Tablighi Jama'at, Students Islamic Movements of India (SIMI), Darul Uloom Nadwatul Ulema Lucknow, and the All India Muslim Personal Law Board (AIMPLB) (Alam 2007b, 33).

39. Darul Uloom Deoband gained notoriety post-9/11, as many Taliban members had studied at Deobandi schools; see Metcalf (2002).

40. Eric Beverley (2015) questions the dominant framing of Hyderabad as a "princely state," arguing that this reinforces colonial discourses that emphasized the importance of the British Raj. He instead insists on Hyderabad's particularity as a Muslim state with a clear position in a wider global, political, and cultural dynamic. For a brief political and cultural history of the state and analysis of Hyderabad's diasporic communities, see Leonard (2007).

41. The history of the violence of "police action" and of the political reconfigurations in Hyderabad during this period has been largely suppressed. Some estimates reveal that as many as 1,000 women committed suicide and an additional 200,000 people died during the police action (Khalidi 1988, x; Sundarlal and Abdulghaffar 1948/1988, 114). Approximately 10 to 20 percent of Muslim men in Hyderabad were killed (Smith 1950, 21). An unofficial government report acknowledged that Muslims constituted the majority of victims. Much of the violence occurred in districts surrounding Hyderabad city. The violence was related to the suppression of a communist uprising in the region that had been building alongside moves for independence. Although Muslims tended to lean toward supporting the Nizam, many aligned themselves with the communist movement. On the eve of the police action, the communists claimed they had liberated 2,000 surrounding villages, canceled debts, and redistributed land. The Indian army eventually crushed the movement (Smith 1950, 14–15), but after nearly six years of armed struggle (Luther 2006, 311–317).

42. Sherman (2015, 92–109).

43. In agricultural areas, the 1949 abolition of the feudal *jagirdari* system of land management affected more than 11 percent of Muslims (Hasan 1997, 183). Smaller landowners faced downward mobility with the fall in agricultural prices and had to sell their lands and homes. A 1954–55 study concluded: "The jagirdar class being ill-educated, untrained, orthodox, feudal in its outlook and inadaptable, has failed to obtain its due share in employment opportunities.... Frustration at present and dark prospects of the future have made them bitter and have created psychological and other problems" (Khusro 1958, 175).

44. Rajan (2014, 10–11).

45. Under the Nizams, charity and philanthropy were major functions of the state, and the last Nizam in particular was known for his financial backing of numerous educational and charitable institutions (Minault 1998). North Indian elites who worked in the state also supported women's charity work and schooling (U. Khalidi 1988, 188–89).

46. In this regard, critics accuse the MIM of communalism. The question of communalization in the case of Hyderabad is controversial. Some argue that the state was always communalized because of an upper caste of Muslims who controlled the princely state while others argue that Hindus in fact controlled private wealth and business and that the two communities had lived harmoniously (see Kooiman 2002).

CHAPTER 3

1. The Hindi equivalent for the concept of "slum" is *basti*. It refers generally to an unplanned, congested neighborhood with infrastructural deficits, absence of sanitation, and poor housing. These are not necessarily squatter settlements marked by improvised or illegal housing indicative of shantytowns, although there are makeshift elements of the houses in the *bastis* I observed.

2. Following decades of administrative complications and court cases, some of which were backed by the Hindu right, the state of Andhra Pradesh passed a 4 percent reservations act for thirteen "backward social groups" of Muslims (Krishnan 2010, 55).

3. In the prevalent interpretation of Islamic law (*fiqh*), charging interest on a loan, known as *riba*, is prohibited. Various interpretations exist, including the idea that the Quran forbids exploitation of the disadvantaged but not necessarily interest; see Saeed (1996).

4. In any given year, *zakat* funds in the city total over a half million U.S. dollars. Because *zakat* is not supposed to accumulate, this amount is spent on the poor throughout the state.

5. *Wakf* refers to property that was permanently dedicated as having pious, religious, or charitable purpose, as recognized in Islamic law. Historically, the setting aside of *wakf* was considered a virtuous act. Since 1995, the Andhra Pradesh (and now Telengana) state Wakf Board has been charged with administering *wakf* properties and lands. *Wakf* property in the state consists of several thousand buildings and half a million acres of land. Hyderabad's *wakf* properties are immensely valuable and in theory belong to the Muslim public. But the board notoriously mismanages the properties, whose real history and wealth remain shrouded in mystery. According to Hasanuddin Ahmed and Ahmedullah Khan (1998, 90–91), a 1990s survey indicated over 35,000 *wakf* properties and 133,000 acres of land in the former state of AP. I failed to obtain an interview with the local Wakf Board, which my companions found unsurprising and amusing.

6. The High Court ruled against the use of loudspeakers for all religious groups, but off-the-record negotiations allow it to continue.
7. Thomas Blom Hansen (1999, 54–55) writes that the tendency to view the masses of "deeply religious" people as potentially irrational and in need of leadership from the "educated sections" of society derives from the fundamentally elitist vision of politics embedded in Indian secularism.
8. The insistence on a private Islam oddly reinforces the Protestant conception of religion as an internal and cognitive state, rather than as bodily disciplines.
9. This in part reflects the demographics of Indian school teachers in general.

CHAPTER 4

1. The precise meaning of the slang use of *pakora* was not clear. For some it might refer more broadly to orthodox forms of practice, while for others it might refer specifically to Wahhabi Islam.
2. Analyzing the success of the Muslim Brotherhood in Egypt, Davis and Robinson (2012, 33) argue that it was "based on a strongly communitarian vision that saw Muslims as mutually responsible for each other and for their community."
3. The liberty with which mosques used loudspeakers is somewhat unique to Hyderabad. Though the city banned the amplification of prayers, a mutual understanding existed between the police and some Muslim neighborhoods so that the law was not enforced. One politician told me that this agreement was in exchange for Muslims' tolerance of a makeshift Hindu temple that worshipers illegally constructed at the floor of the Charminar, the city's central monument built under Muslim rule. Given this arrangement, mosques could make their presence even more public than might otherwise have been the case.
4. I learned of this particular incident second-hand.
5. Zoya Hasan and Ritu Menon (2004) provide a comprehensive analysis of the socioeconomic status of Muslim women in India.
6. Badran (1995) also observed the same story invoked in her study of Egyptian feminist movements.
7. For an analysis of how the Jamaat-e-Islami articulates opposition to neoliberalism, capitalism, and imperialism, see Maidul Islam (2015).
8. In the Hyderabad region in particular, the influx of Gulf labor remittances into Muslim communities fed a consumer culture that supported the practice of dowry (Waheed 2009). The practice of religious and customary gift-giving in marriages has a long history in the sub-Continent that, according to Veena Oldenburg (2002), became severely distorted by colonial interventions in women's property rights regimes. Imperial officers blamed "luxurious weddings" and dowry practices for violence against women that was instead more directly linked to changes in communal property rights that ultimately disempowered women. Today's anti-dowry discourses echo this colonial history. Pointing this

out is not to deny the very real burden that dowry exerts but, rather, to call for a more refined historical understanding of the practice rather than run the risk of blaming Indian culture for the ill effects of marriage expenses and gift-giving.

9. Though there are radical elements to these laws, the effects have been contradictory (Sitaraman 1999).

10. In recent years, the giving of *mehr* has been reduced or undermined (Vatuk 2008b).

11. See Amira Sonbol (2003) for a historical analysis of women and shari'a courts.

12. According to Vatuk (2008b), qazis in India do not have the authority to dissolve a marriage if the husband refuses his consent, although such procedures (known as *faskh*) exist in Islamic countries in cases of cruelty. Thus, in this particular case, the qazi evidently declared a divorce on the grounds of cruelty.

13. In her study of squatter settlements in Calcutta, Roy (2003) discusses how unemployed men appropriate the term *bekar* to signify rejection of menial labor and thereby reconstruct masculinity.

14. This is a loose translation of the Urdu na'at, "Mere Mustafa Aagaye," which is sung in different versions. A na'at is a traditional poem in praise of the Prophet Muhammed.

15. Durkheim (1915/2008).

CHAPTER 5

1. Raphaël Ruffier-Fossoul, "Limogé par Sarkozy, promu officier de la légion d'honneur," *Lyoncapitale*, September 20, 2014, www.lyoncapitale.fr/Journal/Lyon/Actualite/Actualites/Education/Limoge-par-Sarkozy-promu-officier-de-la-legion-d-honneur.

2. This view contrasts with the argument put forth most notably by Olivier Roy that Islamic revival among working-class youth is a rupture from family ties and a rejection of parental values. See "Le djihadisme est une révolte générationnelle et nihiliste," *Le Monde*, November 24, 2015.

3. The themes of burial and honoring one's immigrant parents also arose in interviews Nancy Venel (2005) conducted among Maghrébi young adults from the city of Lille.

4. In 2007, channel M6 aired a documentary on Islam in Lyon. Abbas was interviewed, but the editing made him appear threatening according to him and others who spoke with me about the documentary.

5. This is a common practice in many secular countries.

6. The teachings at the working-class mosque in the banlieue that I attended also on occasion emphasized the importance of respect for neighbors and respect for Muslims and non-Muslims alike.

7. For an exploration of electoral behaviors among Muslims in various European societies, see Nielsen (2013).

8. See Wieviorka (2007, 283–93).

9. I am using Ben-Abbes's real name because he is a public figure.

10. Zahra Ali discusses the tense relationship between secular activist associations and Muslim feminists in an interview conducted by journalist Naima Bouteldja, "France: Voices of the *banlieues*," *Race & Class* 51, no. 1 (2009): 90–99.

11. Ilyas also claimed that these organizations failed to account for millions of euros generated through the halal industry, funeral industry, and other Muslim industries.

12. It is possible that the teachings of Salafist men are different. The only study of Salafi Muslim men in France of which I am aware is Amghar (2011). Amghar conducted eighty-seven interviews with mostly men and a few women across France, Belgium, England, Canada, and the United States. My findings corroborate some of Amghar's findings; however, he argues that Salafism in the West constitutes a sect in the sociological sense, which I find less applicable to the participants in my study.

CHAPTER 6

1. Naima Bouteldja (2014) describes some of these aggressions in a chapter comparing the experiences of women who wear niqabs in France and England.

2. Camille Hamidi cites one of her interviewees in the working-class suburb of Vaulx-en-Velin: "Vaulx-en-Velin is my city. I like saying that I was born in Vaulx-en-Velin, I don't hide it. I remember that I told people in Paris, 'I was born in Vaulx-en-Velin,' and they asked, 'You were born in Vaulx-en-Velin?' and I replied, 'Yeah, yeah, but it's not the Bronx, eh!'" (Hamidi 2010, 151). For an analysis of the social psychological effects of urban desolation and poor infrastructure, see Wacquant (2010).

3. Auyero (2012) presents the extended waiting for state welfare services that low-income people experience in Buenos Aires.

4. Two years later, Sumaiya's husband did relocate to be with her, but their marriage was no less troubled than before.

5. Although Sumaiya was loosely connected to Salafist women, she did not identify as Salafist.

6. The status of smoking in Islam is unclear. Mainstream Muslims do not consider it sinful, but the Salafist community I knew claimed it was sinful for being wasteful and unhealthy.

7. Amghar (2011, 95) estimates between one-fourth and one-third of Salafists are converts, a figure I would agree with based on my research in Lyon.

8. Of Paris, Silverstein and Tetreault (2006) write: "Those [commuter lines] that do connect the suburbs to Paris are heavily surveilled, with fixed cameras and roving patrols of police, military gendarmes, and conductors empowered to make arrests. The result is the relative physical and symbolic separation of *cités* from each other and from Paris proper."

9. This phenomenon is widely reported in newspapers, and I heard about it second-hand. It is unclear to me whether stone-throwing has occurred only in the context of urban riots or also under other circumstances.

10. They were returned to France in 2004 and 2005, convicted in 2007 of criminal association, and released on appeal in 2009.

11. See Fassin (2013) for an ethnographic study of policing in the Parisian banlieues.

12. Abu-Lughod reflects on burqas as "mobile homes" in "Do Muslim Women Really Need Saving?," *American Anthropologist* 104, no. 3 (2002): 783–90.

13. This is in contrast to the antipolitics of Hungary, where, as Joanna Goven (1993) argues, women's domestic work allowed for men to participate in social and intellectual life. Antipolitics, in other words, worked primarily for men.

14. I recorded a number of *qhutbas* at various mosques generally during the early phases of fieldwork. *Qhutbas* in predominantly Maghrébi mosques in the banlieues were delivered in Arabic. Although I was studying Arabic, I understood only minimal content in the moment and had to rely on transcriptions to later understand them in their entirety.

15. Killian (2007) discusses this theme as it arose in her interviews with French North African immigrant women. Her subjects were first-generation Muslim immigrants and they represented a wide range of Islamic practice. They also included those who supported a ban on the headscarf. Thus, they contrasted sharply with the primarily French-born and Salafist women in my study. Killian argues that the importance attributed to "heart" reflected a comfortable compromise, in which the requirements of laïcité (that religion be private and hidden) melded with the women's beliefs that religion is foremost about faith and purity of heart. The women in my study shared this belief about faith but not out of any compromise with the state. Indeed, their belief in the burqa indicates their rejection of this interpretation of *laïcité*. More importantly, they believed that purity of heart comes about *through* external practice.

16. Konrád (1984, 185, 230).

17. Antipolitics, as I have defined it, shares some similarities with black feminist thought, though I have emphasized the idea that it goes against the idea of politics. In contrast, Audre Lorde (1988) wrote of self-preservation as "an act of political warfare."

CHAPTER 7

1. John Esposito's *The Future of Islam* (2010) undoes common misperceptions of Islam and Muslims and provides an accessible overview of major issues confronting the Islamic world.

2. According to a phone survey of 2,450 Americans, 30 percent of respondents said they believe Muslims want to implement shari'a law, 41 percent would be uncomfortable if a teacher at the elementary school in their community were Muslim,

and 47 percent said the values of Islam are at odds with American values. The Public Religion Research Institute conducted the survey and issued a report in conjunction with the Brookings Institution. See "What it means to be American" by Jones et al. (2011). In 2015, according to a YouGov survey, 57 percent of respondents agreed with Republican U.S. presidential candidate Ben Carson's statement, "I would not advocate that we put a Muslim in charge of this nation." See William Jordan, "Most Americans Agree with Ben Carson's Muslim Comments," September 25, 2015, https://today.yougov.com/news/2015/09/25/ben-carsons-muslim-comments/. In Europe, an average of 43 percent of respondents have an unfavorable view of Muslims. Figures are across Britain (26%), France (27%), Germany (33%), Greece (53%), Italy (63%), Poland (50%), and Spain (46%). See Pew Research Center, "A Fragile Rebound for EU Image on Eve of European Parliament Elections," May 12, 2014. http://www.pewglobal.org/2014/05/12/a-fragile-rebound-for-eu-image-on-eve-of-european-parliament-elections/.

3. Patrick Heller (2000, 507), for example, cites the state of Kerala and the Communist Party of India (CPI) as exceptions to India's "identity populism," noting that social transformation occurred in Kerala through cultural venues and associations but ultimately through a "new secular culture."

4. Harriss (2007) links the rise of associations to the postliberalization state and the World Bank agenda of "governance," "empowerment," and "participation." Greater foreign funding for NGOs has driven part of this. It is difficult to say what role this has played in the Islamic revival in Hyderabad, as the World Bank does not encourage foreign donations for Islamic associations.

5. In " 'The Middle Class': Sociological Category or Proper Noun?" Raka Ray (2010) distinguishes between the empirical middle class with all its heterogeneity and the middle class as an ideological construct that serves to obscure inequality and defend privilege. Writing mostly of a Hindu middle class, she argues, "Indeed, at least in the case of India, the cultural dominance of the middle class has effectively undermined and even subverted the democratic possibilities inherent in Indian politics" (321).

6. In 2011, the JIH formed a new political party called the Welfare Party of India (WPI).

7. For a concise overview of common misperceptions of orthodox women across religious traditions, see Avishai (2010).

8. Placing freedom as a practice at the center of feminist theory allows us to move beyond the twin issues that, according to Linda Zerilli (2005), defined and paralyzed American feminist thinking: social rights and subjectivity. The focus on rights and subjectivity originates in two fundamental, interrelated tendencies in Western political theory. These are the view of politics as instrumental and view of freedom as individual. Both of these views have rendered politics as only a means to the ends of social betterment, which comes about incidentally through "women's rights."

9. The quest to explain greater religiosity likely comes from the liberal impulse to critique religion itself. But as Talal Asad (2013, 134) writes, "Critique is no less violent than the law—and no more free."

10. Abdulkader Sinno, in *Muslims in Western Politics* (2009), lists policy recommendations toward greater democracy and security.

11. Writing about theories of cosmopolitan democracy, Craig Calhoun (2002, 89–90) argues that the cosmopolitan disposition, global lifestyle, and identification as "citizen of the world" run the risk of concerning only the lives of elites and further, upholding an effectively capitalist vision of civil society. The danger, he warns, is of emphasizing liberalism rather than democracy.

12. French conceptions of gender justice have been unable to confront this irony. As one example, Elisabeth Badinter is widely considered among the most prominent intellectuals and feminist writers in France. She has published numerous pieces against the burqa in French media. For a profile of her work and background, see Kramer (2011).

APPENDIX A

1. In *The Extended Case Method*, Michael Burawoy (2009, 56–62) also includes the problems of objectification (presenting social forces as external and all-determining) and normalization (reducing a social world to categories in the process of reconstructing theory). In extending out to class relations, state retrenchment, and the global War on Terror, my study also flirts with these "dangers." In this appendix, however, I focus on the power effects in the actual fieldwork.

2. As Erving Goffman wrote, "You can't move down a social system. . . . People at the bottom will know that all along you really were a fink—which is what you are." From "On Fieldwork," in *Contemporary Field Research*, ed. Robert M. Emerson (Long Grove, IL: Waveland Press, 2001), 155.

3. I also wandered around the Mas du Taureau housing projects in the suburb of Vaulx-en-Velin, which I found much livelier and more diverse than Les Minguettes.

4. As it turned out, it was while living in downtown Lyon that he witnessed (in sound only) my neighbor being violently beaten and dragged by the hair across our hall by her boyfriend, prompting me to make a terrified call to the police while frantically hiding my son in the bedroom.

5. See Bogusia Temple, Rosalind Edwards, and Claire Alexander, "Grasping at Context: Cross Language Qualitative Research as Secondary Qualitative Data Analysis," *Qualitative Social Research* 7, no. 4, art. 10 (September 2006). See also Tamara Mose Brown and Erynn Masi de Casanova, "Representing the Language of the 'Other': African American Vernacular English in Ethnography," *Ethnography* 15, no. 2 (2014): 208–31.

6. A case can be made for first building up trust through ethnography before turning to recorded interviews. See Desmond (2007, 295).

7. Duneier (1999, 340) argues for the importance of the recorder in accurately conveying conversations. He appeals to the "Becker principle," that the organized nature of most social processes prevents something like a recorder from having more influence than other pressures and expectations in a given social setting. I suggest that this assessment is culturally specific. In contexts that tend toward anarchic social settings, such as a densely populated slum in India, one cannot apply the same principle. The recorder produces effects, especially in contexts where such technology remains novel.

8. Alice Goffman (2014, 228) describes her subjects' suspicions about her romantic or sexual availability. Some decided she was a lesbian, and others "just seemed to think I was a bit of a loser, unable to make friends with people like myself in the neighborhood I had come from."

9. See Kitts (2003).

10. For an account of developing rapport and "accidental intimacy," à la Geertz, see Emilio Spadola, "Forgive Me Friend: Mohammed and Ibrahim," *Anthropological Quarterly* 84, no. 3 (Summer 2011): 737–56. Spadola reveals his struggles with converting to Islam during his fieldwork in Morocco and the role of forgiveness in salvaging his bond with a primary informant.

11. For a review of anthropological approaches to emotions, including debates on universalism versus relativism, see Catherine Lutz and Geoffrey M. White, "The Anthropology of Emotions," *Annual Review of Anthropology* 15 (1986): 405–36.

12. Paul Rabinow (2007, 45–46) explains how his failure to honor this code turned out to be an important breakthrough in his friendship with Ali, a principle informant. See Judith Stacey, "Can There be a Feminist Ethnography," *Women's Studies International Forum* 11, no. 1 (1988): 21–27, on the emotional risks ethnography imposes on subjects.

13. Kamala Visweswaran calls for feminist ethnographers to approach women's silences as a "central site for an analysis of power between them" and to consider a refusal to speak as resistance. See "Betrayal: An Analysis in Three Acts," in *Fictions of Feminist Ethnography* (Minneapolis: University of Minnesota Press, 1994), 40–59.

14. See *Muslim Girls and the Other France* by Trica Keaton (2006) for a qualitative study of Muslim girls in a banlieue of Paris. Keaton focuses on the girls' experiences in public schools, degraded housing, racism, and to a lesser extent, their varied relationships to Islamic piety, which do not appear so central in their lives.

15. Ayala Fader (2009, 17) writes about similar dynamics in her ethnography of Hasidic women in Brooklyn:

> Like every anthropologist, I explained that the goals of my research were a doctoral degree and, eventually, a book. However, the Hasidic women I worked

with framed my presence in a religious discourse of redemption through return. For them, God had led me to my research topic in order to help me return to the faith. My very presence legitimized their critique of the secular world. That I, who had a liberal Jewish upbringing and such extensive exposure to higher education, might still end up among them was evidence of the power and truth of their Judaism.

16. Robert Bellah (2011, 97) discusses the historical relationship between philosophy, religion, ethics, and science. He writes, "Though 'natural philosophers' criticized forms of myth from ancient times, the war of science and religion is very much a modern phenomenon." See also Elaine Ecklund, *Science vs. Religion: What Scientists Really Think* (New York: Oxford University Press, 2010); Daniel Dubuisson, *The Western Construction of Religion: Myths, Knowledge, and Ideology*, trans. William Sayers (Baltimore: Johns Hopkins University Press, 1998/2003).

17. See McRoberts (2004) for a discussion of this dilemma, unique to ethnographers of religion. McRoberts suggests an "aesthetic approach" to the study of religion, whereby the ethnographer strives to appreciate the rituals and doctrines that worshipers find sublime.

Glossary

The following includes most of the Arabic, French, and Urdu-Hindi terms that appear in the book. The transliterations used correspond with local norms in Lyon and Hyderabad.

Alhamdulillah expression for "praise to God" or "thank God"

alim recognized scholar of Islam

apa respectful Urdu term for sister

ashurkhanas congregation sites or halls for Shia mourning rituals and commemorations especially during the Islamic month of Muharram

azaan the call to prayer made approximately fifteen minutes before the prayer begins

baji Urdu term for sister

banlieue a town peripheral to an urban center and typically connotative of lower-class districts in France

basti Hindi/Urdu equivalent for the concept of "slum," referring generally to an unplanned, congested neighborhood with infrastructural deficits, absence of sanitation, and poor housing

bekar Hindi/Urdu for useless; in some contexts it refers to being unemployed

beur slang term for the French-born children of North African immigrants

bida innovations to Islam that cause deviations from the original teachings and practices of the Prophet Muhammed

chillar slang term in Hyderabad for cheap or petty

cités large estates of deteriorated public housing in areas of urban deprivation in France

converti(e) French term for convert

Dalits term for the "depressed classes" of India, traditionally known as "Untouchables," used interchangeably with Scheduled Castes (SCs)

dargah Sufi shrine constructed over the grave of a saint or religious figure, often housing religious activities and musical offerings in India

da'wa activities toward promoting Islamic piety and inviting others to Islam *djelbab* form of veiling that covers the body except the face and hands

duas prayers of supplication, separate from the five daily obligatory prayers in Islam

Eid/Aïd the celebratory feasts and prayer marking the end of Ramadan or commemorating Abraham's sacrifice

étranger a resident of France without French nationality

hadith traditions related to the teachings and practices of the Prophet Muhammed as recounted by his closest followers in his lifetime

hafiz an individual who has memorized the Quran

hakeem used in Urdu as a title for a traditional Islamic medical practitioner

halal that which is permitted and lawful in Islam

halaqah an Islamic study circle with a teacher, commonly used in France

haram that which is forbidden and unlawful in Islam

hifz training in the memorization of the Quran

hijab the headscarf, understood in both France and India as the veiling of the hair and neck

Hindutva movements that promote Hindu nationalism

iftar evening meal with which one breaks the daily fast during Ramadan

imam in Sunni Islam, the prayer leader or leader of a community

immigré a resident of France who was born abroad to foreign parents

insha Allah expression for "if God wills"

intégriste French term for "fundamentalist"

izzat Hindi/Urdu term for honor or respect

jahez traditional practice of gift-giving to a bride and groom among Indian Muslims

jahil ignorant or untaught

jinns inhabitants of the immaterial world, with some considered benevolent toward humans and others hostile

kafr one who denies the existence of God

khul a form of divorce in Islam based on mutual consent and the wife's renouncing of her *mehr*

kurta pajama traditional men's pant and shirt in South Asia

madrasa center of Islamic learning

Maghrébin an individual of immigrant or ethnic background from Algeria, Morocco, or Tunisia

masha'Allah common expression for "by the grace of God's will"

masjid mosque

mehr gift or monetary amount given by a groom to a bride

milad-un-Nabi birth date of the Prophet Muhammed

mosquées des caves literally "basement mosques," used in France, often pejoratively, for spaces of informal religious gatherings in contrast to structured and more visible mosques

nikah namah Islamic marriage contract

niqab veil that covers the face and is used typically with a *djelbab*

Nizam title for Muslim rulers of princely Hyderabad

orni Hindu/Urdu term for scarf; can be worn in a variety of ways

pardah used in India to refer to the covering or seclusion of women or the segregation of the sexes

qazi judge appointed on the basis of knowledge of Islamic law; commonly performs Muslim marriage rites in India

qhutba sermon given before the Friday congregational prayer

quartiers [sensibles] vulnerable or "at-risk" neighborhoods in France

riba giving or taking of interest on any loan; prohibited in Islam

roqaya incantations and prayers to ward off evil or harm or toward exorcism of *jinns*

sabr patience and fortitude

saheba companions, or close followers of the Prophet during his lifetime; or the companions who had seen him in his lifetime

Salafism a movement originating 100–200 years ago that sought to modernize Islam; it transformed eventually into a movement intended to restore the original teachings and practices of Islam

salwar kameez traditional women's dress in South Asia

sehri predawn meal with which one starts the daily fast during the Islamic month of Ramadan

shari'a judicial practices and moral codes known as Islamic law

sheikh/cheikh title for someone with spiritual or doctrinal authority

sherwani men's garment, knee-length coat, traditionally associated with Indian Muslim aristocracy

soeur French word for sister

sunnah examples, in speech and act, set by the Prophet Muhammed

tafsir explication of the Quran

tajwid science of Quranic recitation

talaq form of Islamic divorce based on verbal repudiation by the husband

tawba repentance

topi Hindi/Urdu for a cap, sometimes used specifically for male Islamic cap

ulema recognized scholars or authorities on religious matters and Islamic law

ummah global community of believers

unani tradition of Islamic medicine based on teachings from ancient Greece

Wahhabism a movement founded in Arabia in the early nineteenth century that technically shunned all traditional schools of Islamic law in favor of strict interpretations of the Prophet's teachings

wakf Islamic trusts and endowments intended for pious and public works

zakat obligatory payment of a portion of one's wealth, usually paid directly to the poor or toward charity

References

Achi, Raberh. 2007. "Laïcité d'empire. Les débats sur l'application du régime de séparation à l'islam impérial." In *Politiques de la laïcité au XXe siècle*, ed. P. Weil, 237–63. Paris: Presses Universitaires de France.

Adraoui, Mohamed-Ali. 2009. "Salafism in France: Ideology, Practices and Contradictions." In *Global Salafism: Islam's New Religious Movement*, ed. R. Meijer, 364–83. New York: Columbia University Press.

Agnes, Flavia. 1999. *Law and Gender Inequality: The Politics of Women's Rights in India*. New Delhi and New York: Oxford University Press.

Ahmad, Irfan. 2009. *Islamism and Democracy in India: The Transformation of Jamaat-e-Islami*. Princeton, NJ: Princeton University Press.

Ahmed, Akbar. 1985. "Muslim Society in South India: The Case of Hyderabad." *Journal Institute of the Muslim Minority Affairs* 6: 317–31.

Ahmed, Hasanuddin, and Ahmedullah Khan. 1998. *Strategies to Develop Waqf Administration in India*. Jeddah: Islamic Development Bank.

Alam, Anwar. 2007a. "Hindutva and Future of Muslims in India." In *Living with Secularism: The Destiny of India's Muslims*, ed. M. Hasan, 137–54. New Delhi: Manohar.

Alam, Anwar. 2007b. "Political Management of Islamic Fundamentalism: A View from India." *Ethnicities* 7(1): 30–60.

Ali, Syed. 2007. "'Go West Young Man': The Culture of Migration among Muslims in Hyderabad, India." *Journal of Ethnic and Migration Studies* 33(1): 37–58.

Ali, Zahra, ed. 2012. *Féminismes islamiques*. Paris: La fabrique editions.

Amghar, Samir. 2011. *Le salafisme d'aujourd'hui: mouvements sectaires en Occident*. Paris: Michalon.

Amiraux, Valérie, and Patrick Simon. 2006. "There are no Minorities Here: Cultures of Scholarship and Public Debate on Immigrants and Integration in France." *International Journal of Comparative Sociology* 47(3–4): 191–215.

Ansell, Aaron Michael. 2014. *Zero Hunger Political Culture and Antipoverty Policy in Northeast Brazil*. Chapel Hill: University of North Carolina Press.

"AP Tops in NRI Remittances." *Hindu Business Line*, August 9, 2006. At www.thehindubusinessline.com/2006/08/09/stories/2006080590591900.htm.

Arato, Andrew, and Jean L. Cohen. 2010. "Banishing the Sovereign? Internal and External Sovereignty in Arendt." In *Politics in Dark Times: Encounters with Hannah Arendt*, ed. Seyla Benhabib, 137–71. New York: Cambridge University Press.

Arendt, Hannah. 1963. *On Revolution*. London: Penguin Books.

Arendt, Hannah. 1958. *The Human Condition*. Chicago: University of Chicago Press.

Arendt, Hannah. 1951/1979. *The Origins of Totalitarianism*. New York: Harcourt Brace.

Asad, Talal. 2013. "Free Speech, Blasphemy, and Secular Criticism." In *Is Critique Secular?: Blasphemy, Injury and Free Speech*, ed. T. Asad, W. Brown, D. J. Butler, and S. Mahmood, 14–58. New York: Fordham University Press.

Asad, Talal. 2009. "The Idea of an Anthropology of Islam." *Qui Parle* 17(2): 1–30.

Asad, Talal. 1993. *Genealogies of Religion: Discipline and Reasons of Power in Christianity and Islam*. Baltimore: Johns Hopkins University Press.

Assemblée Nationale. 2009. Mission d'information sur la pratique du port du voile intégral sur le territoire National. At www.assemblee-nationale.fr/13/cr-miburqa/08-09/index.asp.

Auyero, Javier. 2012. *Patients of the State: The Politics of Waiting in Argentina*. Durham, NC: Duke University Press.

Auyero, Javier. 2002. *Poor People's Politics: Peronist Survival Networks and the Legacy of Evita*. Durham, NC: Duke University Press.

Avishai, Orit. 2010. "Women of God." *Contexts* 9(4): 46–51.

Baber, Zaheer. 2004. "'Race,' Religion and Riots: The 'Racialization' of Communal Identity and Conflict in India." *Sociology* 38(4): 701–18.

Badran, Margot. 1995. *Feminists, Islam, and Nation: Gender and the Making of Modern Egypt*. Princeton, NJ: Princeton University Press.

Baillet, G. Dominique. 2001. *Militantisme politique et intégration des jeunes d'origine maghrébine*. Paris: L'Harmattan.

Balibar, Étienne. 2004. "Dissonances within Laicite." *Constellations* 11(3): 353–67.

Basu, Amrita. 2015. *Violent Conjunctures in Democratic India*. New York: Cambridge University Press.

Basu, Ipshita. 2012. "The Politics of Recognition and Redistribution: Development, Tribal Identity Politics and Distributive Justice in India's Jharkhand." *Development and Change* 43(6): 1291–312.

Baubérot, Jean. 2000. *Histoire de la laïcité en France*. Paris: Presses Universitaires de France.

Baubérot, Jean. 1998. "Two Thresholds of Laicization." In *Secularism and Its Critics*, ed. Rajeev Bhargava, 94–136. Delhi: Oxford University Press.

Baubérot, Jean. 1990. *Vers une nouvelle pacte laïque?* Paris: Seuil.

Bayat, Asef. 2010. "Muslim Youth and the Claim of Youthfulness." In *Being Young and Muslim: New Cultural Politics in the Global South and North*, ed. Linda Herrera and Asef Bayat, 26–47. Oxford: Oxford University Press.

Bayat, Asef. 2007. *Making Islam Democratic: Social Movements and the Post-Islamist Turn.* Stanford, CA: Stanford University Press.

Bayly, Christopher. 1983. *Rulers, Townsmen, and Bazaars: North Indian Society in the Age of British Expansion, 1770–1870.* Cambridge: Cambridge University Press.

Béatrix, Asma. 1988. "Attitudes culturelles et positions sociales dans la population musulmane en France." In *Les Musulmans dans la Société Française,* ed. R. Leveau and G. Kepel, 89–97. Paris: Presses de la Fondation Nationale des Sciences Politiques.

Begag, Azouz. 1986/2007. *Le Gone du Châaba (Shantytown Kid).* Trans. by Naïma Wolf and Alec G. Hargreaves. Lincoln: University of Nebraska Press.

Beinart, Peter. 2014. *Bill Maher's Dangerous Critique of Islam.* At www.theatlantic. com/international/archive/2014/10/bill-maher-dangerous-critique-of-islam-ben-affleck/381266/.

Belbahri, A. 1984. "Les Minguettes ou la surlocalisation du social." *Espaces et sociétés* 45: 101–108.

Bellah, Robert N. 2011. *Religion in Human Evolution.* Cambridge, MA: Harvard University Press.

Bellah, Robert N. 1970. *Beyond Belief: Essays on Religion in a Post-Traditional World.* New York: Harper & Row.

Berezin, Mabel. 2013. "The Normalization of the Right in Post-Security Europe." In *Politics in the Age of Austerity,* ed. A. Schäfer and W. Streeck, 239–61. Cambridge, UK: Polity Press.

Berezin, Mabel. 2009. *Illiberal Politics in Neoliberal Times: Culture, Security and Populism in the New Europe.* Cambridge and New York: Cambridge University Press.

Berger, Peter. 1967. *The Sacred Canopy: Elements of a Sociological Theory of Religion.* Garden City, NY: Doubleday.

Bernardot, Marc. 2008. *Loger les immigrés: La Sonacotra, 1956–2006.* Bellecombe-en-Bauges: Croquant.

Beverley, Eric Lewis. 2015. *Hyderabad, British India, and the World: Muslim Networks and Minor Sovereignty, c. 1850–1950.* Cambridge: Cambridge University Press.

Bhargava, Rajeev. 2011. *States, Religious Diversity, and the Crisis of Secularism.* At www.opendemocracy.net/rajeev-bhargava/states-religious-diversity-and-crisis-of-secularism-0.

Bigo, Didier, et al. 2013. "Mass Surveillance of Personal Data by EU Member States and Its Compatibility with EU Law." *Liberty and Security in Europe Papers* 61. At www.ceps.be/ceps/dld/8565/pdf.

Bilgrami, Akeel. 1994. "Two Concepts of Secularism: Reason, Modernity and Archimedean Ideal." *Economic and Political Weekly* 29(28): 1749–61.

Birnbaum, Pierre. 1996. *The Jews of the Republic: A Political History of State Jews in France from Gambetta to Vichy.* Stanford, CA: Stanford University Press.

Blua, A. 2013. "Muslims in France Warn of Rising 'Islamophobia.'" *Radio Free Europe,* August 14. At www.rferl.org/content/france-muslims-islamophobia/25075616. html.

Boggs, Carl. 1977. "Marxism, Prefigurative Communism, and the Problem of Workers' Control." *Radical America* 11(6): 99–122.

Borrel, Catherine. 2006. *Enquêtes annuelles de recensement 2004 et 2005.* National Institute of Statistics and Economic Studies (INSEE). Report no. 1098. At http://www.insee.fr/fr/themes/document.asp?ref_id=ip1098&reg_id=0.

Bourgois, Philippe. 1990. "Confronting Anthropological Ethics: Ethnographic Lessons from Central America." *Journal of Peace Research* 27(1): 43–54.

Bouteldja, Naima. 2014. "France vs. England." In *The Experiences of Face Veil Wearers in Europe and the Law*, ed. Eva Brems, 115–60. Cambridge: Cambridge University Press.

Bouvet, Laurent. 2007. *Le communautarisme: mythes et réalités.* Gambais (Yvelines): Lignes de repères.

Bowen, John Richard. 2010. *Can Islam Be French? Pluralism and Pragmatism in a Secularist State.* Princeton, NJ: Princeton University Press.

Bowen, John Richard. 2007. *Why the French Don't like Headscarves: Islam, the State, and Public Space.* Princeton, NJ: Princeton University Press.

Bozzo, Anna. 2005. "Islam et République: une longue histoire de méfiance." In *La Fracture coloniale, la société française au prisme de l'héritage colonial*, ed. Nicolas Bancel, Pascal Blanchard, Sandrine Lemaire, 75–82. Paris: La Découverte.

Brouard, Sylvain, and Vincent Tiberj. 2011. *As French as Everyone Else? A Survey of French Citizens of Maghrébin, African, and Turkish Origin.* Philadelphia: Temple University Press.

Browers, Michaelle, and Charles Kurzman, eds. 2004. *An Islamic Reformation?* Lanham, MD: Lexington Books.

Brubaker, Rogers, and Frederick Cooper. 2000. "Beyond 'Identity.'" *Theory and Society* 29: 1–47.

Burawoy, Michael. 2009. *The Extended Case Method: Four Countries, Four Decades, Four Great Transformations, and One Theoretical Tradition.* Berkeley: University of California Press.

Burgwal, Gerrit. 1995. *Struggle of the Poor: Neighborhood Organization and Clientelist Practice in a Quito Squatter Settlement.* Amsterdam: CEDLA.

Calhoun, Craig. 2002. "Imagining Solidarity: Cosmopolitanism, Constitutional Patriotism, and the Public Sphere." *Public Culture* 14(1): 147–71.

Calhoun, Craig. 1997. *Nationalism and the Public Sphere.* Chicago: University of Chicago Press.

Calhoun, Craig, Mark Jeurgensmeyer, and Jonathan VanAntwerpen, eds. 2011. *Rethinking Secularism.* New York: Oxford University Press.

Casanova, José. 2009. "The Secular and Secularisms." *Social Research* 76(4): 1049–66.

Césari, Jocelyne. 2013. *Why the West Fears Islam: An Exploration of Muslims in Liberal Democracies.* New York: Palgrave Macmillan.

Césari, Jocelyne. 2005. "Ethnicity, Islam, and les banlieues: Confusing the issues." *Social Science Research Council.* At http://riotsfrance.ssrc.org/Cesari.

Césari, Jocelyne. 2002. "Demande de l'Islam en banlieue: un défi à la citoyenneté." *Cahiers d'études sur la Méditeraanée orientale et le monde turco-iranien* 33: 39–48.

Chakrabarty, Dipesh. 1995. "Modernity and Ethnicity in India: A History for the Present." *Economic and Political Weekly* 30(52): 3373–80.

Chatterjee, Partha. 2004. *The Politics of the Governed: Reflections on Popular Politics in Most of the World.* New York: Columbia University Press.

Chatterjee, Partha. 1994. "Secularism and Tolerance." In *Secularism and Its Critics*, ed. R. Bhargava, 345–79. Reprint. Delhi: Oxford University Press.

Chaturvedi, Vinayak, ed. 2012. *Mapping Subaltern Studies and the Postcolonial.* Mappings Series. London: Verso Books.

Cohen, Jean L., and Andrew Arato. 1994. *Civil Society and Political Theory.* Cambridge, MA: MIT Press.

Collett, J. L., and O. Lizardo. 2009. "A Power-Control Theory of Gender and Religiosity." *Journal for the Scientific Study of Religion-JSSR* 48(2): 213–31.

Connolly, William E. 1974/1983. *The Terms of Political Discourse.* Princeton, NJ: Princeton University Press.

Copland, Ian. 2010. "What's in a Name? India's Tryst with Secularism." *Commonwealth & Comparative Politics* 48(2): 123–47.

Courtois, Stéphane, and Gilles Kepel. 1988. "Musulmans et prolétaires." In *Les Musulmans dans la Société Française*, ed. R. Leveau and G. Kepel, 27–38. Paris: Presses de la Fondation Nationale des Sciences Politiques.

Crenson, Matthew A. 1983. *Neighborhood Politics.* Cambridge, MA: Harvard University Press.

Davidson, Naomi. 2012. *Only Muslim: Embodying Islam in Twentieth-Century France.* Ithaca, NY: Cornell University Press.

Davis, Nancy Jean, and Robert V. Robinson. 2012. *Claiming Society for God Religious Movements and Social Welfare: Egypt, Israel, Italy and the United States.* Bloomington: Indiana University Press.

Dean, John, and William Whyte. 1958. "How Do You Know If the Informant Is Telling the Truth?" *Human Organization* 17(2): 34–38.

de Barros, Françoise. 2006. "Contours d'un reseau administratif 'algerien' et construction d'une competence en 'affaires musulmanes.'" *Politix* 19(76): 97–117.

de Barros, Françoise. 2005. "Des 'Français musulmans d'Algérie' aux 'immigrés'. L'importation de classifications coloniales dans les politiques du logement en France (1950–1970)." *Actes de la Recherche en Sciences Sociales* 4(159): 26–53.

Deeb, Lara. 2006. *An Enchanted Modern: Gender and Public Piety in Shi'i Lebanon.* Princeton, NJ: Princeton University Press.

Desmond, Matthew. 2014. "Relational Ethnography." *Theory and Society* 43(5): 547–79.

Desmond, Matthew. 2007. *On the Fireline: Living and Dying with Wildland Firefighters.* Chicago: University of Chicago Press.

Dessertine, Dominique. 2007. "Former une jeunesse laïque. Les amicales, entre éducation populaire et civilisation des loisirs (1894–1939)." In *Politiques de la laïcité au XXe siècle*, ed. P. Weil, 303–25. Paris: Presses Universitaires de France.

Dessertine, Dominique, and Bernard Maradan. 2001. *L'Âge d'or des patronages, 1919–1939: la socialisation de l'enfance par des loisirs.* Paris: Ministère de la Justice.

Dikeç, Mustafa. 2007. *Badlands of the Republic: Space, Politics and Urban Policy.* Malden, MA, and Oxford: Blackwell.

Diop, M. 1988. "Stéréotypes et stratégies dans la communauté musulmane de France." In *Les musulmans dans la Société Française*, ed. R. Leveau and G. Kepel, 77–87. Paris: Presses de la Fondation Nationale des Sciences Politiques.

Duneier, Mitchell. 1999. *Sidewalk.* New York: Macmillan.

Dupret, Baudouin, and Jean-Noël Ferrié. 2005. "Constructing the Private/Public Distinction in Muslim Majority Societies: A Praxiological Approach." In *Religion, Social Practice, and Contested Hegemonies: Reconstructing the Public Sphere in Muslim Majority Societies*, ed. A. Salvatore, M. Le Vine, and M. L. Vine, 135–53. New York: Palgrave Macmillan.

Durkheim, Emile. 1915/2008. *The Elementary Forms of the Religious Life.* Trans. Joseph Ward Swain. Mineola, NY: Dover Publications, Inc.

Eickelman, Dale F., and James P. Piscatori. 1996/2004. *Muslim Politics.* Princeton, NJ: Princeton University Press.

Eley, Geoff. 1994. "Nations, Publics, and Political Cultures: Placing Habermas in the Nineteenth Century." In *Culture/Power/History: A Reader in Contemporary Social Theory*, ed. N. B. Dirks, G. Eley, and S. B. Ortner, 297–335. Princeton, NJ: Princeton University Press.

Engineer, Asghar Ali. 2010. *Secularism, Democracy, and Muslim Experience in India: Understanding Communalism and Terrorism.* Gurgaon: Hope India Publications.

Engineer, Asghar Ali. 2007. *Communalism in Secular India: A Minority Perspective.* Gurgaon: Hope India Publications.

Esposito, John L. 2010. *The Future of Islam.* New York: Oxford University Press.

Euben, R., and M. Zaman. 2009. "Introduction." In *Princeton Readings in Islamist Thought: Texts and Contexts from al-Banna to Bin Laden*, ed. R. Euben and M. Zaman, 1–41. Princeton, NJ: Princeton University Press.

Fader, Ayala. 2009. *Mitzvah Girls: Bringing up the Next Generation of Hasidic Jews in Brooklyn.* Princeton, NJ: Princeton University Press.

Fassin, Didier. 2013. *Enforcing Order: An Ethnography of Urban Policing.* Cambridge and Malden, MA: Polity Press.

Fassin, Didier. 2006. "Nommer, interpréter. Le sens commun de la question raciale." In *De la Question Sociale à la Question Raciale? Representer la Société Française*, ed. Didier Fassin and Eric Fassin, 19–36. Paris: La Découverte.

Fazal, Tanweer. 2015. *"Nation-State" and Minority Rights in India: Comparative Perspectives on Muslim and Sikh Identities.* London: Routledge.

Ferguson, James. 1990. *The Anti-Politics Machine: Development, Depoliticization and Bureaucratic Power in Lesotho.* Minneapolis: University of Minnesota Press.

Fernando, Mayanthi L. 2015. "That Muslim Question: Islam and Secularism in Europe." *Anthropology Now* 7(3): 125–30.

Fernando, Mayanthi L. 2014. *The Republic Unsettled: Muslim French and the Contradictions of Secularism.* Durham, NC: Duke University Press.

Fine, Gary. 2007. "Rumor, Trust and Civil Society: Collective Memory and Cultures of Judgment." *Diogenes* 54(1): 5–18.

Foley, Frank. 2015. *Countering Terrorism in Britain and France: Institutions, Norms and the Shadow of the Past.* Cambridge: Cambridge University Press.

Fox, Jonathan. 1994. "The Difficult Transition from Clientelism to Citizenship: Lessons from Mexico." *World Politics* 46(02): 151–84.

Frajerman, Laurent. 2007. "Comment défendre la laïcité scolaire à la libération? Les tensions de la FEN." In *Politiques de la laïcité au XXe siècle*, ed. P. Weil, 463–80. Paris: Presses Universitaires de France.

Fraser, Nancy. 2000. "Rethinking Recognition." *New Left Review* 3: 107–20.

Fraser, Nancy. 1998. "Social Justice in the Age of Identity Politics: Redistribution, Recognition, and Participation." In *The Tanner Lectures on Human Values*, vol. 19, ed. Grethe B. Peterson, 1–67. Salt Lake City.

Fraser, Nancy. 1997. *Justice Interruptus: Critical Reflections on the "Post-Socialist" Condition.* New York: Routledge.

Fraser, Nancy. 1990. "Rethinking the Public Sphere: A Contribution to the Critique of Actually Existing Democracy." *Social Text* (25/26): 56–80.

Fraser, Nancy, and Axel Honneth. 2003. *Redistribution or Recognition?: A Political-Philosophical Exchange.* London and New York: Verso.

Fredette, Jennifer. 2014. *Constructing Muslims in France: Discourse, Public Identity, and the Politics of Citizenship.* Philadelphia, PA: Temple University Press.

Frégosi, Franck. 2004. "L'Imam, le conférencier et le jurisconsulte: Retour sur trois figures contemporaines du champ religieux islamique en France." *Archives de sciences sociales des religions* 49(125): 131–46.

Frégosi, Franck. 1998. "Les problèmes d'organisation de la religion musulmane en France." *Esprit* 239(1): 109–36.

Gastaut, Yvan. 1993. "La flambée raciste de 1973 en France." *Revue européenne des migrations internationals* 9(2): 61–75.

Gay, Robert. 1998. "Rethinking Clientelism: Demands, Discourses, and Practices in Contemporary Brazil." *European Review of Latin American and Caribbean Studies* (65): 7–24.

Gayer, Laurent, and Christophe Jaffrelot, eds. 2012. *Muslims in Indian Cities: Trajectories of Marginalisation.* London: Hurst.

Geertz, Clifford. 1973. *The Interpretation of Cultures.* New York: Basic Books.

Geertz, Clifford. 1971. *Islam Observed.* Chicago: University of Chicago Press.

Geisser, Vincent. 1997. *Ethnicité Républicaine: Les elites d'origine maghrébine dans le système politique français.* Paris: Presses de Sciences Po.

Gellner, Ernest, John Waterbury, and Sydel Silverman, eds. 1977. *Patrons and Clients in Mediterranean Societies.* London: Duckworth.

Ghassem-Fachandi, Parvis. 2012. *Pogrom in Gujarat: Hindu Nationalism and Anti-Muslim Violence in India.* Princeton, NJ: Princeton University Press.

Gille, Zsuzsa, and Sean Riain. 2002. "Global Ethnography." *Annual Review of Sociology* 28: 217–95.

Goffman, Alice. 2014. *On the Run: Fugitive Life in an American City.* Chicago: University of Chicago Press.

Göle, Nilufer. 2002. "Islam in Public: New Visibilities and New Imaginaries." *Public Culture* 14(1): 173–90.

Goven, Joanna. 1993. "Gender Politics in Hungary: Autonomy and Antifeminism." In *Gender Politics and Post-Communism: Reflections from Eastern Europe and the Former Soviet Union,* ed. N. Funk and M. Mueller, 224–40. New York: Routledge.

Goven, Joanna. 2000. "New Parliament, Old Discourse? The Parental Leave Debate in Hungary." In *Reproducing Gender: Politics, Publics, and Everyday Life after Socialism,* ed. S. Gal and G. Kligman, 286–306. Princeton, NJ: Princeton University Press.

Gowan, Teresa. 2010. *Hobos, Hustlers, and Backsliders: Homeless in San Francisco.* Minneapolis: University of Minnesota Press.

Graeber, David. 2013. *The Democracy Project: A History, a Crisis, a Movement.* New York: Spiegel & Grau.

Gramsci, Antonio. 1971. *Selections from the Prison Notebooks of Antonio Gramsci.* Trans. Quintin Hoare and Geoffrey Nowell-Smith. London: Lawrence & Wishart.

Grillo, Ralph D. 1985. *Ideologies and Institutions in Urban France: The Representation of Immigrants.* Cambridge and New York: Cambridge University Press.

Haji, S. 2002. "The Status and Rights of Religious Minorities in Contemporary Islamists' Discourse." MA thesis, Institute of Islamic Studies, McGill University, Montreal.

Hajjat, Abdellali. 2010. "'Bons' et 'mauvais' musulmans: L'Etat français face aux candidats 'islamistes' à la nationalité." *Cultures et Conflits* (79/80): 139–59.

Hajjat, Abdellali. 2014. "Rébellions urbaines et déviances policières: Approche configurationnelle des relations entre les 'jeunes' des Minguettes et la police (1981–1983)." *Cultures et Conflits* 93: 11–34.

Hamidi, Camille. 2010. "Everyday Ethnic Categorizations and the Relationship to Politics." *Revue française de science politique* 60(1): 139–63.

Hamidi, Camille. 2009. "Riots and Protest Cycles: Immigrant Mobilization in France, 1968–2008." In *Rioting in the UK and France, 2001–2006: A Comparative Analysis,* ed. D. Waddington, F. Jobard, and M. King, 135–46. London: Willan.

Hansen, Thomas Blom. 1999. *The Saffron Wave: Democracy and Hindu Nationalism in Modern India.* Princeton, NJ: Princeton University Press.

Hargreaves, Alec. 1995/2007. *Multi-ethnic France: Immigration, Politics, Culture and Society.* New York: Routledge.

Harriss, John. 2007. "Antinomies of Empowerment: Observations on Civil Society, Politics and Urban Governance in India." *Economic and Political Weekly* 42(26): 2716–24.

Hasan, Mushirul. 1997. *Legacy of a Divided Nation: India's Muslims Since Independence.* Boulder, CO: Westview.

Hasan, Zoya. 2007. "Competing Interests, Social Conflict and Muslim Reservations." In *Living with Secularism: The Destiny of India's Muslims,* ed. M. Hasan, 15–36. New Delhi: Manohar.

Hasan, Zoya. 1998. *Quest for Power: Oppositional Movements and Post-Congress Politics in Uttar Pradesh.* New Delhi and New York: Oxford University Press.

Hasan, Zoya, and Ritu Menon. 2004. *Unequal Citizens: A Study of Muslim Women in India.* New Delhi: Oxford University Press.

Havel, Václav. 1985. *The Power of the Powerless: Citizens against the State in Central-Eastern Europe.* Armonk, NY: M.E. Sharpe.

Heesterman, J. C. 1985. *The Inner Conflict of Tradition: Essays in Indian Ritual, Kingship, and Society.* Chicago: University of Chicago Press.

Heller, Patrick. 2000. "Degrees of Democracy: Some Comparative Lessons from India." *World Politics* 52(4): 484–519.

Hintze, Andrea. 1997. *The Mughal Empire and Its Decline: An Interpretation of the Sources of Social Power.* Aldershot and Brookfield, VT: Ashgate.

Hirschkind, Charles. 2006. *The Ethical Soundscape: Cassette Sermons and Islamic Counterpublics.* New York: Columbia University Press.

Hourani, A. 1962/1983. *Arabic Thought in the Liberal Age, 1798–1939.* Cambridge: Cambridge University Press.

Houtman, Dick, and Birgit Meyer. 2012. "Introduction: Material Religion—How Things Matter." In *Things: Religion and the Question of Materiality,* ed. D. Houtman and M. Birgit, 1–27. New York: Fordham University Press.

Huntington, Samuel P. 1996. *The Clash of Civilizations and the Remaking of World Order.* New York: Simon & Schuster.

Hyra, Derek S. 2008. *The New Urban Renewal: The Economic Transformation of Harlem and Bronzeville.* Chicago: University of Chicago Press.

Islam, Maidul. 2015. *Limits of Islamism: Jamaat-E-Islami in Contemporary India and Bangladesh.* Cambridge: Cambridge University Press.

Jauneau, Yves, and Solveig Vanovermeir. 2008. *Les jeunes et les ménages modestes surestiment plus souvent le confort de leur logement.* INSEE report no. 1209. Division Études sociales. At www.insee.fr/fr/ffc/ipweb/ip1209/ip1209.pdf.

Jerolmack, Colin, and Shamus Khan. 2014. "Talk Is Cheap: Ethnography and the Attitudinal Fallacy." *Sociological Methods & Research* 43: 178–209.

Jones, Robert P, Daniel Cox, E. J. Dionne, and William A. Galston. 2011. *What It Means to Be an American: Attitudes in an Increasingly Diverse America Ten Years after 9/11.* Brookings Institution and Public Religion Research Institute. At https://www.brookings.edu/research/what-it-means-to-be-an-american-attitudes-in-an-increasingly-diverse-america-ten-years-after-911/.

Joppke, Christian, and John Torpey. 2013. *Legal Integration of Islam: A Transatlantic Comparison.* Cambridge, MA: Harvard University Press.

Joskowicz, A. 2014. *The Modernity of Others: Jewish Anti-Catholicism in Germany and France*. Stanford, CA: Stanford University Press.

Jouili, Jeanette Selma. 2015. *Pious Practice and Secular Constraints: Women in the Islamic Revival in Europe*. Stanford, CA: Stanford University Press.

Karim, Lamia. 2011. *Microfinance and Its Discontents: Women in Debt in Bangladesh*. Minneapolis: University of Minnesota Press.

Katz, Jack. 1997. "Ethnography's Warrants." *Sociological Methods & Research* 25(4): 391–423.

Kawar, Leila. 2014. "Commanding Legality: The Juridification of Immigration Policy Making in France." *Journal of Law and Courts* 2(1): 93–116.

Kawata, Jun'ichi, ed. 2006. *Comparing Political Corruption and Clientelism*. London: Ashgate.

Keaton, Trica Danielle. 2006. *Muslim Girls and the Other France: Race, Identity Politics, & Social Exclusion*. Bloomington: Indiana University Press.

Kepel, Gilles. 1991. *Les banlieues de l'Islam: naissance d'une religion en France*. Paris: Seuil.

Khalidi, Omar. 1988. "Introduction." In *Hyderabad: After the Fall*, ed. O. Khalidi, x–xiii. Wichita, KS: Hyderabad Historical Society.

Khalidi, Usama. 1988. "From Osmania to Birla Mandir: An Uneasy Journey." In *Hyderabad: After the Fall*, ed. O. Khalidi, 188–98. Wichita, KS: Hyderabad Historical Society.

Khan, Rashiduddin. 1971. "Major Aspects of Muslim Problem in Hyderabad." *Economic and Political Weekly* 6(16): 833–40.

Khusro, A. M. 1958. *Economic and Social Effects of Jagirdari Abolition and Land Reforms in Hyderabad*. Hyderabad: Osmania University Press.

Killian, C. 2007. "From a Community of Believers to an Islam of the Heart: 'Conspicuous' Symbols, Muslim Practices, and the Privatization of Religion in France." *Sociology of Religion* 68(3), 305–20.

Kirsch, Thomas G. 2004. "Restaging the Will to Believe: Religious Pluralism, Anti-Syncretism, and the Problem of Belief." *American Anthropologist* 106(4): 699–709.

Kitts, James A. 2003. "Egocentric Bias or Information Management? Selective Disclosure and the Social Roots of Norm Misperception." *Social Psychology Quarterly* 66(3): 222–37.

Klausen, Jytte. 2005. *The Islamic Challenge: Politics and Religion in Western Europe*. Oxford and New York: Oxford University Press.

Konrád, György. 1984. *Antipolitics*. Trans. Richard E. Allen. London: Quartet Books.

Kooiman, Dick. 2002. *Communalism and Indian Princely States: Travancore, Baroda and Hyderabad in the 1930s*. New Delhi: Manohar.

Korteweg, Anna C., and Gökçe Yurdakul. 2014. *The Headscarf Debates: Conflicts of National Belonging*. Stanford, CA: Stanford University Press.

Kozlowski, Gregory C. 1998. *Muslim Endowments and Society in British India*. Cambridge: Cambridge University Press.

Kramer, Jane. 2011. "Against Nature: Elisabeth Badinter's Contrarian Feminism." *The New Yorker*, July 25, 2011, p. 44.

Krishnan, P. S. 2010. "Understanding the Backward Classes of Muslim Society." *Economic & Political Weekly* 45(34): 46–56.

Kuru, Ahmet T. 2009. *Secularism and State Policies Toward Religion: The United States, France, and Turkey.* Cambridge and New York: Cambridge University Press.

Laborde, Cécile. 2010. *Français, encore un effort pour être républicains!* Paris: Seuil.

Laborde, Cécile. 2002. "On Republican Toleration." *Constellations* 9(2): 167–83.

Laborde, Cécile. 2001. "The Culture of the Republic: Nationalism and Multiculturalism in French Republican Thought." *Political Theory* 29(5): 716–35.

Laurence, Jonathan, and Justin Vaisse. 2006. *Integrating Islam: Political and Religious Challenges in Contemporary France.* Washington, DC: Brookings Institution Press.

Leff, Lisa Moses. 2006. *Sacred Bonds of Solidarity: The Rise of Jewish Internationalism in Nineteenth-Century France.* Stanford, CA: Stanford University Press.

Leonard, Karen. 2007. *Locating Home: India's Hyderabadis Abroad.* Stanford, CA: Stanford University Press.

Leonard, Karen. 2003. "Reassessing Indirect Rule in Hyderabad: Rule, Ruler, or Sons-in-Law of the State?" *Modern Asian Studies* 37(2): 363–79.

Leveau, Rémy. 1992. "Les associations musulmanes." *Projet* 231: 78–80.

Leveau, R., and D. Schnapper. 1987. Religion et politiques: Juifs et musulmans maghrébins en France. *Revue Francaise de Science Politique* 37(6): 855–90.

Lewis, Bernard. 2002. *What Went Wrong?: The Clash Between Islam and Modernity in the Middle East.* New York: Oxford University Press.

Lewis, Bernard. 1990. "The Roots of Muslim Rage (Part 1)." *The Atlantic Monthly* 266(3): 47–60.

Lichterman, Paul. 1996. *The Search for Political Community: American Activists Reinventing Commitment.* New York and Cambridge: Cambridge University Press.

Liogier, Raphaël. 2009. "Laïcité on the Edge in France: Between the Theory of Church-State Separation and the Praxis of State-Church Confusion." *Macquarie Law Journal* 9: 25–45.

Lombardo, Philippe, and Jérôme Pujol. 2010. *Niveau de vie et pauvreté des immigrés en 2007.* INSEE report. At www.insee.fr/fr/ffc/docs_ffc/ref/REVPMEN10d.PDF.

Lorde, Audre. 1988. *A Burst of Light: Essays.* Ithaca, NY: Firebrand Books.

Luther, Narendra. 2006. *Hyderabad: A Biography.* New Delhi: Oxford University Press.

Madan, T. N. 1993. "Whither Indian Secularism?" *Modern Asian Studies* 27(3): 667–97.

Madani, Aiysha. 2005. *A Review of Contemporary Thought in Women Rights: With Reference to Amina Wadud and Others.* Islamabad: Poorab Academy.

Madnī, Sayyid Ḥusain Aḥmad. 2005. *Composite Nationalism and Islam (Muttahida Qaumiyat Aur Islam).* Trans. Mohammed Anwar Hussain. New Delhi: Manohar.

Mahmood, Saba. 2005. *Politics of Piety: The Islamic Revival and the Feminist Subject.* Princeton, NJ: Princeton University Press.

"Mapping the Global Muslim Population." 2009. *The Pew Forum on Religion and Public Life*, October 7. At http://www.pewforum.org/2009/10/07/mapping-the-global-muslim-population/.

Markell, Patchen. 2010. "The Rule of the People: Arendt, Archê, and Democracy." In *Politics in Dark Times: Encounters with Hannah Arendt*, ed. Seyla Benhabib, 58–82. New York: Cambridge University Press.

Maussen, Marcel. 2007. "Islamic Presence and Mosque Establishment in France: Colonialism, Arrangements for Guestworkers and Citizenship." *Journal of Ethnic and Migration Studies* 33(6): 981–1002.

Maxwell, Rahsaan. 2010. "Political Participation in France among Non-European-Origin Migrants: Segregation or Integration?" *Journal of Ethnic and Migration Studies* 36(3): 425–43.

Maxwell, Rahsaan, and Erik Bleich. 2014. "What Makes Muslims Feel French?" *Social Forces* 93(1): 155–79.

McClintock, Anne. 1995. *Imperial Leather: Race, Gender, and Sexuality in the Colonial Contest*. New York: Routledge.

McRoberts, Omar M. 2004. "Beyond Mysterium Tremendum: Thoughts toward an Aesthetic Study of Religious Experience." *Annals of the American Academy of Political and Social Science* 595(1): 190–203.

Mehta, Pratap Bhanu. 2004. "Affirmation without Reservation." *Economic and Political Weekly* 39(27): 2951–54.

Menon, Nivedita. 2007. "Living with Secularism." In *The Crisis of Secularism in India*, ed. A. D. Needham and S. R. Rajeswari, 118–41. Durham, NC: Duke University Press.

Messick, Brinkley Morris. 1993. *The Calligraphic State: Textual Domination and History in a Muslim Society*. Berkeley: University of California Press.

Metcalf, Barbara. 2002. "'Traditionalist' Islamic Activism: Deoband, Tablighis, and Talibs." ISIM paper volume 4. Leiden: International Institute for the Study of Islam in the Modern World. At http://hdl.handle.net/1887/10068.

Minault, Gail. 1998. *Secluded Scholars: Women's Education and Muslim Social Reform in Colonial India*. New Delhi and New York: Oxford University Press.

Ministry of Home Affairs, Government of India. 2001 and 2011. *Government of India Census*. At Censusindia.gov.in.

Moghissi, Haideh. 2008. "Islamic Cultural Nationalism and Gender Politics in Iran." *Third World Quarterly* 29(3): 541–54.

Moghissi, Haideh. 1999. *Feminism and Islamic Fundamentalism: The Limits of Postmodern Analysis*. New York: Zed Books.

Molyneux, Maxine. 1998. "Analyzing Women's Movements." *Development and Change* 29(2): 219–45.

Morvaridi, Behrooz. 2015. *New Philanthropy and Social Justice: Debating the Conceptual and Policy Discourse*. Bristol and Chicago: Policy Press.

Nannestad, Peter. 2008. "What Have We Learned About Generalized Trust, If Anything?" *Annual Review of Political Science* 11(1): 413–36.

Needham, Anuradha Dingwaney, and Rajeswari. Sunder Rajan, eds. 2007. *The Crisis of Secularism in India*. Durham, NC: Duke University Press.

Needham, Rodney. 1972. *Belief, Language, and Experience*. Oxford: Blackwell.

Nielsen, Jørgen S., ed. 2013. *Muslim Political Participation in Europe*. Edinburgh: Edinburgh University Press.

Noiriel, Gérard. 2007. *À Quoi sert "l'identité nationale."* Marseille: Agone.

Noiriel, Gérard. 1988/1996. *The French Melting Pot: Immigration, Citizenship, and National Identity*. Minneapolis: University of Minnesota Press.

Observatoire national des zones urbaines sensibles. 2011. *Rapport 2011*. At www.ville.gouv.fr/IMG/pdf/rapport_onzus_2011.pdf.

Oldenburg, Veena Talwar. 2002. *Dowry Murder: the Imperial Origins of a Cultural Crime*. New York: Oxford University Press.

Osella, Filippo, and Caroline Osella. 2008. "Introduction: Islamic Reformism in South Asia." *Modern Asian Studies* 42(2–3): 247–57.

Pan Ké Shon, Jean-Louis. 2011. "La ségrégation des immigrés en France: état des lieux." *Population & Sociétés* 477: 1–4.

Pandey, Gyanendra. 2007. "The Secular State and the Limits of Dialogue." In *The Crisis of Secularism in India,* ed. A. D. Needham and R. S. Rajan, 157–76. Durham, NC: Duke University Press.

Pandey, Gyanendra. 1999. "Can a Muslim Be an Indian?" *Comparative Studies in Society and History* 41(4): 608–29.

Parekh, Bhikhu C. 1995. "Ethnocentricity of the Nationalist Discourse." *Nations and Nationalism* 1(1): 25–52.

Parekh, Bhikhu C. 1991. *Gandhi's Political Philosophy: A Critical Examination*. Basingstoke: Macmillan.

Pattillo, Mary. 2008. *Black on the Block: The Politics of Race and Class in the City*. Chicago: University of Chicago Press.

Pattillo, Mary. 1999. *Black Picket Fences: Privilege and Peril among the Black Middle Class*. Chicago: University of Chicago Press.

Perrin, A. 2007. "Le financement public des églises catholiques. Des relations complexes autour des édifices cultuels." In *Politiques de la laïcité au XXe siècle,* ed. P. Weil, 533–52. Paris: Presses Universitaires de France.

Piliavsky, Anastasia, ed. 2014. *Patronage as Politics in South Asia*. Delhi: Cambridge University Press.

Poulat, Émile. 2003. *Notre laïcité publique: "La France est une République laïque."* Paris: Berg International.

Prakash, Gyan. 2007. "Secular Nationalism, Hindutva, and the Minority." In *The Crisis of Secularism in India,* ed. A. D. Needham and R. S. Rajan, 177–88. Durham, NC: Duke University Press.

Putnam, Robert D. 2000. *Bowling Alone: The Collapse and Revival of American Community*. New York: Simon and Schuster.

Rabinow, Paul. 2007. *Reflections on Fieldwork in Morocco*. Berkeley: University of California Press.

Radhakrishnan, Smitha. 2011. *Appropriately Indian: Gender and Culture in a New Transnational Class*. Durham, NC: Duke University Press.

Rajagopal, Arvind. 2001. *Politics After Television: Religious Nationalism and the Reshaping of the Indian Public*. Cambridge: Cambridge University Press.

Rajan, R. Sunder. 2000. "Women between Community and State: Some Implications of the Uniform Civil Code Debates in India." *Social Text* 65: 55–82.

Rajan, S. Irudaya. 2014. *Emigration from Kerala, Andhra Pradesh and Tamil Nadu: A Mapping of Surveys on International Labour Migration from India*. Migrant Forum in Asia. At www.mfasia.org/india/429-resources-on-indian-labor-migration.

Rao, Badrinath. 2006. "The Variant Meanings of Secularism in India: Notes toward Conceptual Clarifications." *Journal of Church and State* 48(1): 47–82.

Rao, Neena Ambre, and S. Abdul Thaha. 2012. "Muslims of Hyderabad: Land Locked in the Walled City." In *Muslims in Indian Cities: Trajectories of Marginalisation*, ed. L. Gayer and C. Jaffrelot, 189–211. New York: Columbia University Press.

Ray, Raka. 2010. "'The Middle Class': Sociological Category or Proper Noun." *Political Power and Social Theory* 21: 313–22.

Rawls, John, and Erin Kelly. 2001. *Justice as Fairness: A Restatement*. Cambridge, MA: Harvard University Press.

Renwick, Alan. 2006. "Anti-Political or Just Anti-Communist? Varieties of Dissidence in East-Central Europe and Their Implications for the Development of Political Society." *East European Politics & Societies* 20(2): 286–318.

Riesebrodt, Martin. 2000. "Fundamentalism and the Resurgence of Religion." *Numen*. 47(3): 266–87.

Riesebrodt, Martin. 1993. *Pious Passion: The Emergence of Modern Fundamentalism in the United States and Iran*. Berkeley: University of California Press.

Rosaldo, Renato. 1989/1993. "Introduction: Grief and a Headhunter's Rage." In *Culture & Truth: The Remaking of Social Analysis*, 1–21. Boston: Beacon Press.

Rousseau, Stephanie. 2009. *Women's Citizenship in Peru: The Paradoxes of Neopopulism in Latin America*. New York: Palgrave Macmillan.

Roy, Ananya. 2010. *Poverty Capital: Microfinance and the Making of Development*. New York: Routledge.

Roy, Ananya. 2003. *City Requiem, Calcutta: Gender and the Politics of Poverty*. Minneapolis: University of Minnesota Press.

Roy, Ananya, and Nezar AlSayyad. 2004. "Prologue/Dialogue: Urban Informality: Crossing Borders." In *Urban Informality: Transnational Perspectives from the Middle East, Latin America, and South Asia*, ed. A. Roy and N. AlSayyad, 1–6. Lanham, MD: Lexington Books.

Roy, Olivier. 2015. "Le djihadisme est une révolte générationnelle et nihiliste." *Le Monde*, November 24, 2015. At http://www.lemonde.fr/idees/article/2015/11/24/le-djihadisme-une-revolte-generationnelle-et-nihiliste_4815992_3232.html#a44tavs7QmpdVVzr.99.

Roy, Olivier. 2006. "Islam in Europe: Clash of religions or convergence of religiosities?" In *Conditions of European Solidarity, Vol II: Religion in the New Europe*, ed. K. Michalski, 131–44. New York: Central European Press.

Roy, Olivier. 2004. *Globalized Islam: The Search for a New Ummah*. New York: Columbia University Press.

Roy, Olivier. 1994. *The Failure of Political Islam*. Cambridge, MA: Harvard University Press.

Sachar Committee, Government of India. 2006. *Social, Economic and Educational Status of the Muslim Community of India*. New Delhi: Prime Minister's High Level Committee. At http://mhrd.gov.in/sites/upload_files/mhrd/files/sachar_comm.pdf.

Saeed, Abdullah. 1996. *Islamic Banking and Interest: A Study of the Prohibition of Riba and its Contemporary Interpretation*. Leiden: Brill.

Salvatore, Armando. 2007. "Authority in Question: Secularity, Republicanism and 'Communitarianism' in the Emerging Euro-Islamic Public Sphere." *Theory, Culture & Society* 24(2): 135–60.

Sandbrook, Richard, and Judith Barker. 1985. *The Politics of Africa's Economic Stagnation*. Cambridge and New York: Cambridge University Press.

Sayad, Abdelmalek. 2004. "L'immigration en France: une pauvreté 'exotique.'" In *Mémoires algériennes*, ed. A. Kadri and G. Prévost, 121–51. Paris: Editions Syllepse.

Sayad, Abdelmalek. 1991. *L'immigration, ou, Les paradoxes de l'altérité*. Bruxelles: De Boeck/Éditions Universitaires.

Sayad, Abdelmalek. 1984. *L'immigration algérienne en France*. Paris: Editions Entente.

Scott, Joan. 2007. *The Politics of the Veil*. Princeton, NJ: Princeton University Press.

Scott, Joan Wallach, and Debra Keates, eds. 2004. *Going Public: Feminism and the Shifting Boundaries of the Private Sphere*. Urbana: University of Illinois Press.

Sedgwick, Mark. 2015. "Jihadism, Narrow and Wide: The Dangers of Loose Use of an Important Term." *Perspectives on Terrorism* 9(2): 34–41.

Seligman, Adam B. 1992. "Trust and the Meaning of Civil Society." *International Journal of Politics, Culture, and Society* 6(1): 5–21.

Shahidian, Hammed. 1999. "Saving the Savior." *Sociological Inquiry* 69(2): 303–27.

Sherman, Taylor C. 2015. *Muslim Belonging in Secular India: Negotiating Citizenship in Postcolonial Hyderabad*. Cambridge: Cambridge University Press.

Sikand, Yoginder. 2004. *Muslims in India since 1947: Islamic Perspectives on Inter-Faith Relations*. New York: Routledge.

Silverstein, Paul. 2004. *Algeria in France: Transpolitics, Race, and Nation*. Bloomington: Indiana University Press.

Silverstein, Paul A., and Chantal Tetreault. 2006. "Postcolonial Urban Apartheid." *Items and Issues* 5(4): 8–15. At http://riotsfrnace.ssrc.org/Silverstein_Tetreault.

Simon, Patrick. 2012. *French National Identity and Integration: Who Belongs to the National Community*. Washington, DC: Migration Policy Institute.

Simon, Patrick. 1998. "Ghettos, Immigrants, and Integration: the French Dilemma." *Netherlands Journal of Housing and the Built Environment* 13(1): 41–61.

Simon, Patrick, and Vincent Tiberj. 2013. *Sécularisation ou regain religieux: la religiosité des immigrés et de leurs descendants*. No. 196. Institut National D'Études Démographiques. At https://www.ined.fr/fichier/s_rubrique/19585/document_.travail_2013_196_religion.fr.pdf.

Singh, Ujjwal Kumar. 2007. *The State, Democracy and Anti-Terror Laws in India*. New Delhi and Thousand Oaks, CA: Sage.

Sinno, Abdulkader H. 2009. *Muslims in Western Politics*. Bloomington: Indiana University Press.

Sitaraman, Bhavani. 1999. "Law as Ideology: Women, Courts and 'Dowry Deaths' in India." *International Journal of the Sociology of Law* 27: 287–316.

Smith, Wilfred Cantwell. 1950. "Hyderabad: Muslim Tragedy." *Middle East Journal* 4(1): 27–51.

Somers, Margaret R. 2008. *Genealogies of Citizenship: Markets, Statelessness, and the Right to Have Rights*. New York: Cambridge University Press.

Sonbol, Amira. 2003. "Women in Shari'ah Courts: A Historical and Methodological Discussion." *Fordham International Law Journal* 27(1): 225–53.

Sridharan, E. 2014. "Class Voting in the 2014 Lok Sabha Elections." *Economic and Political Weekly* 49(39): 72–76.

Stack, Carol. 1974. *All Our Kin: Strategies for Survival in a Black Community*. New York: Harper & Row.

Steinmetz, George. 2009. "The New Aesthetic-Political Avant-Garde: Linda Zerilli's Feminism and the Abyss of Freedom." *Sociological Theory* 27(1): 85–89.

Stemmann, J. 2006. "Middle East Salafism's Influence and Radicalization of Muslim Communities in Europe." *Middle East Review of International Affairs* 10(3): 1–14.

Stokes, Susan Carol. 2007. "Political Clientelism." In *The Oxford Handbook of Comparative Politics*, ed. S. C. Stokes and C. Boix, 604–28. New York: Oxford University Press.

Subramanian, Narendra. 2008. "Legal Change and Gender Inequality: Changes in Muslim Family Law in India." *Law & Social Inquiry* 33(3): 631–72.

Sundarlal, Pandit, and Qazi Muhammed Abdulghaffar. 1948/1988. "A Report on the Post-Operation Polo Massacres, Rape, and Destruction or Seizure of Property in Hyderabad State." In *Hyderabad: After the Fall*, ed. O. Khalidi, 100–15. Wichita, KS: Hyderabad Historical Society.

Swidler, Ann. 1922/1993. "Foreword." In *The Sociology of Religion* by Max Weber, ix–xix. Boston: Beacon Press.

Tarlau, Rebecca. 2013. "Coproducing Rural Public Schools in Brazil: Contestation, Clientelism, and the Landless Workers Movement." *Politics & Society* 41(3): 395–424.

Taub, Richard P., D. Garth Taylor, and Jan D. Dunham. 1984. *Paths of Neighborhood Change: Race and Crime in Urban America*. Chicago: University of Chicago Press.

Taylor, Charles. 2007. *A Secular Age.* Cambridge, MA: Belknap Press of Harvard University Press.

Tejani, Shabnum. 2013. "Between Inequality and Identity: The Indian Constituent Assembly and Religious Difference, 1946–50." *South Asia Research* 33(3): 205–21.

Tejani, Shabnum. 2008. *Indian Secularism: A Social and Intellectual History, 1890–1950.* Bloomington: Indiana University Press.

Tévanian, Pierre. 2005. *Le voile médiatique: Un faux débat.* Paris: Raisons d'Agir.

Thapar, Romila. 2007. "Secularism, History, and Contemporary Politics in India." In *The Crisis of Secularism in India,* ed. A. D. Needham and R. S. Rajan, 191–207. Durham, NC: Duke University Press.

The Pew Forum on Religion & Public Life. 2009. "Mapping the Global Muslim Population: A Report on the Size and Distribution of the World's Muslim Population." Washington, DC: Pew Research Center.

Tissot, Sylvie. 2006. "Y a-t-il un "problème des quartiers sensibles"? Retour sur une catégorie d'action publique." *French Politics, Culture & Society* 24(3): 42–57.

Tombs, Robert. 1996. *France, 1814–1914.* London and New York: Longman.

Topalov, Christian. 1987. *Le logement en France: histoire d'une marchandise impossible.* Paris: Presses de la Fondation Nationale des Sciences Politiques.

Toth, James. 2003. "Islamism in Southern Egypt: A Case Study of a Radical Religious Movement." *International Journal of Middle East Studies* 35: 547–72.

Tribalat, Michèle. 1995. *Faire France: une grande enquête sur les immigrés et leurs enfants.* Paris: Editions la Découverte.

Tuğal, Cihan. 2009. *Passive Revolution: Absorbing the Islamic Challenge to Capitalism.* Stanford, CA: Stanford University Press.

Turner, Bryan S. 2003. "Class, Generation and Islamism: Towards a Global Sociology of Political Islam." *British Journal of Sociology* 54(1): 139–47.

United Nations Development Programme. 2014. *Human Development Report 2014.* At http://hdr.undp.org/sites/default/files/hdr14-report-en-1.pdf.

Van Maanen, John. 2011. *Tales of the Field: On Writing Ethnography.* Chicago: University of Chicago Press.

Varshney, Ashutosh. 2002. *Ethnic Conflict and Civic Life: Hindus and Muslims in India.* New Haven, CT: Yale University Press.

Vatuk, Sylvia. 2008a. "Islamic Feminism in India: Indian Muslim Women Activists and the Reform of Muslim Personal Law." *Modern Asian Studies* 42(2/3): 489–518.

Vatuk, Sylvia. 2008b. "Divorce at the Wife's Initiative in Muslim Personal Law: What are the Options and What Are Their Implications for Women's Welfare?" In *Redefining Family Law in India: Essays in Honour of B. Sivaramayya,* ed. A. Parashar and A. Dhanda, 200–35. London: Routledge.

Venel, Nancy. 2005. "Francités, Islamités: compositions citoyennes et religieuses des jeunes musulmans français d'origine Maghrébine." *French Politics, Culture & Society* 23(1): 88–100.

Venel, Nancy. 2004. *Musulmans et citoyens.* Paris: Presses Universitaires de France.

Venkatesh, Sudhir Alladi. 2000. *American Project: The Rise and Fall of a Modern Ghetto*. Cambridge, MA: Harvard University Press.

Vergès, Meriam. 1997. "The Young Activists of Algeria's Islamic Salvation Front." In *Political Islam: Essays from Middle East Report*, ed. J. Beinin and J. Stork, 292–305. Berkeley: University of California Press.

Viet, Vincent. 1998. *La France immigrée: construction d'une politique 1914–1997*. Paris: Fayard.

Voisin, Bruno. 2005. "Les Minguettes, un grand ensemble à Vénissieux, troisième ville de l'agglomération lyonnaise." L'Agence d'urbanisme de l'aire métropolitaine lyonnaise. At www.urbalyon.org/sip6Internet/AfficheDocument.aspx?nom Fichier=HistoireMinguettes.pdf&numFiche=63.

Wacquant, Loïc J. 2010. "Urban Desolation and Symbolic Denigration in the Hyperghetto." *Social Psychology Quarterly* 73(3): 215–19.

Wacquant, Loïc J. 2008. *Urban Outcasts: A Comparative Sociology of Advanced Marginality*. Cambridge and Malden, MA: Polity Press.

Wacquant, Loïc J. 2007. "Territorial Stigmatization in the Age of Advanced Marginality." *Thesis Eleven* 91(1): 66–77.

Wacquant, Loïc J. 2004a. *Body & Soul: Notebooks of an Apprentice Boxer*. Oxford and New York: Oxford University Press.

Wacquant, Loïc J. 2004b. "Pointers on Pierre Bourdieu and Democratic Politics." *Constellations* 11(1): 3–15.

Wacquant, Loïc J. 1993. "From Ideology to Symbolic Violence: Culture, Class, and Consciousness in Marx and Bourdieu." *International Journal of Contemporary Sociology* 3(2): 125–42.

Wacquant, Loïc J. 1992. "Toward a Social Praxeology: The Structure and Logic of Bourdieu's Sociology." In *An Invitation to Reflexive Sociology* by Pierre Bourdieu and Loïc J. D. Wacquant, 1–60. Chicago: University of Chicago Press.

Waheed, Abdul. 2009. "Dowry among Indian Muslims: Ideals and Practices." *Indian Journal of Gender Studies* 16(1): 47–75.

Warner, Carolyn M., and Manfred W. Wenner. 2006. "Religion and the Political Organization of Muslims in Europe." *Perspectives on Politics* 4(3): 457–79.

Warren, M. E. 1999. "What Is Political?" *Journal of Theoretical Politics* 11(2): 207–31.

Weber, M. 1978. *Economy and Society: An Outline of Interpretive Sociology*. Berkeley: University of California Press.

Weber, M. 1958. *The Rational and Social Foundations of Music*. Carbondale, IL: Southern Illinois University Press.

Weber, M. 1946. "Politics as a Vocation." In *From Max Weber: Essays in Sociology*, ed. H. H. Gerth and C. Wright Mills, 77–128. New York: Oxford University Press.

Wedeen, Lisa. 2008. *Peripheral Visions: Publics, Power, and Performance in Yemen*. Chicago: University of Chicago Press.

Weil, Patrick. 2007. "Introduction—La Loi de 1905 et son application depuis un siècle." In *Politiques de la laïcité au XXe siècle*, ed. P. Weil, 9–43. Paris: Presses Universitaires de France.

Wieviorka, Michel. 2007. *The Lure of Anti-Semitism Hatred of Jews in Present-Day France*. Leiden: Brill.

Wilson, William J. 1987. *The Truly Disadvantaged: The Inner City, the Underclass, and Public Policy*. Chicago: University of Chicago Press.

Wimmer, Andreas. 1997. "Who Owns the State? Understanding Ethnic Conflict in Post-Colonial Societies." *Nations and Nationalism* 3(4): 631–66.

Winter, Bronwyn. 2001. "Fundamental Misunderstandings: Issues in Feminist Approaches to Islamism." *Journal of Women's History* 13(1): 9–41.

World Values Survey. 2005. World Values Survey Association in Stockholm. At www.worldvaluessurvey.org.

Wright, Erik. 2004. "Social Class." In *Encyclopedia of Social Theory*, ed. G. Ritzer, 718–25. Thousand Oaks, CA: Sage.

Wright, Robin. 2012. "Don't Fear All Islamists, Fear Salafis," *New York Times*, August 20, A19.

Wright, Jr. Theodore. 1963. "Revival of the Majlis Ittihad-ul-Muslimin of Hyderabad." *Muslim World* 53: 234–43.

Wrye, Harriet Kimble. 2009. "The Fourth Wave of Feminism: Psychoanalytic Perspectives Introductory Remarks." *Studies in Gender and Sexuality* 10(4): 185–89.

Wuthnow, Robert. 1987. *Meaning and Moral Order: Explorations in Cultural Analysis*. Berkeley: University of California Press.

Wyatt, Andrew. 2005. "(Re) Imagining the Indian (Inter) National Economy." *New Political Economy* 10(2): 163–79.

Young, Iris Marion. 1997. "Unruly Categories: A Critique of Nancy Fraser's Dual Systems Theory." *New Left Review* 222: 147–60.

Yuval-Davis, Nira. 1997. "Ethnicity, Gender Relations and Multiculturalism." In *Debating Cultural Hybridity: Multicultural Identities and the Politics of Anti-Racism*, ed. P. Werbner and T. Modood, 193–208. London: Zed Books.

Zamindar, Vazira Fazila-Yacoobali. 2007. *The Long Partition and the Making of Modern South Asia: Refugees, Boundaries, Histories*. New York: Columbia University Press.

Zavisca, Jane. 2007. "Ethics in Ethnographic Fieldwork." *Forum for Anthropology and Culture* 4: 127–46.

Zehraoui, Ahsène. 1999. *Familles d'Origine Algérienne en France*. Paris: CIEMI.

Zerilli, Linda M. G. 2005. *Feminism and the Abyss of Freedom*. Chicago: University of Chicago Press.

Zubaida, Sami. 1989. *Islam, the People and the State: Essays on Political Ideas and Movements in the Middle East*. London and New York: Routledge.

Index